THE THEOLOGY OF SEDER ELIAHU
A Study in Organic Thinking

THE THEOLOGY OF SEDER ELIAHU
A Study in Organic Thinking

MAX KADUSHIN

Classics in Judaic Studies
Global Publications, Binghamton University
2001

First printed by Bloch Publishing Company, New York, in 1932.

Library of Congress Cataloging-in-Publication Data:

Max Kadushin, *The Theology of Seder Eliahu: A Study in Organic Thinking*

1. Judaism 2. Seder Eliahu

ISBN 1-586841-00-9

Published and Distributed by:
Classics in Judaic Studies
Global Publications, Binghamton University
State University of New York at Binghamton
Binghamton, New York, USA 13902-6000
Phone: (607) 777-4495 or 777-6104; Fax: (607) 777-6132
Email: pmorewed@binghamton.edu
http://ssips.binghamton.edu

CLASSICS IN JUDAIC STUDIES

Publisher: Global Publications, State University of New York at Binghamton
Address: LNG 99, SUNY-Binghamton, Binghamton, New York 13902-6000

A Short Biography of Max Kadushin

Max Kadushin (1895-1980) grew up in Seattle, Washington, where his father ran an outfitting store for the Klondike Gold Rush. He came to New York in 1912 and received his B.A. from NYU. Ordained by the Jewish Theological Seminary of America in 1920, he earned a Doctor of Hebrew Letters there in 1932 and an honorary D.Litt. in 1952. From 1921 to 1926 he was rabbi of a congregation in New York City and prepared sermons together with Mordechai Kaplan whose Reconstructionist ideas he eventually disowned. From 1926 to 1931 he was rabbi of a congregation in Chicago. A devoté of the revival of the Hebrew language, he spent a sabbatical in 1929 in Palestine.

In the years 1931 to 1942 he was rabbi and director of the Hillel Foundation at the University of Wisconsin. In the days before formal Jewish Studies programs, he gave classes and seminars at Hillel, drawing leading students and creating a salon of university academics. From 1942 to 1952 he was director of the Hebrew High School of Greater New York, also known as the Marshaliah Hebrew High School. The late Gerson Cohen was a teacher; among the students were Yochanan Muffs and Norman Podhoretz. During the next several years he served two congregations in the New York area, and was the first rabbi of Synagogue Adath Israel in Riverdale. From 1958 to 1960 Kadushin was professor of midrash and homiletics at the Academy for Higher Jewish Learning in New York City.

In 1960 Kadushin became visiting professor in ethics and rabbinic thought at the Jewish Theological Seminary. He held this position from 1960 to 1980, the year of his death.

Kaplan introduced him to Evelyn Garfiel (1900–1987) whom Kadushin married in 1923, and who became his life-long muse. Dr Garfiel, who used her maiden name professionally, received her A.B. from Barnard College in 1920 and her Ph.D. in psychology from Columbia University in 1923. She taught at the University of Chicago, the University of Wisconsin, and the Jewish Theological Seminary. She was the author of *The Service of the Heart: A Guide to the Jewish Prayer Book* (1958).

Sources: Ratner Center Archives at JTS; Theodore Steinberg, "Max Kadushin: An Intellectual Biography." Pp. 1–18 in Peter Ochs (ed.), *Understanding The Rabbinic Mind: Essays on the Hermeneutic of Max Kadushin*. Atlanta Georgia: Scholars Press, 1990.

Introduction: The Inquiry of Max Kadushin

Jacob Neusner

In presenting the entire oeuvre of Max Kadushin, I mean to endow a new generation with access to his thought. For he represents a rich resource of insight, both methodological and substantive, into the particular problems of describing, analyzing, and interpreting the theology of Rabbinic Judaism in its formative documents. He penetrated deep into the inner thought-processes of that Judaism, and he produced insights of remarkable depth through methods of high sophistication.

What specifically did he seek to understand? Kadushin tried to show that within the rabbinic canon is present "an articulation of thought and values more complicated than that which can be devised by logic...This type of thinking...is universal, whilst local in content and individualistic in configuration. It is not logical but organismic: Each organismic pattern of thought or organic complex has its own distinctive individuality — each social pattern and each individual variation of it." He claimed, in particular, that rabbinic "thought is concerned with numerous rabbinic concepts...These concepts are certainly not united in logical fashion and their relationship with each other defies diagrammatic representation. Instead, every concept is related to every other concept because every concept is a constituent part of the complex as a whole. Conversely, the complex of concepts as a whole enters into the constitution of every concept; and thus every concept is in constant, dynamic relationship with every other concept. Rabbinic thought, hence, is organismic, for only in an organism are the whole and its parts mutually constitutive...."[1]

In *Worship and Ethics*, moreover, Kadushin moved directly to define "rabbinic value concepts," such as Torah, religious duty, charity, holiness, repentance, man: "Such terms are noun forms, but they have a different character than other types of terms or concepts. These terms are connotative only, and hence are not amenable to formal definition. Again, they refer to matter which are not objects, qualities, or relations in sensory experience. Their function is to endow situations or events with significance. These value concepts are related to each other not logically but organismically. This means that the value concepts are not deduced from one another and that they cannot be placed in a logical order. Instead, the coherence or relatedness of the value concepts is such that they interweave dynamically."[2]

In making these statements, Kadushin intended to take up the study of the concepts of what I call the Judaism of the dual Torah and he called "the Rabbis." His intent is to enter into "the great realm of awareness, the realm of ideas that endow life with significance." While, in general, Kadushin avoided the word "theology," e.g., "The values of Rabbinic Judaism consist of ideas,"[3] in fact, his inquiry, in its terms, aimed at elucidating that system and order, that coherence and proportion and composition and cogency, that the description of the theology of a document or a set of documents lays forth. Kadushin, for his part, insisted that we cannot define value-terms, over and over again maintaining that these are "undefined concepts," gaining their meaning in context:

> We shall find that the value-concepts are not only undefined but non-definable, and that this accords with the dual nature of the task which is accomplished by them. Being non-definable, the value-concepts are extremely flexible, and they

> can, therefore, respond to and express the *differentia* of human personalities.
> At the time, the value-term does convey an abstract, generalized idea of the concept it represents, and this generalized idea is common to all the members of the group.[4]

Clearly, we have at the same time a definition of the theological task and a denial that it can be done. For Kadushin's acute concern for the social locus of thought and his interest in allowing for individual difference, translate theological inquiry into sociological description of the uses, rather than the logic, of language; that would prove quite plausible, if, at the same time, he did not double back and insist that language has no meaning (merely) because different people use different words differently — but we can nonetheless impute to "the value-term" "an abstract, generalized idea of the concept it represents." But that statement sounds very much like the claim that we know the "concept it represents" even though we cannot define any words that express or convey that concept, that is to say, a priori and intuitive definition.

Kadushin took as his task the description of the theology of the canonical documents of Judaism, and that is what makes Kadushin interesting as we now reread his corpus: how he addressed the question of descriptive theology of the Judaism of the dual Torah that seems to me urgent. Not only so, but his interest lay in framing a viable method of description; he recognized, as have very few others who have proposed to do the same work, that prior to inquiry we have to solve the methodological problem of how to inquire. He understood full well the need for self-conscious definition of what we wish to know, how we propose to find it out, and why the methods we use in our study prove both congruent to the task and also appropriate to the sources. Thus he stated quite explicitly, "Every modern presentation of rabbinic thought is also an interpretation."[5] To those who claimed to give "just the facts," he countered that knowing what we mean by a fact, which is to say, defining taxa and utilizing them, itself represents much more than giving just the facts. He criticized Schechter for his pretentious claim, "I considered it advisable not to intrude too much interpretation or paraphrase upon the Rabbis. I let them have their own say in their own words" — as though we could translate into rabbi-talk such categories as "the Kingdom of God (Invisible)," "The Visible Kingdom (Universal," "the Kingdom of God (National)," and on and on; Kadushin insisted in the face of Schechter's anti-intellectual nonsense: "they are interpretative terms."

Then how to proceed? Kadushin framed what he conceived to be a descriptive vocabulary, doing more than merely re-presenting or paraphrasing in translation rabbinic passages: "Once the rabbinic materials are subjected to analysis, an injustice is done if we reckon merely with this or that specific statement; such specific statements then stand unrelated to rabbinic thought as a whole."[6] But the issue then was, how to speak of the whole all together, all at once? And that, of course, forms the centerpiece of theological description: the claim to be able to say, "This is what it was, this is what it meant, and this is what held the whole together: what was important." To solve that problem, Kadushin called upon the concept of "rabbinic value-concepts," as we have already seen. In my judgment, he took a philosophical route to the solution of a theological problem, and that was both sensible and also unseemly. It was sensible because the ultimate goal of the study of a theological system or structure (my concern with the theology of the canon of the Judaism of the dual Torah is to describe the structure, which is choate and stable, rather than the system, which, in the nature of things, proves dialectical and dynamic and hence defies the low-level description of which, at this time, we may with much work prove capable). But it was unseemly because in order to speak of system and to work in an encompassing way, as we have seen, Kadushin defined out of existence the very thing he wished to describe, analyze, and interpret. His error lay in interpreting too soon, describing too little, analyzing altogether too much out of all context. He missed the specificities, but, alas, that is where God lives: only in the details. That simple fact after all is what defines the task to begin with: to find the theology in the literature, God in the details of words.

I believe Kadushin was the only scholar before this writer who took seriously the documentary boundaries of texts. Thus he started with *The Theology of Seder Eliahu* (New York, 1932); he worked on "Aspects of the Rabbinic Concept of Israel in the Mekilta," *Hebrew Union College Annual* 1943-6, 19:57-96; I published his posthumous book, *A Conceptual Commentary on Midrash Leviticus Rabbah; Value Concepts in Jewish Thought* (Atlanta, 1987: Scholars Press for Brown Judaic Studies). Accordingly, we cannot dismiss him as another routine lexical-theologian, imputing uniform meanings to words wherever and whenever they occur, at the same time assuming that lexical paraphrase sufficed to represent the logic, order, coherence, and structure of those sets of words, even comprising sentences, that represent (a) theology through description.

This he did not do, but this still is what emerged. He identified four concepts of special interest, God's justice, love, Torah, and Israel, each with its own sub-concepts, e.g., "God's justice the subconcepts of chastisements, Merit of the Fathers, Merit of the Children, and 'measure for measure;' God's love the sub-concepts of prayer, repentance and atonement...," and so on. Each of these concepts with their sub-concepts he classified and organized and categorized, with this result: "The relation of a general concept to its sub-concepts...is one form of integration to be found then in the complex of the rabbinic value-concepts." Now to what end and what is at stake? That Kadushin proposed a theological description is beyond any doubt: "Ramified into sub-concepts and conceptual phrases, the four concepts...play a large role in integrating the entire complex of concepts."[7] The key word here is "integrating," and the main point clear.

The point of relevance to this book comes at the present turning in Kadushin's argument. Kadushin's result, repeated in all of his books, is that the concepts "combine or interweave with *every* value-concept of the rabbinic complex of concepts." Lest readers suppose that I have imputed to him this confession of the indeterminacy of all language, I point out that the italics of "every" are his, not mine. Kadushin produces an utter chaos with such hermeneutical positions as this one: "In like manner the four concepts also interweave with each other and with all their sub-concepts and conceptual phases...Apparent now is an all-embracing principle of coherence, making by and large for the organization of the rabbinic value-complex, for, since the four concepts combine with one another and with the rest of the concepts, every concept can interseave with every other concept in the complex...."[8] The upshot is that we can never know what anything means in general, because all language is specific to its setting: "The process of integration has enormous bearing on the meaning of the individual concepts.

The conceptual term is only suggestive of the meaning of the value-concept. The idea-content of any particular rabbinic value-concept is a function of the entire complex of concepts as a whole, more specifically, of the process of the integration of the particular concept with the rest of the concepts of the complex. Depending on how we view the process, we can say, therefore, either that a value-concept takes on idea-content, or that its idea-content becomes explicit only as it interweaves with other concepts of the complex."[9] Again and again Kadushin insists that fixed combinations will not serve to impute the meaning of a value-concept: "There is no way to predict, on the basis of the particular concepts involved, precisely what idea any given combination of concepts may be made to express." Then what of coherence, logic, order? Kadushin answers that question, and with this answer we conclude our survey of his method:

> What is the principle of coherence or order which governs the concepts? We have to do here not with a fixed, static form of unity but with a dynamic process. It is a process of integration, on the one hand, in which the four fundamental concepts combine with each other and with the rest of the concepts so that each individual concept is always free to combine with any other concept of the complex; and it is also a process of individuation, on the other hand, in which any particular concept takes on meaning or character in the very process whereby it combines with the other concepts of the complex....The rabbinic complex of value-concepts is an organism...The rabbinic value-complex, since it is composed of concepts and ideas, is a mental organism.... [10]
>
> The organization of the rabbinic value-concepts is...a highly complicated affair, complex enough because of the constant interweaving of all the concepts in their organismal relationship and made still more complex because of further, supplementary types of relationship permitted by the organismic integration...the rabbinic value-complex functions easily, simply, often almost casually...The rabbinic value-concept is not a meaning added or applied to objective facts or situations but inherent in the situations and as easily apprehended..."[11]

It now suffices to repeat that Kadushin has taken a philosophical route to the solution of what is, to begin with, a literary problem — even while, as I said, identifying the importance of the literary evidence read *in situ*. He has taken the language of the rabbinic writings as the probative evidence, the meanings of words read at one and the same time essentially out of all specific context and also wholly and only in discrete and specific context alone. In my view, the result is wholly negative. Kadushin did not succeed in describing the theology of the Judaism of the dual Torah, because he identified as the appropriate evidence the wrong data, words read pretty much every which way, and furthermore having focused upon the right question — the character of documents and the message of documents — he turned away from his own results. What did Kadushin do wrong? Despite his own good method he ignored the bounds of the documents, treating the canon as essentially uniform and limited only by its outer frontiers. So he lept directly into words and their definition. That accounts for the unnuanced character of his results.

Kadushin most certainly identified as his quest a theological description problem, so he knew precisely the problem he wished to solve. What makes me sure it was the problem of the description of theology? I find ample justification in his own words (even while he did not like the word theology at all):

> The problem of the coherence of rabbinic theology [to which he appends the footnote, p. 267, n. 2: "the term 'rabbinic theology' is not an appropriate designation for rabbinic thought"] appears to be precisely that which we have just raised with regard to values in general. Any representation of rabbinic theology as a logical system...is bound to be a distortion. Careful scholars agree with Schechter who says, 'that any attempt at an orderly and complete system of Rabbinic theology is an impossible task.' Instead they aim at 'letting Judaism speak for itself in its own way,' to use Moore's words, and therefore, for the most part, merely offer collected data on rabbinic concepts or attitudes in the form of centos of rabbinic passages on these themes drawn from various sources. The very fact however that disparate passages drawn from rabbinic sources that were composed at different periods

> and under divergent circumstances can yet be brought together so as to elucidate a rabbinic concept — that fact is proof positive that rabbinic theology possessed some kind of unity, some sort of coherence.[12]

There we have it: what is the logic of this logical system? How is it systemic at all? Not only so, but Kadushin points out, all those who have worked in the Western academic idiom have concurred that we may ask such a question of consensus, logic, order, and coherence. He points out, for instance, that Schechter insisted on the presence of "consensus of opinion," and points to remarkable agreement in doctrine; Bacher in his time stressed that both in method and content (in Kadushin's words) "haggadic literature was already well developed at a very early period and that therefore it is more correct to speak of the enlargement rather than the development of the Haggadah." From this, Kadushin concluded, "The principle of coherence of rabbinic theology...must have been such as made for unity of thought over great stretches of time and still gave room for differences due to changed circumstances and to the divergent proclivities of individuals."[13] And that ends up with his organismic thinking, in which we cannot define anything, but know what everything means.

While among philosophically engaged colleagues, Kadushin quite justifiably retains more than antiquarian interest, for the study of religion, his *ouevre* marks only an experiment that failed. He asked the right question; his criticism of his predecessors hit the mark. But in asking questions of coherence and logic, he denied that these questions could be answered; that is, I think, because he did not know how to answer them. He tried to cover everything all at once, even while correctly working through specific documents in concrete ways; it was, then, a failure of nerve. He wanted too much too soon, and he did not do the detailed work that would have yielded results commensurate to the inquiry: what holds the whole together is a question he never in the end answered at all, and the answers that he did give underlined his own failure.

And yet — and yet, for the sheer wit and intelligence, the effort, and the courage and the nobility of the enterprise as he undertook to realize it, Kadushin stands pretty much all by himself. He is the only scholar who has forthrightly and articulately asked the theological question of Judaism in the correct, academic mode.[14] He is the only scholar who has undertaken to set forth a well-crafted method. And he is the only scholar who has provided sustained and well-articulated results. I cannot (yet) describe "the rabbinic mind," but, like Kadushin, I am confident that unless and until we can make sense of that mind (I should prefer the word "theology"), we shall have attained only a very partial, and not a very persuasive or compelling, description of Judaism. But Kadushin has carried us far beyond the elementary stages in the enterprise.

I express thanks to Dr. Charles Kadushin, Brandeis University, for supplying copies of his late father's works for reprinting in this Classics series.

Notes

[1] *Organic Thinking,* pp. v-vi.
[2] *Worship and Ethics,* p. vii.
[3] *Rabbinic Mind,* p. 1.
[4] *Ibid,* p. 2.
[5] *Ibid,* p. 8.
[6] *Ibid,* p. 9.
[7] *Ibid,* p. 18.
[8] *Ibid,* p. 22.
[9] *Ibid,* p. 23.
[10] *Ibid,* p. 24f.
[11] *Ibid*, p. 30.
[12] *Organic Thinking,* p. 2.

[13] *Ibid*, pp. 2-3.

[14] Theologians who have offered normative statements of course are not subject to judgment here. True, I cannot point to theologies of Judaism that have exhibited profound grasp and appreciation of the rabbinic corpus, which commonly serves only to supply undifferentiated proof-texts for propositions formulated not within the dual Torah but within other realms of thought and discourse entirely; to the discourse of theology of Judaism, therefore, the canonical books, while authoritative and critical, prove peripheral and ancillary. The sole exception in any language is Abraham J. Heschel, but his *Torah min hashshamayim*, on the theology of revelation of the sages, Ishmael and Aqiba, the one immanental, the other transcendental (and for Heschel these words bear rather particular and possibly idiosyncratic meanings) cast in merely descriptive language what is, in fact, a prescriptive and normative theory of revelation in the Judaism of the dual Torah; he mixed academic scholarship with theology, and whether the result was theology, as I should claim, certainly it was not scholarship. But beyond Heschel, the theological scene proves barren indeed to those who take their sight by the fixed star of the dual Torah. And, it goes without saying, when the theologizing of avatars of "the tradition," that is, people educated in the Yeshiva-world, gets translated into English, we are presented with either confused meanderings (J. B. Soloveichik's *Halakhic Man* is the outstanding example) of a pseudo-philosophical order or sheer platitude and banality (the cult figure, Adin Steinsaltz, provides the best instance among a great many).

Max Kadushin's "System"

Charles Kadushin

In his sympathetic "Introduction: The Inquiry of Max Kadushin," Jacob Neusner praises Kadushin's quest for a coherent, descriptive theology of Rabbinic Judaism or what Neusner terms Judaism of the Dual Torah. Nonetheless, this important search for a theological systemic account in the end failed, Neusner feels, because the keys to Kadushin's system, "value concepts," cannot be defined and so he "ends up with his organismic thinking, in which we cannot define anything but know what everything means." (p. xvi).

Theology, a term Neusner correctly notes Kadushin "did not like at all," indeed implies an orderly intellectualized coherence marked, as are all philosophic ideas, by neatly defined concepts tied together with a logical nexus. But the construction of this sort of theology was not what Kadushin thought appropriate to the interpretation of Rabbinic texts. Rather, the aim was to describe a culture and impute a psychological sense or experience to various aspects of that culture as exemplified in particular situations each of which was a "concretization" of one or more values concepts. The situations, however, were not "alive" in the sense that a participant observer can perceive the interplay between culture, social structure and personality in an action or situation that unfolds in real time. Instead, the situations were literary. They were described in Midrashic texts, and in the mandated practices of Halachah. For the purpose of illustrating the interplay between cultural symbols and presumed individual psychological reactions, Midrash was privileged over Halachah since the former allowed for more free floating cultural symbolism. Halachah, constrained as all legal systems to at least the appearance of logical consistency, afforded less opportunity to explore the cultural imagination of the Rabbinic period.

Mandated and prescribed prayers ("worship"), on the other hand, were very fruitful grounds for understanding the psychology of long dead individuals, since the interplay between the various value concepts could be investigated in contemporary situations. The system of prayers and worship is of course daily recreated in Jewish life. The interpretation of their significance and meaning has become a minor industry sparked by the Hassidic revolution, though Kadushin explicitly rejected the mysticism of Hasidism in favor of the somewhat more prosaic "normal mysticism" of Rabbinic practice.

The quest for universal coherence, not necessarily the quest for meaning, is held by some post-modern theorists to be an unattainable goal. For social scientists, it suffices to account for the meaning of specific experiences or more generally, to aggregate such accounts into what Merton called "theories of the middle range." All encompassing theories of cultural integration, or total functional explanations of society, or mono-stranded psychological interpretation have not been acceptable in social science for a number of years, though when Kadushin began his quest these kinds of theories were much the fashion. Indeed, he was ridiculed by some for not having a set of overall explanatory principles of Jewish life. He also adopted social science theories that were not yet in vogue. For example, he espoused gestalt psychology when Watson behaviorism was king, because the ideas of gestalt were helpful in organic thinking. The coherence that he did find was always in delimited specific situations that nonetheless drew upon or at least derived sustenance from the patterns of the entire culture. This is what he meant by "organic." The value concepts' lack of pure semantic definition allowed for their application to a variety of situations and their ability to be invoked, often implicitly, in various combinations.

The Kadushin enterprise then was, as he insisted, not the creation of a new theology or even an explication of an old one. Rather, the aim was to create "thick text" anthropological and psychological accounts of phenomena some of which were two thousand years old. Kadushin's models were always social science, not philosophy. He analyzed and described but not, as theology would have it, prescribed.

This was both his strength and his limitation. Culture, but especially religion – to the extent that the Rabbinic cultural system fits the rubric of religion – is prescriptive in its very essence. But no social science account can be prescriptive or it loses much of its validity. On the other hand, theology and "religion" seek prescription, and Kadushin offered none. This is the real source of the difficulty of his oeuvre and a reason it perhaps did not attain the recognition Kadushin hoped it would. Social scientists were and remain largely secular and not interested in close textual analysis of Jewish sources. The "natural" audience for his work, committed Jews, were looking for prescriptions, but none were offered, at least not in his formal writing.

As I said above, the social science enterprise consists of analyzing the interplay between cultural symbols, social structure, and individual psychology. Here Kadushin was at a great disadvantage. By and large, good evidence of the social structural situation of the Rabbinic Period (which Neusner, by the way, denies was a coherent culture over time) was largely absent from the texts he analyzed. True, the Rabbis were neither a priestly caste nor an occupational stratum and this allowed Kadushin to maintain that the value concepts and the Midrash (if not the Talmud) were non-elitist and emanations of the "folk" rather than dicta or arguments supplied by philosophers. Perhaps. But the evidence for this "democratic" tie between the people and the ideas of the Rabbinic period was mostly speculative, for little documentary illustration in the texts elucidate such ties.

Since the situation of contemporary Jewry is of course one in which various social systems vie for legitimacy in representing Jewish ideas, Kadushin is perforce silent on the validity of these claims since his analysis by and large lacks a social structural base. In conversation, he judged these claims by their degree of "authenticity" in conforming to the flexible structure of Rabbinic thinking which in practice meant the invocation of Rabbinic value concepts as applied to contemporary situations. "Pilpul" and Kaplan style "reinterpretation" were both rejected. But he was reluctant to extract structural precepts from his cultural database. He had no "theology" in the conventional sense. All he could do was explicate the past and illustrate the psychology of worship and prayer as suggested by Rabbinic prescription.

The one realm of creative novelty that he felt might emerge in contemporary Jewish life would result from the interplay between the people on the Land of Israel and the new social structural realities of that experience. He had in mind the vitality of the kibbutz movement as he experienced it in the Yishuv in 1930 and during the early years of the State of Israel. What he might have said about the current reactionary cultural and social systems of the Israeli Haredim is anyone's guess. My own view is that he would be less than thrilled.

Preface

In this study of Seder Eliahu, I have endeavored to describe the various rabbinic ideas the book contains, and, in addition, the principle of coherence uniting these ideas. The attempt to discover a coherent unity in rabbinic theology is, I am well aware, a hazardous undertaking. But hazardous as it may be, we ought not to reconcile ourselves to accepting rabbinic theology as a congeries of ideas unrelated to each other, an inarticulated mass of separate concepts.

With the warnings of Schechter and Moore to deter me, I nevertheless attempted for a time to cast the rabbinic concepts in the Seder into some sort of logical order. All this work was, of course, fruitless. At the last, however, a careful analysis yielded the conviction that this Midrash does possess coherence, but of an entirely different kind from that produced by logical, systematic thought. I have called the type of thinking which, it seems to me, characterizes rabbinic theology "organic thinking" or "harmonious thinking." In the light of the organic coherence of rabbinic theology, the individual concepts reveal a structure otherwise not to be discerned.

I wish to acknowledge with deep gratitude my debt to two of my teachers, Professor Louis Ginzberg and Professor Mordecai M. Kaplan of the Jewish Theological Seminary of America. I availed myself of Professor Ginzberg's works, particularly of the Notes to the *Legends of the Jews* and of the *Legends* themselves, indispensable as these books are to the student of rabbinic theology. I was placed still more in his debt when he annotated my manuscript with numerous helpful notes on the text and with other valuable suggestions. These I have largely incorporated in the book and marked with his initials. Of course, the responsibility for the book as a whole must rest with me.

Those who are familiar with the philosophy of Professor Kaplan may find a point of contact between his conception of "Judaism as a Civilization" and my description of rabbinic Theology of Seder Eliahu as "organic thinking." Without committing him to the point of view taken here, I should like to think of it as in line with his general philosophy.

I wish also to thank Miss Tilly Shub and Miss Alice Seltzer for their technical assistance.

In the transliteration of Hebrew words I followed the usage of the Jewish Encyclopedia. The one exception is in the name of the Midrash itself, "Seder Eliahu," where I followed the precedent set by the editor of the critical edition, M. Friedmann.

Max Kadushin
Madison, August, 1932

Contents

TO THE MEMORY OF MY FATHER

ר' שלמה פינחס ב"ר גדליהו קדושין ז"ל

THEOLOGY OF SEDER ELIAHU

CHAPTER I

INTRODUCTORY—ON THE TEXT

I

Editions

THE edition I have used is that of M. Friedmann's *Seder Eliahu Rabba and Seder Eliahu Zuta* (Wien, 1902) and *Pseudo-Seder Eliahu Zuta* (Wien, 1904).[1] This is the only critical edition of our text, and it is accompanied by a very long introduction in which the editor endeavors to solve the problems of authorship, date and land of origin of the Seder Eliahu. He also devotes a chapter to the ideas and theology contained in the book.

The editio princeps was printed in Venice in 1598, under the title תנא דבי אליהו. Its editor, who claims at the end of the book that he was pressed for time, merely printed a MS. of the year 1186, without attempting to restore parts of the text which were sadly mutilated. Although the columns in his MS. were headed by the rubric—סדר אליהו רבא; סדר אליהו זוטא—, (if we can judge by the printed edition), his title page bears the caption תנא דבי אליהו; and this title has to some degree led certain later critics to deny that the book is the original סדר אליהו.

Samuel ben Moses Haida published another edition in Prague in 1677. Haida was a mystic who conceived it as his duty to restore the original text of סדר אליהו. Through fasting, prayer and contemplation, as he states, he received the inspiration, including visits from the prophet Elijah, which enabled him to penetrate into the inner meaning of the book and to correct the editio princeps. The result is a queer version which he calls

[1] Published by "Achiassaf," Warsaw, and bound in one volume.

זקוקין דנורא, and a commentary of his own named בעורין דאושא. He nevertheless kept the Venice edition which he entitled "the old version" distinct from his, "the new version." Several commentators, however, who followed him, confused the texts hopelessly, and their books were current as תנא דבי אליהו. Finally, there appeared the Warsaw edition of 1880 which again gave both texts, the original Venice edition and the זקוקין דנורא side by side.

Friedmann based his new edition on a Vatican MS. of the year 1073, except for the last ten chapters of סדר אליהו זוטא. Where the MS. has proved inadequate, he has used the Venice edition, and, in a few instances, the parallel passages in the Yalḳuṭ Shime'oni. His vast knowledge of rabbinic literature he employed in clarifying obscure statements, in filling up lacunae and in correcting other textual errors. The corrections, except for those supplied by the Venice edition, he has not included in the text, but has placed in his excellent critical commentary.

The last ten chapters of Seder Eliahu Zuta he has called "Pseudo-Seder Eliahu Zuta," for reasons which will appear below. These he edited on the basis of the editio princeps and a Parma MS.

In this work I have relied generally on the text as presented by Friedmann.[2] When the Seder Eliahu is referred to by page,

[2] (a) I took the liberty of correcting the text in several passages: on page 137, this is the text as given: יש בו באדם דברי תורה ויסורין באין עליו. לבו מתמרמר עליו. כאיזה צד יעשה. יצדיק עליו את הדין. היה רעב יאמר: כך וכך כתוב בתורה ברעב. היה צמא יאמר: כך וכך כתוב בתורה בצמא היה עומד ערום יאמר: כך וכך כתוב בתורה בערום. אין לו מזונות שיאכל יאמר: כך וכך כתוב בתורה בחוסר כל (דברים כ"ח מ"ח) [השונא] חי וקיים על פני האדמה יאמר הכתוב עד האבידו אותך (שם נ"א) חי וקיים בעולם. ברוך המקום שנתן לי חיים בעולם. I think the difficulties are evident, and that Friedmann by adding השונא doesn't help much. It seems to me that the text should read: ... כך וכך כתוב בתורה בערום: ועבדת את אויביך ... ברעב ובצמא ... ובחוסר כל ... עד השמידו אותך. (דבר' כ"ח מ"ח)

In Zuta, page 3 ("Additions") the same verse is used, in similar fashion, as a whole. Here אין לו מזונות שיאכל is probably a gloss that crept into the text, and חי וקים על פני האדמה is a dittography.

(b) On page 18, this is the text as given: כתר יפה שמונח להם ולבניהם ולבני בניהם בשביל תורה שעשו הרי הוא מונח לעולם הבא לך ... ושמא תאמר הואיל ונכנס משה לבית עולמו שמא בטל ממנו מאור פניו וכו'. The passage refers to the light of countenance (halo) which Moses, according to the Bible, was given upon descendit is always to his edition. Professor Ginzberg has suggested a number of textual corrections which I have gladly adopted and incorporated in the passages as they are cited in this book.

II

Some Critical Opinions

Friedmann has reviewed the various opinions of the critics who preceded him regarding the date, authorship and land of origin of this book. He discusses and refutes the conclusions of Rapoport, Zunz, Bacher and Oppenheim, and Yawetz. We need only to summarize the views of these authorities, however, to recognize how widely they differ, and how difficult the solution of these problems will prove to be.

(A) Rapoport believes that our text is not the original סדר אליהו, and that its proper name is the one found on the title-page of the editio princeps: תנא דבי אליהו. In the Babylonian Talmud (Ket. 106a) R. 'Anan (c. 280 C. E.) is spoken of as the scholar to whom the prophet Elijah taught "what is called סדר אליהו רבא סדר אליהו זוטא." The 'Aruk[3] knows of this סדר אליהו רבא and describes it as having three large divisions and thirty chapters, also telling us that סדר אליהו זוטא contains twelve chapters. Now our text has no large divisions at all, and the רבא contains thirty-one chapters while the זוטא has twenty-five. Rapoport therefore concludes that our text is a much later work than the original סדר אליהו which the Talmud mentions and which the 'Aruk still knew, and that it was written in Babylon.

ing from Mt. Sinai. It seems to me obvious that the text should read כתר יפה שמונח להם ולבניהם ולבני בניהם לעולם הבא הרי הוא לך.

(c) On page 188, the text is given: והיה מכריז ואומר כל מי שהוא רוצה לעלות לירושלים יבוא ויעלה; I have added the phrase from the Yalḳuṭ, to which Friedmann refers in note 13, but does not quote: ולא אמר הכל יעלו לירושלים.

(d) On page 23 of "Additions," I have accepted Professor Ginzberg's suggestion regarding בפלטרי. The text should read, as he says, בפדרסטי. (Genizah Studies, Vol. I, page 235).

(e) Other textual corrections will be found below in the course of the discussions.

[3] A talmudic dictionary written in the twelfth century by Nathan ben Yeḥiel of Rome.

Rapoport bases his conclusions also on internal evidence. There are some quotations in the Talmud designated as from תנא דבי אליהו that are not found in our text; hence, he says, our text is not the סדר אליהו referred to in the Talmud. The most decisive proof of the book's late origin are the actual dates contained in the book itself: "The entire existence of this world is to be 6,000 years—2,000 years of chaos, 2,000 years of Torah, 2,000 years of the period of the Messiah. Because our sins have multiplied, a period of servitude has encroached upon the period of the Messiah *and has lessened it by more than 700 years*."[4] Now the last 2,000 years (the period of the Messiah) begin with the year 242 C. E., or 172 years after the Destruction. It is apparent, therefore, that our author lived in the middle of the tenth century. In Chapter VI, we are told that the world has existed for 94 Jubilees and 44 years, that is 4744. The date again practically coincides with the first quotation, especially if we regard the 44 extra years as referred to by the phrase "*more* than 700 years." Finally, there occurs this statement: ". . . and from the building of the last Temple until it was destroyed is 420 years; and from its destruction until the present is 900 years."[5] If we recall that the fourth millenium closes 172 years after the Destruction, the date mentioned here is 4728. The difference of 16 years between this and the date mentioned in Chapter VI (4744) need not disturb us, for it is apparent that the author in the last quotation speaks in round numbers. We may be quite certain, therefore, that the book was written after the middle of the tenth century, either in 968 or else in 984, about the time of Sherira Gaon.

Friedmann regards all the evidence that Rapoport adduces as not conclusive. Our text is the original Seder Eliahu, he declares. The dates, he says, are not authentic, having been put in by a later copyist, and that they thus refer merely to the last redaction of our text. He attempts to restore the three large divisions the text had originally, to renumber the chapters, and finally to excise the last ten chapters from the Zuta in order

[4] S. E. R. page 6 (Chapter II).
[5] S. E. R. page 163 (Chapter XXXI).

to make our work coincide with the description of the 'Aruk. He denies that it was written in Babylon, as we shall see, and puts forward the theory that there were many Baraitot current in talmudic times which were designated by the rubric תנא דבי אליהו, and that our Seder Eliahu is but one collection of these Baraitot. For this reason some of the passages in the Talmud that we might expect to find in our text are not included in it.

Zunz agrees in the main with the views of Rapoport, merely adding that the author says that he lived in Babylon. The faulty text which Zunz used misled him, for, on the contrary, as Friedmann points out, the author distinctly says that he came from Jabne.[6]

(B) Bacher and Oppenheim also take our book to be a product of the gaonic period, and attempt to prove that the author was a rabbinic preacher who engaged in disputes with the Karaites. It is true that he does have frequent arguments with those "who know Bible but not Mishnah,"[7] the latter apparently denying that certain rabbinic laws are rooted in the Bible. But as Friedmann and others contend, this situation and these arguments are not confined to the period of the Karaites. That sectaries arose in very early times who accepted the Bible but denied the validity of rabbinic law we know from the Talmud,[8] as well as from the sectarian writings dating from tannaitic times.[9] Moreover, the phrase "who know Bible but not Mishnah" may not refer to sectaries at all since the Talmud employs the same phrase to denote merely stages of learning.[10] It is used similarly by our author, certainly on some occasions,[11] when he

[6] On pp. 95 and 168.

[7] As on pp. 70–75.

[8] Sanhedrin 99a and 99b. Some sects had halakic compilations, different from the Mishnah, but employing a similar method as Professor Louis Ginzberg has demonstrated in his Eine unbekannte judische Sekte, 1922.

[9] The Testaments of the Twelve Patriarchs, Book of Jubilees, and book of the Hebrew sect at Damascus published by Schechter in Documents of Jewish Sectaries, Vol. I, the Halakah of which has been examined by Professor Ginzberg, op. cit.

[10] Ḳiddushin 40b; also Erubin 54b.

[11] As on page 13.

exhibits an intense love for all classes of Jews among which he specifically mentions "those who know Bible but no Mishnah." It is hardly thinkable that he could have had the Karaites in mind or any other group inimical to rabbinic Judaism.

Friedmann feels that he definitely disposes of all attempts to place the author after the talmudic period and in any land outside of Palestine by referring to the following passage (on page 59): "One . . . should not eat with the *'ame ha-areẓ* at table, and should not be overmuch with them at a meal at any place; for the *'ame ha-areẓ* give little heed to tithes and to the seventh year." Tithes and the seventh year need be observed only in Palestine.

(C) Yawetz takes our author to be a man by the name of Eliahu who lived in Palestine in the sixth or seventh century. He places too much weight, however, on very doubtful historical allusions which he finds in the prayer, "Sovereign of the world! Not because of our righteous acts . . ." etc. (On page 118).

All of the authorities assume that our text was written by a single author. There is a definite style throughout the book, a beautiful, flexible Hebrew with a characteristic phraseology.

III

Friedman's Theory

(A) The "Original" Seder Eliahu.

Friedmann has treated the literary and historical problems of our text so exhaustively as to compel us to consider his theories in some detail. Dividing our text as published in the editio princeps into two parts, he regards only the first, consisting of Seder Eliahu Rabba and the first fifteen chapters of Eliahu Zuta, as being the original Seder Eliahu which is mentioned in the Talmud. The second part, consisting of the last ten chapters of the Zuta he calls "Additions to Seder Eliahu Zuta," or "Pseudo-Eliahu Zuta," and assigns it to a later period, in which respect he follows the example of Zunz and Oppenheim. What follows here is a summary of his conclusions with regard to the "original" Seder Eliahu.

He advances the rather unusual theory that Seder Eliahu is the result of direct religious experience on the part of Rabbi 'Anan and others, in which the prophet Elijah appeared to them and acted as their teacher, exactly as if he were one of the authorities in a tannaitic school. To prove that this phenomenon was not unique, he has collected the passages in the Talmud which describe the occasions when Elijah revealed himself in one guise or another to Rabbis and even to less worthy persons.[12] Seder Eliahu was not, however, dictated to R. 'Anan, Friedmann says, but existed long before him, and was merely edited by the school of which 'Anan was the head. The sources of this book were many Baraitot or collections of Baraitot in which were handed down the revelations of many other and earlier disciples of Elijah. The expression תנא דבי אליהו,[13] therefore, might refer either to those "pious men" who were known to have been taught by Elijah, or else to an actual school in Jerusalem or Jabne, named after Elijah, where these sayings and homilies were studied. It is also possible that תנא דבי אליהו might refer to an individual pupil of that school who taught the particular homily introduced by this phrase. The fact that the book is written in mishnaic Hebrew, and not, as we might expect, in the biblical Hebrew of Elijah's day, Friedmann, with good insight, does not regard as damaging to his theory.

If we accept this theory, we have a definite clue as to the time when our text was written. But there is more tangible evidence. Very frequently the Mishnah is mentioned here as one of the branches of the Torah, but only in one doubtful instance is the Talmud so mentioned.[14] Names of Tannaim are

[12] Friedmann more than implies his own faith in such revelations. Those places in our text where the author speaks in the first person, Friedmann includes in the list of the revelations of Elijah in the guise of a scholar, although, apparently, the group of scholars with whom he conversed did not guess his identity. The only exception is the story on page 97, which Friedmann declares is an interpolation.

[13] Literally, "the house (i. e. school) of Elijah taught."

[14] On pages 29, 69, 91 and numerous other places. On page 68 this statement occurs: קרא אדם תנ"כ בילדותו והזקין ושנה משנה מדרש הלכות ו ת ל מ ו ד ואגדות; תלמוד is probably a gloss, for משנה and הלכות are already mentioned; ("תלמוד" also frequently means "Midrash"); otherwise the formula is the same as the one so often employed in this book.

found in our text, but no mention of an Amora. In Bereshit Rabba, Chapter 54, there is a quotation from Seder Eliahu,[15] which is introduced by the phrase תני אליהו. Bereshit Rabba was written about 540 C. E. and the Talmud was closed about 500 C. E., hence our text was composed before the close of the Talmud and after the close of the Mishnah, Friedmann says, contemporary with the Baraitot of R. Ḥiyya and R. Hosha'ya.

The passage in Ketubot referred to above concludes with "and that is what is called Seder Eliahu Rabba Seder Eliahu Zuta." Is it true, as Rapoport holds, that our text is not the original Seder Eliahu, which the Talmud knows? If it can be proved that the great number of passages common to both Seder Eliahu and the Talmud were at least not taken by the former from the latter, there can be little doubt that we have the Seder Eliahu "given" to R. 'Anan, and not a later compilation made from the תנא דבי אליהו passages of the Talmud. The evidence above, including the quotation from Bereshit Rabba, would seem to indicate that our author (or compiler) did not know of Talmud Babli or Yerushalmi. Friedmann undertakes a comparison of the passages, however, in order to determine more exactly the relation between our text and the Talmud:

All but one or two of the passages in the Talmud introduced by the phrase תנא דבי אליהו are found in our Seder Eliahu, but Friedmann does not think that either borrowed from the other. There are many passages in the Talmud introduced by תנו רבנן, for which we have parallels in Seder Eliahu, but again Friedmann declares neither copied from the other in most cases. Of the large number of Baraitot and quotations from individual Tannaim[16] which have parallels in our text, he regards one as being an earlier version than ours, two as having been influenced by Seder Eliahu, one as having the Sifre and Mekilta as its source, and in one case he thinks our text used Abot d'rab Nathan as its source; a comparison of the rest, he concludes, reveals that neither the Talmud nor Seder Eliahu copied from each other.

[15] The song of the oxen bringing the Ark from the Philistines; in S. E. on page 58.

[16] Among which might be counted two statements by R. 'Anan, both of which are also found in Seder Eliahu.

He believes that both used in common earlier sources, probably those Baraitot current among the pupils of the prophet Elijah. And he points to other parallels to our text in the Talmud given anonymously and with no sign of their being Baraitot, as further proof that Agadot, not based on texts (and thus revealed directly by Elijah) were handed down by this group.[17] The majority of the parallels in Talmud Babli and Yerushalmi to which names of Amoraim are attached he similarly believes to have had this common earlier source.[18] The parallel passages in the later Midrashim, Shemot Rabba, Bamidbar Rabba,[19] Pesiḳta d'rab Kahana, and the later interpolation in Wayyiḳra Rabba, Chapter 33, he states, were taken from Seder Eliahu.

There are many parallels to the prayers in the Talmud and early prayer books. Again Friedmann is certain that, except for a few phrases from the *Tefillah*, our text did not borrow either from earlier or later works. His conclusion is, therefore, that in the main Seder Eliahu is an independent work, that it certainly did not borrow from the Talmuds, that it is the book by that name already known to the Talmud, and that it must have been written before the close of the Talmud and after the composition of the Mishnah.

Further evidence of the antiquity of Seder Eliahu, Friedmann finds in passages that reflect the ideas and conditions of the age in which they were written. Our author has a long discussion with a fire-worshipping Persian priest;[20] Nimrod, the king, avows himself to be a fire-worshipper;[21] Abraham, condemned to be burnt, is surrounded by wood that is placed 500 ells away from him in all directions, a measure of precaution against contaminat-

[17] It is almost unnecessary to add that he again feels that neither the Talmud nor Seder Eliahu copied or took from each other, though in one case he thinks the latter the source of the former.

[18] Several passages in the Talmuds he thinks were taken from Seder Eliahu. In only one instance did our text borrow from the Talmud—on page 95, "When God blessed Israel" . . . etc., and this, of course, he regards as a later interpolation.

[19] In Chapter 4 and Chapter 5. In Chapter 4, the passage is introduced "Eliahu says."

[20] Page 6.

[21] Page 27.

ing fire by a dead body that might be practiced by fire-worshipping Persians.[22] Without doubt these passages indicate that our author lived when the Persian religion of fire-worship was reigning, and hence our text must have been written no later than the sixth century, and may have been written in the third. The question is raised as to why the world has been divided between two kingdoms,[23] another allusion to Persia (and Rome). Marrying the daughter of one's sister is held to be a virtue,[24] for which there is no authority in Jewish tradition, but which was highly regarded among the ancient Persians. Friedmann also calls attention to the names of the fourteen species of lice which God brought upon Egypt;[25] they are partly Aramaic and partly Hebrew, and thus denote that the language of the Jews of that time was Hebrew mixed with Aramaic. Our author tells "the house of David" to judge with righteousness;[26] and so he must have lived at a time when either the Patriarchate or Exilarchate still had power.

The 'Aruk, as has been mentioned above, describes Seder Eliahu Rabba as having three large divisions (בבות) and thirty chapters, and Zuta as having twelve chapters. Friedmann attempts to arrange the text so as to coincide with this description. He reconstructs the divisions (that are missing in our text) on the basis of logical coherence and continuity of biblical texts, and therefore regards the sections from pages 88–118 and pages 147–156 as later interpolations. On the basis of his MS. he corrects the numbering of the chapters, and claims that in Eliahu Rabba, Chapters 5 and 6 were originally one chapter. Thus the Rabba is made to agree with the 'Aruk's description. He does not succeed quite so well with the Zuta. Claiming that collections were later made from Seder Eliahu, he says we have one such before us in Chapter 15 of Zuta[27] (which he believes is the last in the Seder proper) and that Chapter 1 of Zuta was also added

[22] Page 27.
[23] Page 113.
[24] Page 78.
[25] Page 41.
[26] Page 53.
[27] It is introduced by אמר אבא אליהו.

later.[28] Nevertheless, this would still give the Zuta thirteen chapters, whereas the 'Aruk says it contains twelve.

Of course, all the statements wherein dates are definitely mentioned, Friedmann also insists are later interpolations by a copyist. The book, according to him, was written a short time after the Mishnah was completed, but additions crept in until it was finally redacted in the tenth century.

(B) The Last Ten Chapters of Zuta (Chapters 16–25).

Friedmann, following others, does not regard this section as belonging to Seder Eliahu proper, but as having been appended to it in the course of time. The 'Aruk speaks of only twelve chapters; moreover, internal evidence shows this section to have been written in Babylon and at a later period than the "original" Seder Eliahu; finally, his Vatican MS. ends with Chapter 15, another indication that Chapters 16–25 were added later.

He divides the section further into two parts: Chapters 16–18 he calls פרקי דרך ארץ, and Chapters 19–25 פרקי דר' אליעזר, and he sees no inherent relationship between the two parts. For the second part he uses a Parma MS. which begins with Chapter 19, and after Chapter 25, continues with material found in Chapters 30, 31, 40, and 41 of P. R. E. Friedmann, therefore, concludes that the whole MS. is a collection of passages dealing with statements of Rabbi Eliezer, since that is also the characteristic of Chapters 19–25. The MS., nevertheless, does call these seven chapters "Seder Eliahu Zuta." Eliezer Roḳeaḥ, in quoting a statement from Chapter 22,[29] prefaces it by "and we read in Pirke R. Eliezer"; the Yalḳuṭ Shime'oni which contains many quotations from these seven chapters, marks two of them[30] as being from Pirke R. Eliezer; these instances, Friedmann believes, are additional proofs that these chapters were once independent of our text. There remain, therefore, Chapters 16–18 to be considered. After a very long discourse on the tractates Kallah and Derek Ereẓ, he claims that these three chapters

[28] It is introduced by משום דבי אליהו הנביא.

[29] See note 17 on p. 38 of "Additions."

[30] See "Additions," p. 27, note 18; and on p. 46, note 15.

are similar to them in content and thus have earned the name פרקי דרך ארץ.

Evidence that the last ten chapters were indeed written at a late period is not lacking:

In Chapter 19[31] there occurs the statement, "But our masters in the land of Israel," which indicates that the author was not in the land of Israel. In Chapter 21[32] it is told that all the nations (except Israel) will be compelled to cross the bridge over Gehenna; this figure, Friedmann states, is to be found only in Zoroastrianism, and thus the book may have been written in Persia or Babylon. There are also almost direct references to the Arabic empire. In Chapter 20,[33] Abraham declines to make the blessing over the wine at the great feast of the righteous, even though asked to do so by God, because, he says, there went forth from him seed that provoked God. This must refer to Ishmael who is quite innocent in biblical and rabbinic accounts, but, who, when standing for the Arabs after Mohammed, is an enemy of Israel. In Chapter 21, it is foretold that darkness is in store for the sons of Esau and the sons of Ishmael; the two great world-empires, Rome and Islam, which oppressed Israel are thus given in their historical order.[34]

[31] "Additions," p. 28.

[32] Ibid, p. 34.

[33] Ibid, p. 32.

[34] Mann, Changes in the Divine Service, Hebrew Union College Annual, Vol. IV, pp. 302–310 and pp. 250–1, declares that S. E. was written in Babylon in the second half of the fifth century. He brings forward all the internal evidence in S. E. R. presented above; and in addition the prayer used by Yawetz (above, p. 6), to prove that the *Shem'a* was prohibited in public prayer when the magi persecuted the Jews. But Mann also takes it for granted that the last ten chapters of the Zuta are not to be accepted as part of Seder Eliahu. For that reason he takes no cognizance of the evidence that these chapters contain. Moreover, he ignores the patent reference brought forward by Friedmann and given here above on p. 6, which is found in the "original" S. E. (He explains away the reference to Jabne and Jerusalem). The real contradictions offered by the historical background of our text cannot be so easily dismissed. See note 152 on p. 147 below, where the prayer in question is discussed, and also Professor Ginzberg's remark there.

IV

Ginzberg's Theory

We are at liberty to accept or reject Friedmann's theory that our text was inspired by the prophet Elijah, according to our convictions on these matters. Unfortunately, however, Friedmann erects his whole critical structure on this so dubious a foundation. He starts with the assumption that Seder Eliahu was written by "pupils" of Elijah a little after the close of the Mishnah. Since the dates in the book contradict this he dismisses them all too easily as interpolations. He offers absolutely no proof of his contention that the parallels to our text in the Talmud are not borrowed from the latter, or for the hypothetical existence of earlier Baraitot which he claims were the original source. In attempting to adjust the text to the description of the 'Aruk, he throws out large sections similar in style and content to the rest of the book. He proves that the last seven chapters were written at a later period; and he deduces from that, since he is convinced that Seder Eliahu came from the post-mishnaic period, that they do not belong to the book. His own MS. plainly indicates that these chapters belong to Eliahu Zuta; the Yalḳuṭ also marks all but two passages as from S. E., and the citation in the case of those two, as well as the one by Roḳeaḥ, may well refer to a smaller section of the S. E. known as "P. R. E."[35] He excludes the so-called פרקי דרך ארץ from the book simply to shorten the Zuta in order to fit the statement in the 'Aruk.

Yet the book, if taken as a unit, does present this contradiction: Some parts of it seem, on the basis of evidence reviewed above, to have been written before and some parts after the close of the Talmud, some passages refer to an author in Palestine and other passages certainly imply a land outside of Palestine. If we accept our present text as the authentic S. E. the puzzling

[35] It is also possible that since these seven chapters all contain homilies of R. Eliezer that they were sometimes included in collections from the authentic P. R. E., and that Roḳeaḥ and the Yalḳuṭ possessed such MSS. The Parma MS. used by Friedmann seems to be a collection of this kind—see a description of it on page 11.

question as to the nature of the text known by the 'Aruk still remains.

New light is shed on the composition of our book by Professor Ginzberg in the short introduction to Sections 22 and 23 (Chapters on Repentance and Gehenna) of his Genizah Studies, Vol. I.[36] In Section 22 occur the following rubrics: סליק פרקא . . . זה סליק;[38] סליק פרקא והסדר מן אליה רבה תלמוד גדול;[37] הסדר מן תלמוד רבא פרקא . . . [ ]ל הקטן.[39] These rubrics can only mean that they either close or begin quotations from the "Talmud" of Seder Eliahu, the first two from the "Talmud" on Rabba, the third possibly from the one on Zuta. Seder Eliahu, Professor Ginzberg states, once contained a Mishnah, or rather Baraita, which was composed early and a Talmud which was added later, certainly after the Talmud Babli.[40] Our text, however, no longer has the Baraita and the Talmud separate, but offers a confused mixture of both.

The fact that the material either following or preceding the rubrics is not found in our Seder Eliahu does not weaken this theory, Professor Ginzberg holds. He states that Seder Eliahu was once much larger than the text we have received, and cites as proof a longer parallel to our text found in Section 22.[41] Further corroboration is found in Section 29,[42] which is a collection from Seder Eliahu, and where he discovers two long passages of the original "Talmud," now missing from our own version. In the

[36] Genizah Studies in Memory of Doctor Solomon Shechter, Vol. I (Midrash and Haggadah) by Louis Ginzberg, Jewish Theological Seminary of America, New York, 1928 (Hebrew), pp. 188–191.

[37] Folio 3b, line 10.

[38] Folio 5a, rubric.

[39] Folio 2b, line 7; Professor Ginzberg, in the text, supplies the missing letters so that the words are שמואל הקטן; in the introduction he suggests that it may have read אליה קטן. Friedmann tells us that he received this fragment from Schechter but that he felt the ancient copyist had added these rubrics so that the collection might thus be more highly prized. We see once more how Friedmann was misled by his theory. Incidentally, he states that the rubrics in his MS. read מאליה קטן. (Introd. p. 88).

[40] Professor Ginzberg reminds us of the similar Baraita and Talmud in the tractate Kallah.

[41] Folio 1b, line 12; Seder Eliahu, page 105, agadah on Isaiah 44:5.

[42] Opus, cit. See introduction to this section, pages 235–238.

same collection there is a haggadah, telling of how R. 'Aḳiba rescued a man from the punishment of Gehenna. In all the other places where this haggadah is found the name of the Rabbi is, as here, 'Aḳiba, except in the parallel passage in Eliahu Zuta, Chapter 17,[43] where the story refers to R. Joḥanan ben Zakkai. Now in Section 22,[44] Rabbi Joḥanan is also the authority for another haggadah on Gehenna, from which Professor Ginzberg deduces that the "Talmud" of Eliahu Zuta may originally have had a number of haggadot on Gehenna with R. Joḥanan as the authority. This is the more likely, since, as he states, the last ten chapters of Zuta[45] appear to be a section of the original "Talmud" dealing with Redemption, Paradise and Gehenna.

"The problem of this Midrash can therefore not be solved so long as we have not succeeded in separating the earlier material from the later, the text from the commentary."[46] Nevertheless, several important matters have been established: Seder Eliahu once contained a Baraita, composed at an early period shortly after the close of the Mishnah and a commentary, "Talmud" that was written much later;[47] the final redaction took place in the tenth century, if the dates in the text are not interpolations. We should not be surprised, therefore, if some passages reveal an earlier and some a later origin. There is no need, also, to posit a common source from which both the Talmud and Seder Eliahu drew haggadot, since it may well be that the Talmud borrowed from the Baraita of our Seder, and the Seder

[43] "Additions" page 22.

[44] Folio 3b, line 13.

[45] Those which Friedmann has called "Additions."

[46] Opus cit., Introduction (English) page xv. Professor Ginzberg (page 190) has given us another instance of the "commentary" to Rabba, the passage dealing with "Israel is the Lord's vineyard" on page 43 of our text. It seems to me that we have frequent proofs of his theory in those passages which give terse mishnah-like haggadot which are then amplified by lengthy commentary. These are often broken up by other perhaps misplaced passages. Example: on page 128: במה קונה אדם את אביו שבשמים ... קונהו מתוך אהבה מתוך אחוה ... מתוך השלום; page 139: מתוך האהבה כיצד ...; p. 143: מתוך הרחמים כיצד ...; p. 156: מתוך השלום וכו'.

[47] On page 190, opus cit. Professor Ginzberg states that S. E. made use of the Talmud Babli, and gives evidence of such use.

later borrowed homilies from the Talmud. Finally, it is impossible to dismiss whole sections, including the last ten chapters of Zuta as not belonging to Seder Eliahu. Our text not only confuses Baraita with "Talmud," but is very much shorter than the original Seder, so that on the basis of textual criticism it is no longer possible to establish the old textual coherence. The "Additions" are no additions at all, but, as Professor Ginzberg has suggested, probably a section from the original "Talmud" on Zuta.

In the light of the facts supplied by Professor Ginzberg, we can understand more clearly the description of Seder Eliahu contained in the 'Aruk (v. סדר): "Seder Eliahu Rabba and Seder Eliahu Zuta—they are outside Mishnayot (i. e., Baraitot, Mishnayot not included in the Mishnah edited by Rabbi). And the Rabba contains three 'gates' (בבי), and thirty chapters; and the Zuta twelve chapters." The original, uncorrupted text of Seder Eliahu, to which no doubt the 'Aruk refers, was easily seen to be based on Baraitot, and the mention of "gates" indicates that the text was very much larger than it is now, large enough really to merit the name of "Seder," order. For that reason, any attempt to square our chapters with the number mentioned in the 'Aruk is fruitless.

CHAPTER II

RABBINIC THEOLOGY: ORGANIC THINKING

I

Rabbinic Theology

Those who attempt to find some organizing principle in rabbinic theology, to discover the mold into which it has been cast, are well-nigh baffled by the problem. Rabbinic theology certainly presents no nicely elaborated system of religious creeds, built up by logic, ordered, and definitely arranged. Such a system may, conceivably, be imposed upon rabbinic theology; if so, the violence done to rabbinic thought—wholly gratuitous points of emphasis, wholesale lifting of statements without their contexts, and the elision of rabbinic opinion contrary to the thesis —can be laid to the door of one who has a special plea to make. Weber, for instance, in whose *System der Altsynagogalen Palastinenischen Theologie* these faults are found in abundance, undertakes to prove the dominance of legalism in rabbinic theology.[1] Careful students of rabbinic theology, therefore, take occasion to deny that it can be reduced to anything resembling a system. "It will, therefore, suggest itself," says Schechter, "that any attempt at an orderly and complete system of Rabbinic theology is an impossible task."[2]

The only other alternative, if we would judge from the foremost works on rabbinic theology, is to offer collected data on rabbinic concepts, doctrines or attitudes in the form of centos of rabbinic passages on these themes. Illuminating these passages here and there with penetrating and helpful interpretations, modern authorities have nevertheless been content to let the

[1] Weber, System der Altsynagogalen Palastinenischen Theologie, (Leipzig, 1880).

[2] S. Schechter, Some Aspects of Rabbinic Theology (New York, 1910), p. 16.

Rabbis "have their own say in their own words and even their own phraseology." This remark by Schechter[3] explains his general treatment of rabbinic concepts no less than his way of phrasing them. He organizes his material so that the very headings are, for the most part, the concepts by means of which the Rabbis thought: "The Kingdom of God," "The Law," "The Joy of the Law," "The Zachuth of the Fathers," "The Evil Yezer," "Repentance." Since he ranged over the whole field of rabbinic theology but culled only such statements as fitted his plan, he insisted that his work be regarded as only "Some Aspects of Rabbinic Theology," a view which is justified by the limited number of concepts chosen as well as by the necessarily limited number of statements considered.

Moore's monumental work is devoted to a representation of the institutions and theology of Judaism in the age of the Tannaim.[4] At first sight, Moore seems to have gone beyond Schechter in drawing forth from rabbinic theology organizing principles integrating otherwise amorphous material. Thus he lays down "the fundamental principle of Judaism and some of the ways in which it was applied."[5] The fundamental principle consists in "the twofold character of nationality and universality which had been inseparably impressed upon it by its history;"[6] and the ways in which it was applied are to be discerned, apparently, in the interpretation of Scriptures, in the unwritten Law, in the Synagogue and Schools and in the attitude toward Gentiles.[7] He treats further of the Idea of God; the Nature of Man, and his relation to God; the Observances of Religion; Morals; Piety; and the Hereafter. Manifestly, the idea of God, the nature of man, observances, piety, etc. are categories which we of the present think in and as such they are useful in helping us collate and classify the ideas and attitudes of the Rabbis. But they are not the characteristic categories in which the

[3] Ibid, Preface, p. viii.

[4] G. F. Moore, Judaism in the First Centuries of the Christian Era (3 Vols., Cambridge 1927).

[5] Ibid, Preface, p. viii.

[6] Ibid, Vol. I, p. 219.

[7] Ibid, pp. 219–353.

Rabbis themselves thought, as Moore himself would probably have been the first to grant. Nay, it is extremely doubtful if "the fundamental principle" itself would have been recognized as such by the Rabbis under the highly modern guise of "nationality and universality." The point made here is not that the material is falsely classified nor is it that the interpretation is wrong but only that the organizing principles are not, in the terms they are stated, basic to rabbinic thinking. Indeed, it is very probable that Moore did not intend them to be more than convenient classifications for us. He, like Schechter, declares: "I have avoided imposing on the matter a systematic disposition which is foreign to it and to the Jewish thought of the times;"[8] and, again like Schechter, he states his intention to have been that of "letting Judaism speak for itself in its own way."[9] If we disregard the nomenclature of his larger divisions, he, as well as Schechter, achieved his object by arranging centos of rabbinic passages illustrative of rabbinic concepts.

Kohler's *Jewish Theology* is not confined to the rabbinic period, attempting to lead from rabbinic theology through medieval thought to a Jewish theology adjusted to suit our day.[10] It is not, therefore, germane to our study which limits itself to rabbinic theology. In passing, however, it may be stated, that here, too, no organizing principle is drawn from the materials of rabbinic theology proper.

From the works on rabbinic theology it does not appear that any principle of coherence can be discovered in rabbinic thinking. Baldly put, this inference is neither likely nor attractive; yet what else are we to conclude from presentations of rabbinic concepts among which there is no necessary relation? But this conclusion is negated by some pertinent considerations. For one thing, students of rabbinic theology have been impressed by the remarkable agreement in theologic view, not alone among Rabbis of the same generation, but even between Palestinian teachers of the first and second centuries and Babylonian authorities of the fifth and tenth. It is Schechter whose unusual insight

[8] Schechter, opus cit., Preface, p. viii.

[9] Ibid.

[10] K. Kohler, Jewish Theology, (New York, 1918).

enables him to penetrate to this basic unity: "It should be noted that Rabbinic literature is, as far as doctrine and dogma are concerned, more distinguished by the consensus of opinion than by its dissensions. On the whole, it may be safely maintained that there is little in the dogmatic teachings of the Palestinian authorities of the first and second centuries to which, for instance, R. Ashi of the fifth and even R. Sherira of the tenth century, both leaders of Rabbinic opinion in Babylon, would have refused their consent, though the emphasis put on the one or the other doctrine may have differed widely as a result of changed conditions and surroundings. On the other hand, a careful study of the Agadic sayings, for instance, of R. 'Akiba and R. Meir of the second century, will sufficiently prove that there is little or nothing in the dicta of these great teachers which would have prevented them from subscribing to the same general theological beliefs that inspired the homilies contained in the *Seder Elijah* and the *Agadath Bereshith* compiled in the seventh or in the eighth century, if not much later."[11] Surely, if there exists such unity in thought over so many centuries, there must be some kind of coherence whereby the characteristic modes of the theology are kept intact despite differences in time, circumstances and personalities.

Schechter rightly recognizes, however, as Moore and others do later, that the rabbinic indifference to logical consistency precludes finding the basis of their unity in a logical system of theology. At one time the Rabbis emphasize one doctrine, on other occasions, another doctrine;[12] and sometimes there is complacent acceptance of downright inconsistencies.[13] Now Schechter and later authorities conclude from all this that rabbinic theology does not contain a logical system. That much is obvious. But is there no alternative between amorphous concepts and a logical system? Can we not perhaps find a principle of coherence in rabbinic theology that may account for its unity and yet allow for the differences of opinion and for logical inconsistencies?

[11] K. Kohler, Opus cit., Preface, pp. xi–xii.
[12] Ibid., pp. 11–13.
[13] Ibib., pp. 15–16.

II

Organic Thinking

In this monograph on the theology of Seder Eliahu a definite coherence will be shown to exist among all the rabbinic concepts in the Seder. To guard against the possibility of imposing an arbitrary or subjective organization upon the material, I have utilized every available statement in this Midrash. The few passages not available are those where the text is hopelessly corrupt;[14] or that are so fragmentary as not to convey a complete thought;[15] or that are purely halakic in character and thus not relevant to our purpose here.[16] Such unutilized passages are in fact so few in number that they need not be taken into account when considering the theologic ideas of the Midrash. For all practical purposes, the Midrash has been carefully sifted, and every statement examined and classified according to the concepts involved. There is, it seems to me, an advantage in this treatment over the method of culling rabbinic literature for the purpose of explaining and illustrating rabbinic concepts. The concepts stand out as in the latter method; and, in addition, we are at the same time forced to reckon with other factors, among them the inherent relationship between the concepts, that may easily slip us by when we pick and choose our passages as we please.

[14] Passages not used because of corrupt text are—pp. 110–11: "By the Temple service . . . It is as though in answer to Benjamin my brother . . . you would not allow him to remain in your house for a moment;" p. 122: "I said to them, 'My masters, a judge that slew . . . 'an eye for an eye;' ', p. 137: " 'That thou hide not thyself from thine own flesh'. . . but should honor them equally."

[15] Passages not used because too fragmentary, are—p. 162: "The sages have taught regarding the Chariot . . . and sins against God;" Additions, p. 12: "Rabbi Jose . . . says . . . and has not returned;" ibid, p. 13:" Joḥanan . . . says . . . Ikruria also."

[16] Passages not used because halakic only, are—pp. 34–5: "R. Simon, the son of Gamaliel said . . . those declared unfit;" p. 36: "Of the bullock it says . . . the woof and warp (walk);" pp. 146–7: "This is a warning to the judge . . . to teach you that a court of thirty is necessary in cases of corporal or capital punishment". (Partly used).

The claim that there is an inherent relationship among rabbinic concepts can be made with justice, on the basis of the present work, only with regard to Seder Eliahu. Whenever subsequently I use the term "rabbinic theology" or like generalizations it should be understood that I have reference only to rabbinic theology as exemplified in this Midrash. Whether the same principle of coherence extends to rabbinic theologic literature at large could be verified only upon painstaking examination of other Midrashim, on which task I hope sometime later to venture. Nevertheless, there are indications that our conclusions here are not without bearing on rabbinic theology in general. According to Professor Ginzberg, as we have seen above, Seder Eliahu once contained a "Baraita," composed at an early period shortly after the close of the Mishnah and a "Talmud" that was written much later.[17] The coherent relation between the rabbinic concepts in the Seder can, therefore, be due to either of two causes: Either the "Baraita" determined the cast of ideas and thus made for the basic unity to be found in its "Talmud" as well, or else the same principle of coherence holds true generally of rabbinic theology. Favorable to the second assumption is the fact that there are many homilies in Seder Eliahu that are found in both Talmuds and in other Midrashim.[18] We ought recall, moreover, the conviction expressed by Schechter that a basic unity of thought exists between the earliest Tannaim and the latest Midrashim, among which he specifically mentions Seder Eliahu. Granted the assumption that our principle of coherence holds good for rabbinic theology in general, development of individual concepts or changes in them due to new circumstances are by no means precluded.

The nature of the coherent relationship of rabbinic concepts differs in so many ways from that inherent in the types of thinking to which we are accustomed, that I have been forced to apply to it a new name, "organic thinking." We may best begin the definition of this term and its application to rabbinic theology by stating that there are four fundamental rabbinic concepts: God's loving-kindness, His absolute justice, Torah, and Israel.

[17] Above, p. 15.

[18] See above, pp. 8, 9 and 14–15.

They are fundamental not in the sense in which certain articles of a creed are fundamental by being given a position of primary importance while other beliefs are relegated to secondary rank. The Rabbis believed just as implicitly in other than these fundamental concepts—such as The World to Come, the Sovereignty of God, the Sanctification of the Name, etc., concepts that were as much a part of their world outlook as those we have called fundamental. God's loving-kindness, His justice, Torah, and Israel are fundamental, however, in the literal sense that all the other ideas, beliefs, concepts of the Seder are built upon, or rather out of, these four.

The constitutive elements of every concept are the four fundamental ones. Let us take, as examples, the concepts cited above. The Sanctification of the Name occurs, that is, God is recognized by the world as one God, when Israel demonstrate their readiness to die as martyrs for this truth, when Torah is exalted before men, when God's absolute justice or His love is vindicated.[19] Likewise, *Malkut Shamayim*, the sovereignty of God, is accepted by Israel upon themselves by declaration, and by the study of Torah and by the recognition of His love and justice;[20] mankind at large will perforce recognize the sovereignty of God *L'atid la-bo*, in the time to come.[21] The World to Come, which is most often conceived by the Rabbis as a perfect world-order that will take place on this earth, is a belief similarly composed of the four fundamental concepts: the good and bad of the earth will be judged, and rewarded or punished at that time, Israel will be the inhabitants of the new world-order in which God's love will reign, and the occupation of all will consist in the spiritual pursuit and study of Torah.[22] Even the Rabbis' conception of nature[23] and their use of angelology[24] conform to the four fundamental concepts. Additional instances of the same character are furnished by the concept of the Nations of the

[19] See below, pp. 64–71.
[20] See below, pp. 58–61.
[21] Below, pp. 61–64.
[22] Below, Vol. II.
[23] See below, pp. 83–88.
[24] See below, pp. 88–101.

World, the ethical motives, and other aspects of rabbinic theology discussed in the body of the book.

It is characteristic of the fundamental concepts that, besides being the constitutive elements of the rest, they are constitutive of each other, inextricably intertwining with one another. But one illustration out of many possible examples will suffice here. The ability to repent is given man because of God's love; if he repents, he is rewarded, if not, he is punished; in either case, there is the infallible operation of God's justice. The means of his repentance are to be found in Torah and association with Israel and the Patriarchs.[25]

Rabbinic theology, it can now be seen, represents a type of thinking quite different from that which we associate with religious dogmas as the latter appear in creeds of the church, or, for that matter, in Jewish formularies like that of Maimonides. Creeds proceed from a rational process which, starting with certain premises, builds upon them deductively by successive inferences, step by step, until at the top of the pyramidal structure we have the conclusion, that is, the religious creed. To dislodge but one step of the pyramid is to cause the whole structure to tumble down in ruins. In other words, religious creeds are the product of systematic thought, bear a logical relation to one another, and can be arranged in ordered systematic form. In rabbinic theology it were vain to look for a logical, systematic order for the reason that its basic unity is of another type entirely. Here the *whole* enters into each one of the parts, every individual concept independently exhibits all the characteristic qualities of rabbinic theology, yet all concepts are interrelated with one another by very reason of their common constitutive elements. This kind of thinking can only be described as "organic." Only organisms possess this character of mutual interrelation between the whole and its parts.

The organic quality of rabbinic theology accounts for that paradox, observed long ago by students, which allows differences of opinion to exist without thereby causing the basic unity of rabbinic thought to suffer. Fluid rather than crystallized thought,

[25] See below, pp. 118–137.

it gives room for differences in temperament and degree of ethical sensitiveness among individuals, and even for different moods in the same individual. This is possible because on one occasion one of the fundamental concepts may be stressed, and on another occasion, another. At one time, for example, the plea is made that Israel survive lest otherwise Torah should disappear;[26] at another time, in answer to a direct question, Israel is given precedence over Torah.[27] When in one homily, there is disapproval that the gift of prophecy was given to a Gentile, Balaam,[28] it is Israel that is emphasized; whilst in the homily that states that, whether Israelite or Gentile, prophecy rests upon anyone according to his deserts,[29] it is God's justice that is emphasized. Since the four fundamental concepts enter into all the other concepts, it follows that within every concept there is room for many contradictory statements, depending upon which one of the four is stressed. Yet, by the same token, the coherent unity of rabbinic theology remains unaffected for the fundamental concepts by their interrelation with all the concepts and with each other make for the organic coherence of the whole. Organic coherence is, therefore, not the same as logical consistency: strict logical consistency is required when one statement must square with another in a hard-and-fast, crystallized system. Organic thinking has that elastic quality inherent in life itself which permits of manifold inconsistencies while yet retaining its essential character.[30]

The Rabbis by no means always expressed their ideas in terms of the organic complex of rabbinic theology. Individual Rabbis sometimes offer observations on nature which are completely apart from theology, as when one author declares that the whole world lives under the Scorpion, giving as proof that anyone travelling from Palestine to Rome will always find him-

[26] P. 112; had Israel not accepted the Torah, they would have all been destroyed—p. 85.

[27] P. 71. [28] P. 191. [29] P. 48.

[30] Another principle, which we cannot discuss here, also accounts for some of the contradictions: Some Rabbis have a tendency to abstraction, and others are content to speak in very graphic and corporeal figures. This principle and its illustrations will be taken up in the body of the book.

self under the same constellation;[31] or, as when some Rabbis, in speaking of the plagues sent upon Egypt, remark that there are fourteen species of lice,[32] whilst another individual affirms, apparently from observation, that the frog exhibits intelligence by his peculiar call which has the effect of a signal to the birds of the locality.[33] In some instances, the observation of natural phenomena by individuals may lead to theological deductions, but these deductions have none of the earmarks of organic thinking. Thus, one author sees in the aesthetic arrangement of the Pleiades proof that God has designed the world,[34] and another finds the element of divine design in the individuality he has observed in all creatures, none being exactly like the others of his species.[35]

Clearly the observations of natural phenomena and the conclusions derived from them represent a different type of thinking from that which we have called organic thinking. The former is solely the product of individual minds. It takes an individual to observe the arrangement of the Pleiades and to derive from them a personal aesthetic satisfaction, or to notice the varieties of species and the variety within a species, or to notice the effect of a creature's call. Such observation partakes of the character of scientific investigation. It demands—and this is important—a degree of effort, concentration, strain. All thinking which is the creation of individual minds has this feature of effort and concentration about it, whether it be the pragmatic observation of facts, or speculative and deductive reasoning, or a combination of both. Scientific thinking demands continuous effort on the part of the individual because it calls for an unceasing check-up of the facts; speculative and deductive thinking likewise demands effort of the individual because it calls for strict, logical consistency whereby every statement must square with every other in the system. Thinking that is individualistic is effortful.

Organic thinking is, on the other hand, the product of group life. It belongs to those phenomena that develop in the group and that are handed down by social transmission, phenomena

[31] P. 9.
[32] P. 41.
[33] Ibid.
[34] P. 9.
[35] P. 10.

that include language and other social symbols and institutions. The distinctive qualities of any complex of organic thinking arise in ways no more mysterious—and no less—than do the distinctive qualities of any entity, animate or inanimate. We can break up water, for example, into hydrogen and oxygen; but the properties of neither can in any way account for the distinctive qualities of water. In the same way, investigators may have found that some of the rabbinic concepts have historical antecedents; but these antecedents do not exhibit the characteristics possessed by the concepts within the organic complex of rabbinic theology. The Jewish people certainly "borrowed" concepts from other peoples with whom they came into cultural contact, but the special connotation, the new and distinctive meaning these concepts have in rabbinic theology are the product of Jewish group life, pure and simple. In organic thinking, then, the sum of the "parts" does not equal the "whole." The truth seems to be that with organic thinking as with all, particularly living, wholes, the generative process is one where the whole and its elements are "reciprocally generative and constitutive."[36] Without regard to the origin or sources of the concepts, rabbinic theology was the complex of organic thinking evolved by the Jewish people.

What is essentially human, it is now widely recognized, is the product of untold generations of group life. What is essentially human is, also, the personality of the individual man. May we not be getting nearer here to the heart of those secret springs of human nature whence arises the integrated personality of the individual? We know that man reacts to the world by means of concepts, and we know, too, that he reacts as a whole, integrated, functioning self, not with a bundle of unrelated concepts. But it is the peculiar virtue of organic thinking that it functions as a *whole*, that it is an integrated, fluid complex of concepts. Thus we can infer that the group, when it supplies the individual with its own distinctive organic thinking, endows him with that integrated self lacking which he is not human. The individual self, then, and organic thinking are one; and it

[36] Ritter and Bailey, The Organismal Conception, (U. of Cal. Press, 1928), p. 303.

is as natural for a man, as effortless, to think in terms of the organic complex of his group as it is for him to breathe. Here we are at the root of the main distinction between organic and individualistic thinking. The latter we have said is featured by effort and strain. Organic thinking is as effortless as language —this may be more than an analogy—for it is as integrally a part of the individual. The organically interrelated concepts are the instruments with which the individual naively and unpremeditatively grasps the world. Thus it was that rabbinic theology was the mental equipment of many generations of Jews, their unpremeditated and spontaneous reaction to the world, which functioned for them at all times, and by which the world was continually made intelligible to them. Rabbinic theology was not, as is the case with all effortful thinking, their occupation for an hour devoted to concentration upon a problem, but rather their normal habit of thought. To say that it was their normal habit of thought, that it was effortless, is to say not only that they were, of course, not aware of the organic nature of their thinking, but that the outstanding fact about the Rabbis was, in the apt words of Schechter, "to have a theology without being aware of it."[37]

The distinction just made between organic and individualistic, between effortless and effortful, thinking, should not lead us to suppose that an impregnable wall forever divides them. If the Rabbis were largely dominated by the first, they were, nevertheless, as we have seen above, also capable of the second type of thought. But even more important is the fact that both organic and individualistic thinking are two aspects of a functioning individual's thinking. When the individual acquires the complex of organic thought, it functions as a learned or acquired reaction to his environment, and, as such, is subject to individualistic differentia. Individualistic thinking, different reflections on the problems of life as these arose out of the varying circumstances facing every individual and even the same individual at different times, no doubt contributed largely to those differing opinions we noticed to have been a characteristic of rabbinic

[37] Schechter, opus cit., p. 12.

theology. Moreover, organic thinking was indebted to effortful, individualistic thinking both for the form and the remarkable concreteness in which rabbinic theology is couched. Rabbinic statements usually take the form of interpretations of biblical texts; and although the use of these texts may sometimes appear to us as ingenious and even fantastic, the interpretations are the result of careful training in the rabbinical method of biblical exegesis. And that concreteness which is so marked in rabbinic theology can only be the product of an alert attention to ever wider applications of the rabbinic concepts. Finally, it is even possible—though that may not be established even after a very careful scrutiny of rabbinic theology and its historical backgrounds—that individualistic thinking may have had something to do with the antecedents of the concepts which finally evolved in the complex of rabbinic theology. It may well be that individual thinkers created or refined a conception that was later absorbed and integrated into rabbinic theology by the Jewish people.

We have endeavored to describe, in this section, rabbinic theology as an organic complex of concepts. It has coherence, but not the kind that depends on logical sequence. Instead of logical, rabbinic theology offers harmonious, thought; and, consequently, instead of being featured by effortful, discursive speculation, its character appears to be unpremeditative, naive, effortless. It is harmonious because in every part, in every concept, there is always implicit the whole, all the concepts at once. The term "harmonious thinking" puts us in mind immediately of aesthetic harmonies which, while amenable to analysis, yet are beyond logical necessity. Perhaps it is in this sphere also that rabbinic theology belongs.

III

"The Organismal Conception"

This is the name given by Ritter and Bailey to the conception of "wholes" which today is the dominant hypothesis in so many fields of science. To quote them, it is "the conclusion that, in all parts of nature and in nature itself as one gigantic whole, wholes are so related to their parts that not only does the existence of the whole depend on the orderly cooperation and interdependence of its parts, but the whole exercises a measure of determinative control over its parts."[38] Because organic thinking is an example and a verification of this hypothesis we are justified in straying from the strict limits of rabbinic theology and in adding this short excursus to this chapter.[39]

Ritter and Bailey demonstrate that the organismal conception has proved to be a most fruitful hypothesis in eight branches of scientific research, including besides the biological sciences even the sciences of inanimate nature. The theory of evolution itself is now being restated by various thinkers who, in one form or another, have adopted the organismal conception. Patrick, for instance, speaks of the formation of "unitary complexes" in evolution: "Evolution is a series of stages. At each stage a new form of relatedness supervenes, and from this new relatedness something new emerges, and this new relatedness is effective in determining the 'go of events' in the next higher level. It is what we have called the formation of unitary complexes, each with its characteristic reaction. Evolution is thus characteristically 'jumpy,' proceeding with a step-like advance with the sudden appearance of new characteristics at each step."[40]

Now, man, too, is a unitary complex. His body is an organism. For some time now two important psychological schools have worked under the assumption that man's psychic life is also a unitary complex. Psycho-analysis has looked upon man's emotional life as a unit, emotional disturbances and conflicts resulting, according to its terminology, in the disintegration of

[38] Ritter and Bailey, The Organismal Conception: Its Place in Science and its Bearing on Philosophy (U. of California Press, Berkeley, California, 1928) p. 307.

[39] Long before I had read or heard of the organismal conception in its wider implications, I completed my analysis of rabbinic theology and, on the basis of a minute examination of the data, found it to be an organic complex of thought, and applied to it the term "organic thinking." After the material on the organismal conception was called to my attention by Dr. H. M. Kallen, it seemed to me all the more significant as corroborating both the method employed and the basic conclusions reached.

[40] G. T. W. Patrick, What Is the Mind? (Macmillan, New York, 1929), p. 174.

personality. Gestalt psychology has largely undertaken to show that man's sense-perceptions are always part of a dynamic, organic configuration. What of man's concepts? If it is true that man as a whole is an organism, is it not true that he must also think organically?

Rabbinic theology appears to be one indication that man thinks organically, or, at least, that the Jews did think organically. The structure of rabbinic theology is organic. The common recognition that the antecedents of the rabbinic concepts do not account for the qualities these concepts exhibit when in the rabbinic organic complex also seems to point to a characteristic of "unitary complexes." Patrick describes their emergence as of a "jumpy" character, "proceeding with a step-like advance with the sudden appearance of new characteristics at each step;" and Ritter and Bailey point out that there is a "reciprocally generative and constitutive relation of a whole to its elements." If, in addition, our assumption that this organically integrated thinking and the individual self are one—which seems to be borne out by the effortlessness accompanying organic thinking —we have some kind of solution to that puzzling problem of what it is that makes for the integration of personality. For the sources of that integration, and for examples of organic thinking, we ought to look to the social products and folk-literature of the group.

Is organic thinking a matter confined to the past? There are a great many people who, although they no longer completely possess the organic complex of the past, are nevertheless influenced by it. In some way, they discard unacceptable features and reinterpret the concepts for themselves so that they maintain a measure of serenity. Probably most of us are in this category. What is highly desirable, then, is that these reinterpretations be not haphazard, but guided by a real knowledge of the organic pattern as well as by works on interpretation, another service individualistic thinking can and should render to organic thinking. Yet undoubtedly the widespread and popular diffusion today of general philosophic and scientific, that is to say, individualistic, thinking has weakened the hold of effortless organic thinking. "Individualistic" thought and investigations have for many broken up organic complexes and their constitutive concepts have correspondingly suffered. More, the very standard of thought runs counter to organic thinking: the desideratum in science has been extended to religion, ethics and morals, even to folk-ways and customs, and the individual is always bidden to investigate and analyze, to exercise conscious choice, effortful thought, conscious action. This, to be sure, should and probably does make for progress, and, in view of the completely new world of technology and political and social forces we live in, is no doubt now absolutely necessary. And yet are we not becoming more and more perplexed, uneasy, torn with internal strife, and totally unsatisfied? Can we exercise choice and effortful thinking all the time? Is the human being doomed to sit forever on the hot frying-pan of individualistic thinking? We must hope that the various conclusions of present individualistic thinking and the reinterpretations of socially inherited organic complexes are the antecedents of an organic complex yet to be; that, when the time is ripe and all social and intellectual circumstances are favorable, these individualistic thoughts and reinterpretations will once again "click" together into a new organic complex more in conformity with our present knowledge of the world.

And then the process will be repeated as it always has been. Individualistic thought will break away from the organic dynamic pattern, and again new vistas be opened for further evolution in man's mental life.

CHAPTER III

THE CONCEPTION OF GOD

I

The Four Fundamental Concepts

The theology of the Seder, in common with that of the other haggadic Midrashim, cannot be reduced to a logical system, to be sure. Yet there are four concepts in the Seder—God's loving-kindness, His justice, Torah, and Israel—which appear to be fundamental. "They are fundamental not in the sense in which certain articles of a creed are fundamental by being given a position of primary importance while other beliefs are relegated to secondary rank;"[1] there are concepts other than these four named, e. g., *'Olam habba*, which are believed in just as implicitly. They are fundamental, however, "in the literal sense that most of the other ideas, beliefs, concepts of the Seder are built upon, or rather out of, these four."[2] Thus, the homilies concerning *'Olam habba*, to use the example cited, describe the World to Come largely from the point of view of God's loving-kindness, His justice, Torah and Israel. These fundamental concepts seem to be the vantage points from which the authors of Seder Eliahu looked upon the world and by means of which they solved the ethical and theologic problems that faced them. Obviously, some of the facts which confronted them could be viewed and interpreted from any one of these several vantage points, depending upon the author's choice. If Israel be the concept emphasized, then the *'am ha-areẓ*, for example, is regarded with leniency; if Torah, the *'am ha-areẓ* fares badly. So-called differences of opinion or contradictions can, therefore, be traced to the emphasis at one time upon one and at another time upon another of these

[1] Above, p. 23.
[2] Ibid.

fundamental concepts. But it must not be supposed from this that we shall find four tight and mutually exclusive compartments in the theology of this book; on the contrary, the fundamental concepts often affect and color each other so that a single passage may be a compound of several concepts, as indeed is frequently the case. All such characteristics are sufficient to distinguish them from creeds, and since the term "fundamental concepts" is so reminiscent of credal theology, I have discarded it as a rule for the less ideological though perhaps equally cumbersome one of "points of reference."

II

Independent Attributes

It is enough merely to read Seder Eliahu to conclude that the book contains little that is not theology. It is a homiletic exposition by the Rabbis on how God has created the world, how He has governed it in the past, how He rules it in the present, and in what manner He will perfect it in the future. The four points of reference, "the vantage points from which the Rabbis viewed the world," are, by the same token, the vantage points from which they view the activity of God. That is to say, they conceived of God mainly as ordering the world in accordance with His loving-kindness, His justice, His affection for and choice of Israel and the observance or neglect of His Torah. To say this, however, by no means implies that the Rabbis' conception of God was limited by these vantage points. The latter define His activity, His relations with the world of individuals and nations, animals, natural forces and angels, but statements about God's nature independent of His activity are also to be found. Eternity, holiness, truth, omniscience, humility, creativeness and omnipotence, as well as transcendance and immanence, are the independent attributes of God mentioned in Seder Eliahu.

Now the outstanding characteristic of rabbinic theology is its concreteness. The four points of reference, bulking so large in the rabbinic view of the scheme of things, infuse warmth into the theology, render it relevant to history and to their own life and expectations. God's love and justice, and the fate of Israel, and the influence of Torah—all are vital and effective agents in the drama of man's life on earth, not matters that are spun out of speculation and remain abstract ideas only. By themselves the *independent* attributes of God are abstract—or at least as abstract as rabbinic theology can be; in a few passages, where they do appear by themselves, they remain abstract. But there are few homilies indeed where the Rabbis allow an independent quality of God to be untied to a point of reference. In most of the cases—and we shall consider all the passages in which independent attributes are mentioned—there is a tendency to run over into the concretely-phrased points of reference, as though the Rabbis seemed anxious to make all attributes of God relate to His active direction of man and of the world.

The eternity of God is the theme of the following passage: "I was before the world was created; I am since the world was created; I am in this world (עוה"ז), I shall be in the World to Come (עוה"ב)."[3] To which is added, "I kill and make alive" (Deut. 32:39),[4] a reference to God's justice in this world and the next. In answering a man who is apparently a Persian priest, one of the authors of the Seder says: "God is a judge; God is holy, righteous, gracious and true forever and ever. He knoweth the beginning and the end, and telleth the latter end from the beginning and from the beginning that which has not yet happened,[5] knoweth what has happened and what will happen, and hopes for good and not for evil (actions by men), and is rich and findeth joy in His portion (Israel)."[6] Here the independent attributes of God are holiness, truth and omniscience. Omniscience, however, is attached to His loving-kindness to form a paradox—though God knows everything, all the actions of men even before they have been committed, yet He hopes, expects only good deeds and not evil. His omniscience does not interfere, therefore, with man's freedom of will or of choice. God's omniscience

[3] Page 130.

[4] Ibid.

[5] This phrase after Isaiah 46:10.

[6] Page 3 and page 6. That Israel is "God's portion" is brought out by passages on pp. 10 and 173. See below in chapter on "Israel."

stands out in relief against the needs of a king of flesh and blood: A king who sits on his throne gets a word of wisdom from one elder, a word of knowledge from another, of understanding from another . . . but God is not so.[7] God, instead, out of His knowledge provides the righteous and the learned (ת"ח) with wisdom, discernment, knowledge and understanding.[8] "He giveth wisdom to the wise" (Dan. 2:21)—to Moses; "and knowledge to them that know understanding"—to Joshua, the son of Nun. He is the source of mystic knowledge, for "He revealeth the deep" (*ibid*)—the depth of the Merkabah; "and secret things"—the knowledge of how the world was created.[9]

The attribute of omniscience seldom stands alone in the Seder as can be seen from the instances given above.[10] A particularly clear example is in the following passage:

"And with His wisdom and understanding He created His world and established it, and after that He created Adam and caused him to rule (over the world) before Him. And He had minute knowledge of him to the end of all generations, and He foresaw that his progeny would anger Him. (Thereupon) He said: 'If I will hold against him the early sins, the world will not stand; I must cause the early sins to pass away.' "[11] Thus, God employs His omniscience to aid His mercy and loving-kindness—an independent attribute being absorbed by a point of reference.[12]

[7] Page 84.

[8] Ibid. His wisdom in contrast to man's, even Moses', is the subject of a homily on page 44 of "Additions."

[9] Page 85. Here and in the preceding passage the connection with Torah is obvious.

[10] God's omniscience is also indicated when He showed Moses "every generation with its learned men, every generation with its prophets, every generation with its interpreters (of Torah), every generation with its leaders (פרנסין), every generation with its men gifted in practical affairs (אנשי מעשה)." —p. 183. And this passage is concerned primarily with God's justice and with God's love. See below, pp. 114, 164.

[11] Page 3. As a proof text, "And the Lord passed by before him" (Exod. 34:6) is given. "Read not ויעבֹר but ויעביר—from which we learn that He caused all their wickedness to pass away from before His eyes."

[12] No less than His mercy, His justice is also informed by His omniscience: R. Joshua proves to the Caesar that the lame, the blind and the deaf from

Humility is an attribute of God, but it is so woven around the fundamental concept of Torah as to be inextricable from it: David, when he taught in his academy "was neither on a cushion nor on a bench, but sat on the ground and taught the Torah in public for the sake of Heaven. *Shekinah* came and stood above him and said, 'Speak, my son, how came you by these things? They are mine. Thou art described with a 'ת' (for it says 'Those that sit at the academy of תחכמוני')[13] and Torah with a 'ת'."[14]

Another independent attribute of God is truth. David praises Him with the word "truth."[15] Despite proof-texts, the word is made to connote little since it remains unattached in this passage to any point of reference. Yet, in another place where it is incidental to the fundamental concept of justice, the attribute of truth takes on far more content.[16]

God is the Creator—"with His wisdom He created His world and established it, and after that He created man and brought him into the world."[17] Because creativeness is an activity as well as an attribute—and hence it was always excluded from among God's attributes in classical philosophy—it has a wider application in the Seder than any other "independent" quality standing alone. It is, indeed, so largely influenced by the fundamental concepts that it is given separate treatment below.

Associated with the creativeness is the universality of God.

birth have already been judged and therefore afflicted because "a man's deeds are revealed to Him, whether they will be good or bad before He intends to create (the man);" and proof is supplied in the instance of the duplicity of a certain blind man. (Page 41 of "Additions.") See below, p. 202–203.

Because, also, God knew from the start that "the Nations of the World will in the future provoke Him," He hid the light of the first three days of creation, reserving it for the righteous in the World to Come. (Page 33 of "Additions.")

[13] II Sam. 23:7 interpreted with שבת understood as academy.

[14] Page 15. Since ת is the last letter in the alphabet, it is a symbol for humility. Humility is thus a quality of Torah since it begins with ת. By innuendo God is also associated here with this quality. תחכמוני is the name given to David.

[15] Page 39.

[16] The passage refered to is on page 40 of "Additions." See below, here, p. 167.

[17] Pp. 6 and 3.

"All is His and the work of His Hands."[18] He is the "King from one end of the world to the other and the entire world is His."[19] Yet the universality of God and His election of Israel seem to offer no contradiction to the Rabbis. In the very same passage they state that His reward and portion in the world which He created is Israel,[20] once more an independent attribute joined to a point of reference. His omnipotence is naturally taken for granted since He is the Creator of the universe and its King.[21]

To sum up: Eternity, holiness, truth, omniscience, humility, creativeness, universality and omnipotence, the independent attributes of God mentioned in the Seder take on concreteness as they are linked to points of reference.[22]

III

The Question of Anthropomorphism

Concreteness in the expression of religious thought, application of the conception of God to their own life and that of their people inevitably led the Rabbis to the use of anthropomorphism. How did they express their belief that Torah is divine and that God continually exercises His qualities of justice and loving-kindness? "From the day the world was created down to the present hour, I sit upon My throne of glory: one-third of the day I study Bible and Mishnah (אני קורא ושונה), one-third of the day I judge the world and one-third of the day I do charity (צדקה) and provide for and feed and sustain the whole world and all that I have created in the world."[23] As with this passage, an analysis of *all*

[18] Page 115; a similar expression on page 91. All wealth and riches are His, page 44, "Additions."

[19] Page 172.

[20] Ibid.

[21] The strength of man, even of a Samson, ceased and disappeared, "but let God glory . . . for all the might is His." (Page 44, "Additions").

[22] Two more attributes are to be added: His transcendence is discussed below, page 47; and His immanence on pages 50–56.

[23] Page 130; with slight variations of text on pp. 62 (twice) and 90; on page 84 (twice) and on page 162 as a statement about God.

the striking cases of anthropomorphism[24] reveals this very significant fact: The anthropomorphisms occur exclusively in connection with points of reference or with independent attributes when these are joined to points of reference. (There are two exceptions which will be mentioned and accounted for later.) So important is this fact for the understanding of rabbinic theology that it would not be amiss to present all these cases and to indicate how they naturally classify themselves under one or the other of the fundamental concepts.

God's loving-kindness, His concern over mankind, stands out in bold relief in the following graphic figures: God is not anxious to punish evil-doers and when punishment is necessary He does so only "with sighing."[25] When Moses wonders why God is so forbearing when He is continually being forsaken, "the Holy One, blessed be He, was silent and answered not."[26] There are wicked men against whom a decree of untimely death had been issued, but who repented before they died. God grieves over them. "Out of that grief there is no comfort to the Holy One, blessed be He, except if He raises them out of the dust upon their feet, and places them between His knees, fondling and embracing and kissing them and bringing them into the life of the World to Come."[27] The time that God brought the deluge upon the world was one of mourning before Him, hence He ceased from study, refrained from work.[28] When Abraham was cast into the fiery furnace, "the compassion of the Holy One, blessed be He, was aroused and He went down from His highest heaven of heavens from the place of His glory, greatness, magnificence (the holiness of His great name) and rescued Abraham our father."[29] God Himself taught Moses the text and order of the prayers of forgiveness with which Israel must come before God

[24] I have selected only such passages in which the anthropomorphism is bold enough to attract attention. The conclusion holds as well, however, for all casual expressions such as "God said" etc.

[25] Pp. 98–99.

[26] Page 144.

[27] Page 21.

[28] Page 162. The laws of mourning forbid work and study.

[29] Page 27; also on page 49 of "Additions," where it simply says, "The Holy One, blessed be He, went down to rescue him."

when troubles meet them. "The Holy One, blessed be He, went down His thick, dark cloud like the ש"ץ who is wrapped in His *talit*, and revealed to him the order and text of the prayers of forgiveness."[30] And, always, "God's hands are stretched forth to receive those that repent . . . stretched forth under the wings of the *Ḥayyot*."[31]

That God's justice, though delayed, is certain is brought out by this passage: "There is laughter (before God) (i. e. God laughs) only one hour, and that is when the Nations of the World in their pride say, 'Let Him come against us with a thousand thousand horsemen and with a thousand thousand swords.' "[32] The halo, which the Bible says, Moses received upon coming down from Mt. Sinai was, according to the Rabbis, a just reward. He had saved Israel by standing in prayer before God on several occasions in their behalf. God's reward was permanent: "Just as the Face above is forever and ever so the light of the face of Moses entered with him to the house of his eternal rest (בית עולמו)."[33]

The reward of the righteous is limitless, and the anthropomorphisms correspondingly unrestrained. David will invite God to eat with the righteous in Paradise, and He will consent to walk with them in the garden, and afterward call upon David to say grace.[34] "And the Holy One, blessed be He, will sit at the head of the righteous . . . (and) say to them, 'Now you have seen My countenance.' "[35]

The Torah is of transcendent importance to the world. This is conveyed by means of homilies fraught with anthropomorphisms: "When our ancestors stood at Mt. Sinai . . . the Holy One, blessed be He, was watching and came to the world . . . When Israel received the yoke of Heaven with joy, He also went

[30] Page 42, "Additions."

[31] Page 37, "Additions."

[32] Page 62. In a very daring anthropomorphism, the angels go looking for God and find Him with "His garments red as scarlet" after He visits vengeance upon Edom. (Page 29, "Additions.")

[33] Page 18.

[34] Page 32, "Additions."

[35] Page 35, "Additions."

down from His place of glory, from the highest heavens."[36] How is it made plain that Torah is the eternal study? "(In the World to Come) the Holy One blessed be He will sit in His *bet ha-midrash* and the righteous of the world will be sitting before Him and they will engage in discussions upon Bible, Mishnah, Halakot and Agadot . . ."[37]

Israel occupies a place in the economy of the world that is unique. Whatever happens to this people is of cosmic importance, cosmic consequence. When Jacob left his father's house to go to Laban, "*Shekinah* came and stood above him and said to Jacob, 'My son, lift up now thine eyes and look toward heaven and see the twelve stars and constellations in the firmament—twelve hours the day, twelve hours the night—as against the twelve tribes that I will give you!' "[38] Israel is God's portion "and He is rich and satisfied with His portion."[39] He swore by His great name "that the Torah will be given them" and He "swore to His people that He would not exchange them for another people and would not change them for another nation."[40] The righteous are especially beloved of God and when He recalls their deeds He "strikes His hands one against the other."[41] When God spoke to Moses, "He did not speak in terms of imperative command, but in terms of joy." Psalms 133:1, "Behold how good and how pleasant it is for brethren to dwell together in unity" is used to describe His relationship with Moses,[42] a very bold use indeed. The verse is similarly applied to His relations with Aaron.[43] Concerning Israel, God said to Moses, "Am I not He that ye are My children and I am your Father, ye are My brothers and I am your Brother, ye are My friends and I am your Friend, ye are My beloved and I am your Beloved?"[44]

[36] Page 85.

[37] Pp. 15 and 19.

[38] Page 29.

[39] Page 3. This expression is a cliche and used figuratively, of course. See above, page 35, note 6.

[40] Page 127. Again, on page 181, the expression is found, "I swear by My great name."

[41] Page 32.

[42] Page 68.

[43] Ibid.

[44] Page 65.

Sometimes the Rabbis use an imagery, in portraying God's love for Israel and His joy in the people, that to the modern ear seems almost gross: "At that time the Holy One blessed be He hugged and kissed His hands over His wisdom and understanding, saying, 'This is My reward from you: That I speak with you so frequently.' "[45] "If they (Israel) had repented from the destruction of the last Temple until this day all the more would (God) have fondled and embraced and kissed them and held them in His bosom forever."[46] God is immanent within Israel, even during battle: "In the days of Samuel . . . the Holy One blessed be He went down from His place of glory . . . and dwelt with them in battle."[47] Israel's misfortunes, and especially the sufferings of the righteous, are lifted to cosmic tragedies: When Nebuchadnezzer conquered Israel, "He went down from the highest heavens, from the place of His honor, greatness, kingdom . . . and lifted up a lamentation over them;" and the Rabbis add, "All their days they were idol-worshippers, yet as soon as they repented somewhat, He immediately wept over them."[48] "In every generation in which you find men who are righteous, pious and upright, He strikes His hands one against the other and places them across His heart and again He places them on His arms (gestures of mourning) and weeps over them whether in secret or openly. Why does He weep over them in secret? It is undignified for a lion to weep before a jackal . . ."[49] When Pharaoh decreed that those who did not finish their measure of brick should be put in between the bricks of the buildings, God let His voice be heard in Egypt (in mourning) over the Israelites that were dying.[50] When Balaam, the son of Beor, came to Balak, the son of Zippor, king of Moab, "The Holy One blessed be He caused sorrow and grief to enter so that no creature could

[45] Page 103. בכל שעה ושעה. Similarly God rejoices over Abraham, page 45, "Additions."

[46] Page 83. The same figure is employed on page 194. There it occurs in a parable which is confused with the application.

[47] Page 87.

[48] Page 154.

[49] Ibid.

[50] Page 44.

recognize Him";[51] and similarly when Israel fainted for hunger in the academies.[52] Rabbi Ẓadoḳ saw the Temple in ruins and, in his anguish, cried out against God. "Thereupon Rabbi Ẓadoḳ fell into a slumber and he saw the Holy One blessed be He as He was standing in mourning and the angels mourning after Him."[53] "In another place also the Holy One blessed be He wept over them and established a weeping (time) for generations."[54]

There are a great number of passages in which the anthropomorphism is mitigated by a precautionary stereotype phrase or term. Frequently either before or after an anthropomorphism the Rabbis insert the phrase, "Were this not written (in the Torah) it could not have been said," and then proceed to give the warrant from the Bible.[55] In one place they strengthen the phrase: Declaring that every ת"ח sitting by himself and studying Bible and Mishnah has God opposite him studying Bible and Mishnah (and arguing) with him, they add, "Were this not written (analogy between Lam. 2:19 and I Kings 20:29), it could not have been said, and he who would say it would be guilty of the death penalty."[56] The precautionary term with which the Rabbis sometimes introduce an anthropomorphism is כביכול, which may be rendered, "if it could be said" or, "as it were," or, "so to speak:"[57] כביכול, e. g., The Temple was not built by the hands of man but only by His hand.[58] Such terms would

[51] Page 115. A similar expression used in a parable, however, on page 18; there it reads, "and caused sorrow and grief to enter his heart."

[52] Ibid. (p. 115).

[53] Page 149.

[54] Page 154. וקבעה בכייה לדורות—the weeping time, it is explained further, is in the night.

In the Age to Come, God will tell Israel, "From the day that I destroyed My house below, I did not go up and dwell in My house above; but I was sitting in the dew and the rain. And if you do not believe Me, put your hands upon My head and see the dew that is upon My head." Biblical warrant is found in Song of Songs, 5:2 (page 36, "Additions."). God will blow a horn when He gathers the Dispersions of Israel (page 38, "Additions.")

[55] Pages 160, 155, 172, 60, and elsewhere—אלמלא דבר כתוב אי אפשר לאמרו (or אלולי); on page 185—אלמלא מקרא כתוב.

[56] Page 89—אילולי הדבר כתוב אי אפשר לאומרו וכל האומרו נתחייב עליו מיתה.

[57] Pages 150, 148, 134, 154, 185 and elsewhere.

[58] Page 150.

seem to indicate that the Rabbis were reluctant to ascribe physical movements or manlike feelings to God. But Professor M. M. Kaplan has pointed out that this reluctance does not indicate that the Rabbis had any abstract notion of God; it is most likely merely an aversion to ascribe to God any activity that would tend to lower His dignity or to infringe upon His absolute majesty.[59] Dr. Bacher states that כביכול and similar terms are always employed, where "a strong expression" is used concerning God, as a way of showing reverence or by way of apology for the "strong expression."[60] Professor Ginzberg says that כביכול is most often used in conversation in which a corporeal description of God appears, and emphatically adds that "the Rabbis certainly did object to a corporeal God." Any of these explanations will also account for the fact that, instead of the natural expression, "Moses said to Him," the Rabbis employ the circumlocution: "Moses said before Him" (לפניו);[61] and that instead of "Habakkuk asked God," the text is: "Habakkuk asked before the Holy One blessed be He (מלפני)[62]—to take a few instances out of very many.

All of the passages in which the precautionary stereotypes and circumlocutions are used will reveal, upon examination, that they, too, fall under one or the other of the points of reference, as is the case with those homilies where the anthropomorphism was unsoftened.[63]

It is by now quite evident that rabbinic theology teems with anthropomorphisms. But if we recall that it is one of the central

[59] Unpublished lectures.

[60] Bacher's Terminologie (Hebrew translation by A. Z. Rabinowitz), I, p. 50 and II, p. 200. On p. 50, note 10, he declares that the word כביכול in the Tosefta of Sota, end of Chapter 14, is a late addition, and that it is missing in Zuckermandel's edition. He goes on to say that there is no room there for כביכול because the matter concerns not God but Israel. Ginzberg, however, not in this connection, it is true, says that the word also occurs when a strong expression with regard to Israel is used, and points to an instance in the Pesiḳta, ed. Buber, 15b.

[61] P. 127. Also in the dialogue between God and Hosea on p. 187, and in numerous other places.

[62] P. 194, and similarly frequently elsewhere.

[63] "The same in all other sources where כביכול is used!" (L. G.)

problems in all religious thought—modern as well as ancient —we shall at least not misconstrue the rabbinic use of colorful imagery. In philosophy, the conception of God is an abstraction which can have no continuous relation with the world; in religion, the conception of God gives meaning to history, comfort to the individual in sorrow, direction and purpose in life, conviction that this is a moral universe. How can this belief that God cares for man be expressed in terms other than concrete? However that belief is expressed, its expression must be anthropomorphic and the more concrete and warm the expression, the more anthropomorphic. The Rabbis understood God's relations with mankind in terms of His loving-kindness, His justice, Israel and Torah. Within these realities they saw His activity and His intervention, His projection, as it were, into the world of their ken. They readily perceive, we have seen, that God has a host of attributes. It is only when they describe His relations with the world that their expression becomes concrete and that these attributes melt into a point of reference. Again, we have seen that anthropomorphism occurs only when these points of reference, the foci of His activity, are involved. Then it is that they affirm God's kindness or His love for Israel in the strongest terms of solicitude possible, His justice in figures drawn from life, His insistence on Torah in an extension of their own experience. So absorbed were they in these points of reference that little of their theology remains abstract, that is, philosophic, but is largely drawn into the circle of the concrete, reenforcing wherever possible the active belief in God's direction of the world.

We have noted that anthropomorphisms are *confined* to the four points of reference and to the independent attributes when joined to them; in other words, that there is no anthropomorphic ascription to God's being but only to His activity. This conclusion cannot be too greatly stressed. It is true enough that the Rabbis themselves make no such distinction between being and activity, for these terms are entirely lacking in rabbinic theology which never indulges in sheer philosophical analysis. It may even be possible that in the imagination of some Rabbis, the conception of God was always clothed with anthropomorphic figures. But the fact remains that descriptions of God's being or essence are never given concreteness, if such descriptions are given at all. And it is this quality in rabbinic theology that renders it possible for individuals today, as in the past, to possess philosophical conceptions of God whilst reverencing rabbinic theology as a source for inspiration.

Seder Eliahu contains three homilies in which reference is made to the countenance of God, apparently in violation of what has been said above. Two are attached to a point of reference, however, and neither contains more than the bare reference itself: "Just as the Face above is forever and ever so the light of the face of Moses entered with him to the house of eternal rest;"[64] and the reward of the righteous will consist in God sitting at the head of the righteous "and He will say to them, 'Now you have seen My countenance.' "[65] On the other hand, the third homily, when the three are placed side by side, seems entirely to negate the effect of the other two: The angels say "Holy" three times (in praising God) "because men do not see Him, because the ministering angels do not see Him, because even the *Ḥayyot* carrying His throne do not see the glory."[66] And this last, it should be noted, is not attached to a point of reference. There is little doubt, in the first place, that some Rabbis possessed a more abstract conception of God and of spiritual experience generally than others, as will be shown below.[67] In the "Additions," from which one of the homilies was taken, anthropomorphisms are bolder than in the rest of the book; and Professor Ginzberg's suggestion that these ten chapters are a selection from the later "Talmud" and unified in their theme of Redemption, Paradise and Gehenna[68] would confirm, perhaps, the impression that the later author (or authors) was inclined to a freer and bolder use of anthropomorphisms than his predecessors. Nevertheless, even these authors would do no more than hint at a more concrete conception of God when that is independent of the fundamental concepts.

At superficial glance, one "independent" passage seems to present in so many words an anthropomorphic conception of

[64] Page 18. [65] "Additions," page 35. See above page 40.
[66] Page 163. [67] See pp. 99–100.
[68] See above Chapter I, page 15.

God: The famous story of Hannah and her seven sons[69] is here given in the version of Miriam, the daughter of Tanḥum, and her seven sons who are brought before Emperor Hadrian. Six sons refuse to bow down to the idol and are killed. The youngest son engages in a discussion with the emperor, who asks him if there is indeed a God in the world, which naturally the lad affirms. Then there follows this dialogue: Emperor—"Has your God a head?" Boy—"It has been said of old (כבר) 'His head is as the most fine gold' " (Song of Songs 5:11). "Has your God ears?"—"It has been said of old, 'And the Lord hearkened and heard.' " (Mal. 3:16)—"Has your God eyes?"—"It has been said of old, 'They are the eyes of the Lord that run to and fro . . .' " (Zech. 4:10). "Has your God a nose?"—"It has been said of old, 'And the Lord smelled the sweet savor.' " (Gen. 8:21). The Emperor continues to ask whether God has a mouth, palate, hands, feet, might; the boy always affirms with biblical references.[70] Now it is peculiar that in a polemic against idol-worship a degree of anthropomorphism really approaching the objectification denounced should be employed. But this very peculiarity contains the answer to the question it raises. The anthropomorphism here —in a story which has regard for artistic verisimilitude—is, no doubt, a pedagogic device to place before an idol-worshipper a conception of God which he can grasp. Moreover, the fact that the Rabbis refrain from direct description and use only biblical verses indicates that the anthropomorphisms here are a device merely and that the Rabbis are, on the contrary, anxious to avoid a direct description of God.

The second anthropomorphism unattached to a point of reference is the one which assigns to God a fixed dwelling-place: Manasseh made an idol of four faces and placed it in the Temple in order that no one should pray there. Whereupon God said to Isaiah, "Go tell that (man of) flesh and blood: 'Thus saith the Lord: The heaven is My throne and the earth is My footstool'

[69] II Maccabees, Chapter 7; IV Macc.

[70] Pp. 151–153. Friedmann cites parallels in Gittin 57b, Lamentations R. Chapter I, Pesiḳta Rabbati, Chapter 3, Yalḳuṭ Shime'oni on Lamentations, ibid. on section *Tabo*. He also mentions Joseppon but omits II Maccabees, and IV Maccabees.

(Is. 66:1)—and not the heaven alone but וילון ורקיע ושחקים וזבול ומעון ומכון וערבות (the names of the seven heavens derived from biblical allusions to God's abode), and I sit above them all. 'Where is the house that ye may build unto Me? And where is the place that may be My resting-place?' (*ibid*)."[71] Here again the Rabbis commit an anthropomorphism in the very endeavor to contrast the worship of God with idol-worship. But their motive is apparent: What they wish to express is the idea of God's transcendence and therefore they employ the imagery of "the highest heaven of heavens."[72] Manifestly, therefore, their anthropomorphism in this case has a purpose—that of emphasizing His transcendence to such a degree as to make the worship even of a symbol, the mistaking of the function even of the Temple itself, impossible.

It is no more easy for us to escape using anthropomorphisms than it was for the Rabbis. As long as we believe in prayer—to speak of only one of the religious attitudes—we shall be forced to employ anthropomorphisms. Although we fully appreciate the sincere religious convinction that prompted them, many of the rabbinic anthropomorphisms strike us today as being too bold and perhaps even gross. These we interpret, endeavoring to retain the abiding value of that conviction whilst we remove the figure in which it was expressed. Interpretation, therefore, in some degree, consists in rendering more general, more abstract, that which is given us in more concrete form. Thus we might interpret the Rabbis' statement that God studies Torah one-third of the day as meaning (to us) that the Torah is inherent in the world's economy. So conceived, interpretation involves both a gain and a loss: A gain in that we have rendered a religious truth more in harmony with modern taste, influenced as the latter has been by philosophic tradition; a loss in that we have removed, together with the anthropomorphisms, much of the virility, warmth and concreteness that made rabbinic theology so effective.

[71] Page 188. On page 160, similarly: Above the myriads of angels is the throne of glory, "and the sapphire above that, and God dwells in the highest heaven of heavens."

[72] Also on pp. 27 and 172.

IV

Terms for God

The biblical terms for God do not occur at all in Seder Eliahu except, of course, in biblical quotations. The term most commonly used in the book is "The Holy One blessed be He."[73] It is employed just as we use the term God and in no special connection or peculiar sense. The same is true of *Maḳom*, literally "The Place," which, though less common, is often to be found especially in the phrase "Blessed be the *Maḳom*, blessed be He."[74]

"Heaven" usually occurs in stereotype terms: "Fear of Heaven,"[75] "for the sake of Heaven,"[76] "the name of Heaven,"[77] "the Kingship of Heaven,"[78] "for the honor (or glory) of Heaven."[79] It is found also by itself, e. g., "I love Heaven."[80]

The Seder frequently uses the phrase "He who spake and the world came into being."[81] It is used generally, and not as we might imagine, in passages only referring to creation.

Two terms usually stand at the beginning of a petition or prayer, "Master of the universe,"[82] and "Father in heaven." The former is also found, however, when God is addressed on other occasions.[83] "Father in heaven"[84] besides in prayers, is found in the phrase, "the will of his (or their) Father in heaven,"[85] and is used also generally.[86] Twice the term "Father of mercy"

[73] הקדוש ברוך הוא—pp. 3, 4, 5, etc.

[74] ברוך המקום ברוך הוא—pp. 21, 14, 137, 8, 50, 89 and elsewhere. Schechter translates מקום as "Omnipresent" in his Aspects of Rabbinic Theology.

[75] Page 70 and elsewhere.

[76] Pp. 15, 121 and elsewhere.

[77] Page 140 and elsewhere.

[78] Page 82 and elsewhere.

[79] Page 19 and elsewhere.

[80] Page 132.

[81] מי שאמר והיה העולם—pp. 69, 105, 133, 139, 179 and elsewhere.

[82] רבונו של עולם—pp. 15, 17, 127 and elsewhere.

[83] Pages 143, 146 and elsewhere.

[84] אבי שבשמים or אבינו—pp. 83, 149, 112, 89 and elsewhere.

[85] Pages 17 and 123.

[86] Pages 81, 82, 123, 195 and elsewhere.

occurs, in connection with God's mercy, of course,[87] and once, "their Father."[88]

"The King of the kings of kings" is used not in a special situation, except perhaps in contrast to human kings, but generally.[89] "Above" is found in two phrases—"beloved of Above"[90] and "against the Above," the latter usually as part of the larger phrase, "reviling against (or blaspheming) the Above,"[91] though also by itself.[92] "The God of gods and the Lord of lords,"[93] "the righteous Judge,"[94] and "the Might,"[95] each occur only once. "The Name" is found in this book usually in the concept of "sanctification of the Name" and "profanation of the Name."[96]

There are two terms—the "Holy Spirit" and *Shekinah*—which medieval Jewish philosophy regarded as aspects of God that were not wholly to be identified with Him, and that view has lingered on. In our text the "Holy Spirit" is used unequivocally as but another term for God, though, to be sure, in a special sense. Where the Bible states explicitly, "And *the Lord* said to him, 'Go return on thy way to the wilderness of Damascus' " etc. (I Kings 19:15), Seder Eliahu, quoting the same passage introduces it as follows: "When *the Holy Spirit* said to Elijah, 'Go return on thy way to the wilderness of Damascus' " etc.[97] In the following passages from our Seder, also, the iden-

[87] Pages 69 and 188—אב הרחמים.

[88] Page 153—אביהם של אילו.

[89] מלך מלכי המלכים—Pages 13, 84; in contrast to human kings, page 152. On page 10 (and elsewhere)—מלך מלכי המלכים הקב"ה.

[90] Pages 167 and 197—אהוב מלמעלה.

[91] כלפי מעלה—Pages 121, 189, and "Additions," page 45.

[92] Page 85.

[93] אלהי האלהים ואדוני האדונים—page 27; found in Deut. 10:17 and Psalms 136:2–3.

[94] שופט צדק—page 25.

[95] מפי הגבורה—page 171.

[96] קדוש השם and חלול השם—page 114; "Additions," pages 37, 40, 41, 47. "His name" is found on page 83 and elsewhere frequently.

[97] רוח הקודש—p. 22; repeated with a phrase added to the biblical statement by the author on p. 186.

Comp. Bacher, opus cit., pp. 123–4, 290–4, s. v. רוח הקודש, who also defines the term in a manner similar to ours. Professor Ginzberg feels that the translation "Holy Spirit" is not an accurate rendering, and prefers, instead, "the

tification of the Holy Spirit with God is unmistakable: "When (the exiles) reached the waters of the Euphrates and drank, more were killed than the Chaldeans had slain. Walking on the way, they said, 'O God keep Thou not silence, O God keep Thou not silence' (Ps. 83:2). The Holy Spirit answered them and said, 'Fools that you are, when you worshipped idols on the mountains and hills you did not say' " etc.[98] "On that occasion the compassion of the Holy One blessed be He was moved toward them, and the Holy Spirit brought them good tidings and comfort; and He said to them, 'My sons, I swear by My great name that this weeping shall be unto you a weeping of joy.' "[99] That "My sons" of the preceding passage refers to the Holy Spirit is proved from a similar use in the following: "Thus would the Holy Spirit bring good tidings to the learned (ת"ח), and say to them, 'My sons, even though I have given you a good Torah in this world . . . you shall have a double reward in this world.' "[100] "The Holy Spirit" is, then, a term for God.[101]

Verses from the Bible are described as having been uttered by the Holy Spirit, usually through the medium of the traditional author of the book from which the verse is taken. To give one example: "To this verse (i. e., to an introductory verse given previously) refers what has been said by the Holy Spirit through Isaiah the prophet, 'Come now, and let us reason together, saith the Lord'—of whom did Isaiah say this verse?"[102] The Holy

Spirit of Holiness." Bacher, on the other hand, also regards *Ḳodesh* here as an adjective, offering Ps. 51:13 as analogy (p. 123). He looks upon "the Holy Spirit" as grammatically at one with "the holy tongue"—לשון הקודש (p. 116), and with "the holy writings"—כתבי הקודש (p. 61). See also Dalman's Die Worte Jesu, I, p. 166, which he cites.

[98] P. 154.

[99] P. 181—referring to the time when Moses was about to return from Mt. Sinai the second time.

[100] Page 196.

[101] The Rabbis employed the word "spirit" in their terminology for Divinity in another connection also. " 'A voice is heard in Ramah, lamentation and bitter weeping, Rachel weeping for her children'—read not רחל but רוח אל (the spirit of God) weeping for her children." (Page 148.)

[102] "Additions" page 37. Similarly a verse from the Psalms is uttered by the Holy Spirit through David ("Additions," page 45), and from the Song of Songs, through Solomon ("Additions," page 40).

Spirit is by no means confined to the Bible, however; we have seen above, and there are other instances as well, where the Holy Spirit gives new utterances independently, and some that are even messages of the hour, designed to cheer and fortify the learned (ת"ח) of Israel.[103] It often uses man as its medium, formerly the prophets, Patriarchs and righteous,[104] and now the learned (ת"ח) who are qualified by their knowledge of the Torah,[105] their ethical qualities and their concern for God's glory and Israel's redemption.[106] Indeed, anyone, "whether Gentile or Israelite, man or woman, male slave or female slave, according to the deeds done (i. e. if one is worthy), the Holy Spirit rests upon him."[107] We are forced to conclude, from the function which the Holy Spirit exercises, that whilst it is another term for God, it is a term for a special activity of God. When He communicates with man, He does so as the Holy Spirit, whether directly without any medium or whether through the instrumentality of prophet, Patriarch or the learned of the rabbinic period. To be sure, the Rabbis do not consistently use the term "Holy Spirit" whenever, in their homilies, God speaks to man; He speaks as "the Holy One blessed be He" frequently,[108] and in some places as *Shekinah*.[109] From this fact we may infer, again, that the Holy Spirit is but another term for God. Its special connotation, included in its general function, is that God speaks through the divinely inspired words of men. The Rabbis' belief that those in their own day who are properly qualified speak with divine sanction is at one with their basic conviction, sometimes lost sight of, that God's rule and manifestation is in the present, not only in the past and future.[110]

Related to the conception of "the Holy Spirit" is that of the *Bat-Ḳol*, which may be literally but inadequately translated as

[103] Page 196. Other extra-biblical utterances are on pages 13, 154, 181.

[104] Pages 7, 48.

[105] Page 167.

[106] Pages 63, 19.

[107] Page 48.

[108] Page 130; numerous other instances.

[109] As on page 94.

[110] See below the chapter on God's justice, and, in this chapter, below, the section on God's Kingship.

"the echo of the Voice," a term again no doubt prompted by circumspection. It was conceived apparently as coming from heaven and thus as being God's direct word. The story of Miriam, the daughter of Tanḥum, who, when the last of her seven sons was slain, jumped down from the roof and died, concludes with this statement: A *Bat-Ḳol* went forth and said to her, "Of you it is written, 'The mother of sons is joyful' (Ps. 113:9)."[111] Here the *Bat-Ḳol* uses a biblical verse, but, be it noted, in the form of a verdict. The verdict-like quality of the *Bat-Ḳol* which this time does not employ a Bible text, is even clearer in the pronouncement at the end of the incident related of the reformed harlot and one of the learned: "A *Bat-Ḳol* went forth and said, 'Such-and-such (the woman) and so-and-so (the man) are destined for the life of the World to Come.' "[112] If we are to judge by these passages, the *Bat-Ḳol* frequently utters a decision of some kind.

Shekinah, as used in Seder Eliahu, is also a term for God. In the following passage David addresses *Shekinah* as "My Father in heaven," which we have seen is a general term for God: "When David heard this (that he was not to build the Temple) he bowed his full height to the ground and came and sat before *Shekinah* and said, 'My Father in heaven, may Thy great name be blessed for ever and ever . . .' "[113] *Shekinah* and "The Holy One blessed be He" are apparently identical in another passage: When God will judge the world, including the nations and Israel, He will gather all Israel; "and *Shekinah* will be *in front* of them, and the prophets behind them, and the Torah on their right, and the ministering angels on their left, and they will lead them to the valley of Jehoshaphat, the king;" after describing how the Nations of the World and their idols will fall from the bridge over Gehenna into Gehenna, and how the Patriarchs testify for Israel, the passage continues, "Then the Holy One blessed be He will pass over (the bridge) before them (i. e. before Israel), and they after Him; as it says, 'And their King is passed on before them, and the Lord at the head

[111] בת קול—p. 153.

[112] "Additions," p. 40.

[113] שכינה—p. 89.

of them' (Micah 2:13)."[114] The same figure is maintained throughout the passage—*Shekinah* is in front when Israel is assembled; it therefore leads them over the bridge of Gehenna, except that since both *Shekinah* and "the Holy One blessed be He" are terms for God, they are here used interchangeably.

Shekinah particularly denotes God's in-dwelling within Israel, His immanence amongst His chosen people. His Presence is localized in the tabernacle or Temple,[115] in the sense that He withdrew His *Shekinah* when He destroyed His house and burnt His Temple.[116] The catastrophe of exile and the destruction of the Temple are in this book associated with the withdrawal of *Shekinah*.[117] The *Shekinah* extends its presence over the whole people when they are worthy, Israel being gathered, the figure is, "under the wings of the *Shekinah*."[118] One who desires to become a proselyte out of conviction is therefore described as longing "to come under the wings of the *Shekinah*." But the *Shekinah* is not irrevocably always with Israel, as they realized,[119] and in the wilderness the corruption of their ways was tantamount, apparently, to a refusal "to come underneath the wings of the *Shekinah*."[120] God's immanence within Israel, hence, necessarily depends upon Israel itself and even upon individuals, for the wicked of Israel by committing transgressions "crowd off the feet of the *Shekinah*," a vivid figure indeed.[121]

Since *Shekinah* is the term for God's immanence, it is sometimes interchanged for "the Holy Spirit," the presence of God's word within individuals and an aspect of His immanence. The Rabbis were extolling the power of a piece of bread, and ask, "And whence do we know that it caused the *Shekinah* to rest on false prophets?" Quoting I Kings 13:18–20, they conclude,

[114] "Additions," pp. 34–5.

[115] P. 148.

[116] "Additions," p. 29.

[117] Ibid, pp. 30–1.

[118] תחת כנפי השכינה—p. 146. God loved Abraham because "he watched over people and brought them in under the wings of the *Shekinah*"—p. 29.

[119] Page 122. See the version of the Venice edition in Friedmann's note No. 10, and his correction of our text there.

[120] Page 32.

[121] דוחקין רגלי השכינה—page 194.

"Even though he lied to him, nevertheless the *Holy Spirit* rested upon him"—interchanging, as we can see, the two terms.[122] Another passage declares "that he who speaks disparagingly of the blemishes of the learned (תלמידי חכמים), it is as though he speaks disparagingly of the *Shekinah*;"[123] and this analogy, again, is possible because the learned are regarded as the embodiment of the Holy Spirit, an aspect of *Shekinah*.

From the special meaning of *Shekinah* as God's immanent presence in man, it lends itself to the expression of the cognate idea of God's nearness to man. A man's deeds cause him to be far or else bring him near to the *Shekinah*.[124] That man's bliss in the World to Come consists in his nearness to the Divine Presence is an oft-recurring theme in the Midrash; and our Seder puts it thus: "Everyone that has regard for goodness merits and receives the presence of *Shekinah*."[125] The angels naturally enjoy this bliss continually, but man too, if he has kept himself free from transgression and iniquity and sin and has learned Torah, "becomes prepared to receive *Shekinah* even as the ministering angels."[126]

Shekinah has all these special meanings but it is also employed as a *general* term for God, again, however, often with a slight connotation of a Presence, a vague personification. This is illustrated by the two passages quoted at the beginning of our discussion on *Shekinah*,[127] and by the following: "And when he (i. e. Jacob) went forth from his father's house to go to the house of Laban, *Shekinah* came and stood above him and said to Jacob, 'My son, lift up now thine eyes and look toward

[122] Pages 60–1.

[123] Page 16.

[124] Page 104.

[125] מקבל פני שכינה—page 16. David, because of his many good deeds, will be seated at the right of the *Shekinah*—page 90.

[126] Page 52. The angels enjoy the bliss of the presence of *Shekinah*—p. 161; the *Ḥayyot* within the throne of glory itself have even a greater measure of bliss (ibid). Under "angels" in the chapter on creation the relation of the angels' bliss to the conception of justice is elaborated.

[127] Above, page 53. In the Seder the passages are on pages 89 and "Additions," page 34.

heaven' " etc.[128] We have found, therefore, that *Shekinah* is a general term for God, that in a special sense it stands for God immanent within Israel, that thus it is associated with the Holy Spirit, and that it sometimes conveys the idea of God's near presence particularly in the World to Come. We should add God's immanence among His attributes, though it cannot be classified among the independent attributes but is rather one peculiarly suited, as can easily be seen, to the four fundamental concepts.[129]

Shekinah and "the Holy Spirit" have this in common: They both express, on occasion, God's immanence in man; and in this sense only the former includes the latter. Both demand that man be qualified thus to act as a divine instrument; both depart when man sins,[130] and *Shekinah*, since it descends upon the whole congregation of Israel, can be crowded off by the actions of the sinners among Israel. On the other hand, *Shekinah* is also a general term for God, whereas "the Holy Spirit" stands always for a special activity of His, with or without man as an instrument.

The question as to why rabbinic theology possesses so many terms for God is one that cannot be fully answered here. Yet it may be that some light has been thrown on it by some of the matters treated thus far. Ehrlich has demonstrated that the substitution of *Adonai* and *Elohim* for the tetragrammaton was the result of reverence and not because of any prohibition derived from Exodus 20:7.[131] This reverence was extended, as we know, to the terms *Adonai* and *Elohim* themselves, and the Rabbis refrained out of this motive from employing

[128] Page 29. The same expression occurs when *Shekinah* speaks to David: "*Shekinah* came and stood above him, and said to him, 'Speak, my son, how come you by these things?' "—on page 15.

[129] For that very reason it harbors within itself anthropomorphic tendencies even when employed as a general term. The phrases "God withdrew His *Shekinah*" and "He allowed His *Shekinah* to rest on them" are an attempt to soften the anthropomorphism by temporarily dissociating, as it were, God and *Shekinah*.

[130] The Holy Spirit, in the case of David for 22 years—page 7; *Shekinah* withdrew from Israel, above, p. 54.

[131] Mikra Ki-pheshuto, Vol. III, pages 168–171. Whether his other conclusions in that section are correct does not concern us here.

them even in theological discussions.[132] Now the Rabbis' major interest lay in describing how God was continually affecting and governing the world, how, in other words, He acted with respect to the four points of reference. What was more natural, therefore, than for them to find terms for God that would exactly express His activity when viewed from these four vantage points, since they were bound not to refer to God by His biblical names? Thus, "the Holy Spirit" derives from Torah, *Shekinah*, from God's choice of Israel, "Father in heaven" and other parental appellations from His loving-kindness, and "King of the kings of kings" from His governance or justice. It is reasonable to infer that, once this tendency to find terms for God expressive of particular aspects of His activity or descriptive of His qualities was established, it would envelop independent attributes as well: Since He is holy, He is "The Holy One blessed be He;" Creator, He is "He who spake and the world came into being;" universal, He is "The Master of the universe;"[133] omnipotent, He is "Might;" transcendant, He is "Heaven," "Above;" "The Name" is the very expression for reverence itself.

After the terms acquired current usage, they became *general* terms for God, regardless of the particular attributes or activity in which they had their origin; (except, of course, such terms as "the Holy Spirit" and perhaps "Father of mercy" which refer so patently to specific aspects of God). Instead, some of the terms got to be crystallized together with certain set phrases, as the result of usage,[134] some were favored as the inauguration of prayers,[135] and some became popular terms for God in almost every context.[136]

[132] There is one exception in this book, on p. 6. But it can be explained: Our author is talking to a Persian magus; in speaking of God, he must use the term *Elohim*, since the peculiarly rabbinic terms would be unfamiliar to a non-Jew.

[133] The attribute of Kingship has, of course, a similar connotation—see above, page 38. מקום "The Place" may also have this attribute as its origin. Schechter who translates it "The Omnipresent" probably had in mind the famous homily of God's being "The Place of the Universe."

[134] E. g., קדוש השם, כלפי מעלה, לכבוד שמים—See above, pages 49 and 50.

[135] אבי שבשמים, רבונו של עולם, רבון העולמים—(ibid.)

[136] מי שאמר והיה העולם, מקום, הקדוש ברוך הוא—(ibid.

V

God's Kingship

Malkut Shamayim is not, contrary to some writers on Jewish theology, the belief in the future establishment of the Kingdom of God. These authors translate the phrase as "The Kingdom of God" or "The Kingdom of Heaven," terms more than reminiscent of Christian theology. They insist, however, that, whereas Christian theology teaches that into this Kingdom of Heaven those who are "saved" will enter only after death, the Rabbis taught that the Kingdom of God (or of Heaven—the terms are synonymous), which is the reign of perfect justice and peace under God as King, will take place on earth.[137] Now this distinction is correct if made between the Christian conception of "The Kingdom of Heaven" and the rabbinic conception of the *'Olam Habba*, the World to Come, provided we bear in mind the rabbinic belief that those already dead who are worthy will be revived and share the World to Come with those then living who are worthy.[138] But *'Olam Habba* is not *Malkut Shamayim*. The fact is that the Rabbis believed that the Kingdom of God is right here and now, always was and will be in the future. They voice their belief in the answer Abraham is said to have given Nimrod who asked whom he should worship: "The God of gods, the Lord of lords, whose kingship is established in heaven and earth and in the highest heavens"[139]—God whose kingship *is* established, not "whose kingdom come." On this earth and now He rules with perfect justice, and aught that happens to individuals and nations is in exact measure to their deeds.

Malkut Shamayim means "the Kingship of God;" it is an abstract noun;[140] and it is usually given in the phrase: "They

[137] See K. Kohler's Jewish Theology, Chapter XLIX. Among others, Mann, for example, speaks of "the hope of the ultimate restoration of Israel when the eschatological 'kingdom of heaven' would become supreme on earth"—Changes in the Divine Service, Hebrew Union College Annual, Vol. IV, p. 246. See below, note 142, p. 59.

[138] Below, chapter on The World to Come. [139] Page 27.

[140] מלכות שמים—מלכות is an abstract form; "The Kingdom of God" would be ממלכת שמים, just as ממלכת כהנים is properly translated, "a kingdom of priests" in Exod. 19:6.

accepted (or, he accepted) the Kingship of God."[141] "To accept the Kingship of God" means to acknowledge that God rules now.[142] But how does He manifest His rule? Through His governance of the world, through His loving-kindness for man, through His giving of the Torah, through His choice of Israel, primarily through the ways in which the Rabbis saw Him as affecting the world. That God rules may be acknowledged as a general proposition or else may be affirmed by an act demonstrating conscious obedience to His will. The latter, in view of the Rabbis' predilection for the concrete, is the more frequently met with in this Midrash. Seldom, however, can there be concrete occasions in which God's choice of Israel can be acknowledged; more often, the possibility for acknowledging His justice and loving-kindness; most often, indeed daily, is it given to study and practice His Torah and thus to acknowledge His sovereignty. For that reason we find that accepting the Kingship of God is usually associated with Torah.

It was at Sinai that all Israel acknowledged, with the acceptance of the Torah, the Kingship or sovereignty of God.[143]

[141] קבלו . . . מלכות שמים—pages 85, 83, 179, 82, 132, 86.

[142] The trend of the authorities on rabbinic theology toward this view of *Malkut Shamayim* is unmistakable. Schechter, though he retains the translation "Kingdom of God," declares that it is established in the consciousness of the individual and that "the idea of the Kingdom may thus be conceived as ethical (not exactly eschatological)"—Aspects, pp. 89–90. Moore directly states that by *Malkut Shamayim* "is to be understood not the realm over which God rules, but his *Kingship*, his character of king"—Judaism, II, p. 372. Ginzberg likewise states that "the idea of the Kingdom of Heaven was . . . neither eschatological nor political but the rule of God in the heart of the individual"—Students, Scholars and Saints, p. 96. Foakes-Jackson and Lake define *Malkut Shamayim* unequivocably as "the sovereignty of God"—Beginnings of Christianity, I, pp. 269–280. And Dalman writes, "Es kann kein Zweifel daruber obwalten dass sowohl im Alten Testament als in der judischen Literatur das auf Gott bezogene מלכות stets 'Konigsregiment,' niemals 'Konigreich' bedeutet . . ."—Die Worte Jesu I, p. 77; cf. also, ibid, p. 312. They also see, of course, the relation between *Malkut Shamayim* and Torah in rabbinic literature but do not account for it as we do here on the basis of the four points of reference.

[143] I translate מלכות שמים as "sovereignty of God" since it is a less awkward term than "the Kingship of God" used here previously in order to differentiate "Kingship" from "Kingdom."

Then "Israel accepted the sovereignty of Heaven with joy, saying, 'All that the Lord hath spoken will we do and obey' (Exod. 24:7)."[144] To "accept the sovereignty of God with joy" is to attain to an emotional exaltation, more than conviction or acknowledgment. They were prepared for that experience for "they stood at Mt. Sinai to accept the sovereignty of Heaven with free-will."[145]

It was not enough for Israel once to have accepted the sovereignty of God: every generation must accept it anew. "In the days of Joshua, the son of Nun, Israel accepted upon themselves with love the sovereignty of Heaven,"[146] and "in the days of Samuel, the prophet, Israel accepted upon themselves with fear the sovereignty of Heaven."[147] While it is not wise, perhaps, to labor the point, we ought to take account of the phrases "with love" and "with fear," since they are certainly employed deliberately. The love of God and fear of God, it will be shown later, are man's reactions to God's loving-kindness and to His justice, respectively.[148] Hence, in these statements there seems to be a hint that God's sovereignty was acknowledged by Israel when they were convinced of God's loving-kindness or else of His justice.

The individual, no less than the nation, must acknowledge in both word and deed the sovereignty of God. The affirmation of faith in God, repeated at every period of prayer and in the death-bed confessional—"Hear, O Israel, the Lord our God, the Lord is One" (Deut. 6:4)—is also the classic declaration of His sovereignty,[149] and as such is "a grave *mizwah*."[150] Another assertion of the sovereignty of God is the first commandment.[151]

[144] Page 85; similarly twice on page 179.

[145] בנדבה—page 83. The giving of the Torah and the sovereignty of Heaven are again associated in interpreting Ezek. 16:8—on page 139; and when the Nations of the World refused the Torah, "they refused to accept Thy sovereignty"—p. 127.

[146] באהבה—page 86. [147] ביראה, ibid.

[148] See below, chapter on motives.

[149] Page 132 and 140.

[150] Page 132.

[151] Ibid: " 'Thou shalt not take the name of the Lord thy God in vain;' 'Remember the Sabbath day.' What have these statements to do with one

The prophets, apparently, accepted God's sovereignty with the acceptance of their mission, the Rabbis stating that Isaiah "accepted the sovereignty of Heaven with joy" when he said, "Here am I, send me" (Is. 6:8).[152] The learned and their pupils acknowledge His sovereignty when they study Torah, of course, when "they study Bible and Mishnah (קורין ושונין) . . . and accept upon themselves the yoke of Heaven."[153] Torah includes practice as well as study; the breaking of a commandment is an indication that the sovereignty of God is not accepted, be the affirmation in word never so strong: "Every one that is accustomed to vain oaths and false swearing does not accept upon himself the complete sovereignty of Heaven (מלכות שמים שלימה), and he that is not accustomed to vain oaths and false swearing does accept upon himself the complete sovereignty of Heaven . . . A man should not say to himself, 'I love Heaven and am afraid of Heaven' in order (to permit himself) to transgress any of the *mizwot* in the Torah . . . But he should say to himself, 'I love Heaven and am afraid of Heaven' in order not to transgress any of the *mizwot* in the Torah."[154]

In the passage above we again find that the declaration "I love and fear Heaven" is tantamount to the affirmation of *Malkut Shamayim*. This is proved by the conclusion of the passage,

another?" The midrash explains that he who swears falsely does not accept the Kingship of God. But the two commandments as given have no relation to one another, although later a hint of a different interpretation is implied. The Third Commandment, that against false swearing, is no doubt coupled with the First, as in the paragraph of the text immediately preceding.

[152] Page 82. See Friedmann's note No. 16.

[153] Page 97—עול שמים, "the yoke of Heaven": I take this to be equivalent to "the yoke of the sovereignty of Heaven," since on page 85 the same expression is used and is soon followed by the statement, "when Israel accepted the sovereignty of Heaven with joy." In both cases "the yoke of Heaven" is associated with Torah.

This association between *Malkut Shamayim* and Torah makes those who interpret the former as being the future establishment of the Kingdom of Heaven hard put to it to explain passages in which this conjunction occurs. Kohler (l. c. p. 339) says that "studying and practicing the law . . . was tantamount to 'placing himself under the Kingdom of God' "—without any explanation as to why it should be tantamount.

[154] Page 132. The passage probably refers to sectarian antinomians.

which sums up the entire argument that merely to affirm love or fear of God without performing His *mizwot* is not to accept His sovereignty: "Therefore they placed this (*mizwah* of *zizit*) near the grave one of *Malkut Shamayim*—'Hear O Israel' is followed by 'that they put upon the fringe of each corner' (i. e., arranged so in the prayers). Thus you learn that the lightest *mizwah* is like the grave one, and the grave one like the light one."[155] And again in another passage it is remarked that the injunction in the Bible to love God has "at its side *Malkut Shamayim*."[156] Assuming that love and fear of God are the respective reactions of man to God's loving-kindness and His justice, as is shown below,[157] and that the latter are manifestations of His sovereignty, expressions of love and fear of God are really affirmations or acknowledgments of His sovereignty.

On one occasion, God's sovereignty was manifest to the whole world, and that was when He gave the Torah on Mt. Sinai. There was no need to infer from His justice or love or anything else that He rules, for He revealed Himself. "At that moment the whole world trembled, saying, 'Perhaps He has come to the world to destroy it.' The Holy Spirit answered them, saying, 'The King of the kings of kings came only to have a feast with His sons.' And He said, 'I came to reign. Why do I reign and because of what do I reign.' "[158] There is a parallel passage in the Mekilta with the same proof-texts which says that the Nations of the World feared then that He had come to destroy them.[159] At one point in history, the Rabbis thus believed, God's majesty was visible to all. But the time will come again, in the World to Come, when His sovereignty will once more unmistakably be made known to the whole world, and thenceforth it will be acknowledged by everybody forever. "Just as we shall go to bow down (before God), so shall all the Nations of

[155] Ibid.

[156] Page 140.

[157] Below in chapter on motives.

[158] Page 13. The text here is a bit obscure, but the Mekilta parallel helps us to understand the proof-texts.

[159] Mekilta, beginning of *Yitro*, Weiss edition, page 65; cited by Friedmann.

the World, in the future, go to bow down to the King of the kings of kings, the Holy One blessed be He."[160] Those who identify *the 'Olam Habba* and *Malkut Shamayim* are justified to the extent that in the *'Olam Habba*, the Rabbis believed, the whole world will accept His sovereignty. But it is incorrect to state that the Kingdom of God is to exist only in the World to Come. According to the Rabbis it always exists, and will exist in the World to Come when history has run its course.

Appendix to "God's Kingship"

Those who claim that belief in *Malkut Shamayim* is the belief in the future establishment of the Kingdom of God base their opinion on the passages in the prayer-book referring to it. My contention is that they mistranslate the term and thus misinterpret the prayers. Actually, it seems to me, the prayers refer to the *acknowledgment* of God's sovereignty by the whole world when He will reveal Himself again. A few examples will suffice, I think, to make this clear:

In the *'Amidah* for *Rosh Hashanah*: "Our God and God of our fathers reign Thou in Thy glory over the whole world . . . and appear in Thy splendor and excellence of Thy might upon all the inhabitants of Thy world—(והופע בהדר גאון . . .), that whatsoever hath breath in its nostrils may say, The Lord God of Israel is King, and His sovereignty ruleth over all (ומלכותו בכל משלה)."[161] In the famous *'Alenu* prayer: "We therefore hope in Thee, O Lord our God, that we may speedily behold the glory of Thy might, when Thou wilt remove the abominations . . . when Thou wilt perfect the world in the sovereignty of God (לתקן עולם במלכות שדי) and all the children of flesh will call upon Thy name . . . Before Thee, O Lord our God, will they bow and fall (יכרעו ויפולו); and unto Thy glorious name will they give honor (יקר יתנו); and they will all accept (ויקבלו כלם) the yoke of Thy sovereignty (עול מלכותך), and Thou wilt reign over

[160] Page 81.

[161] Singer's Prayer Book (Bloch Pub. Co.), page 353. Where my translation differs from his, I supply the Hebrew as my warrant; and so throughout these quotations. It is the mistranslations that have aided the misconception.

them speedily (ותמלוך עליהם), and forever and ever. For the sovereignty is Thine, and to all eternity wilt Thou reign in glory." In the *Ḳaddish*: "May His great name be magnified and sanctified (יתגדל ויתקדש שמה רבה) in the world which He hath created according to His will; and may He cause His sovereignty to rule (וימליך מלכותה) during your life and during your days . . ." God's name will be magnified, in other words, when the whole world accepts His sovereignty.

VI

Ḳiddush Hashem and Ḥillul Hashem

The acknowledgment that God is sovereign of the world, expressed by declaration or implicitly by the acceptance of the four fundamental concepts, is the affirmation of faith in Him by individual or nation. It is limited to that only, quite without regard to the affirmation's effect upon others or upon the world in general. The points of reference, however, are God's manifestation in the world. As such, they bear witness to Him: If they are true to their function, they glorify God; if not, they, as it were, discredit Him. The rabbinic term for the former is *Ḳiddush Hashem*—the sanctification of the Name, and for the latter, *Ḥillul Hashem*—the profanation of the Name. If Israel demonstrates its loyalty, Torah its efficacy and God's justice and love their universal sway, then they sanctify the Name; any deviation by Israel, inefficacy of Torah or instance of favoritism or cruelty by God would profane the Name.[162]

How the terms, *Ḳiddush Hashem* and *Ḥillul Hashem*, came to have this meaning in rabbinic theology cannot be altogether ascertained. Certainly it is not very helpful in this connection

[162] קדוש השם and חלול השם. "קדוש השם in its original meaning is limited to an act of a heroic character by which man makes the holiness of God known to others. Compare b. San. 84a–74b."—(L.G.). In this Midrash regardless of the original limitation of the term, it conforms, as do all the other concepts, to the points of reference. May it not be also that the passage in Sanhedrin deals with only one aspect of the concept, which, incidentally is treated here as well?

to go back to the original meaning of the word *ḳadosh*, and to try to trace its various connotations: for, by the time of the Rabbis, primitive and even biblical meanings of fundamental religious terms had given place to new denotations, in some cases drawn from biblical contexts and almost wholly fortuitous juxtaposition of biblical verses and phrases. If this is true, it is just possible that the rabbinic concept of *Ḳiddush Hashem* was derived from Isaiah 6:3: "Holy, holy, holy is the Lord of hosts; the whole earth is full of His glory." Holiness, they may have argued from this verse, is thus equivalent to the whole earth being "full with His glory;" that is, He is made holy, sanctified, when He is being glorified. That this explanation is by no means unjustified is suggested by the very manner the Rabbis use the verse in Seder Eliahu. "Two rows (of angels) standing before Him *sanctify* His great name every day: From the rising of the sun until the setting of the sun, they say, 'Holy, holy, holy.' "[163] Reciting "Holy, holy, holy" is sanctifying the Name. To the same verse, perhaps, the following statement refers: "But (the people of) Israel rise from their beds early in the morning and *sanctify* My name twice every day continually."[164] Of course, this explanation of the origin of the rabbinic significance of the term *Ḳiddush Hashem* is put forward

[163] Pp. 163, 193, 84, 156. On pp. 34 and 84 the declaration quoted above is assigned the angels "from the rising of the sun until the setting thereof." At night, another text from the Bible is used: "From the setting of the sun until its rising, they say, 'Blessed be the glory of the Lord from His place' (Ezek. 3:12)." It is this sanctifying of the Name which constitutes the "song" of the angels before God—"Additions," p. 28.

[164] "Additions," p. 37. It is more than doubtful whether this statement does refer to Is. 6:3, which is recited in the *Ḳedushah*. See Prof. Ginzberg's opinion below, p. 149, note 162. He regards ומקדשין ("and sanctify") as a textual error, and with very good warrant. Nevertheless, this does not entirely rule out the possibility that this verse may have been the source, textually anyhow, of the concept. In this connection, Prof. Ginzberg warns: "The *Ḳedushah* is of comparatively late origin and cannot be the source for *Ḳiddush Hashem*." But I do not mean to say that the *Ḳedushah* is the source, but rather that the verse later incorporated in the *Ḳedushah* may be the source. The prooftext in Lev. 22:32 used in b. San. 74a, though containing the roots *ḥallel* and *ḳaddesh* hardly connotes the much wider interpretation of the idea in rabbinic theology.

tentatively, being merely a suggestion that this possibility ought not be ruled out.

The passages quoted in the preceding paragraph indicate that, as with *Malkut Shamayim*, *Ḳiddush Hashem* is affirmed by a declaration. But, whereas, in the case of the former, "Hear, O Israel, the Lord our God the Lord is One" is directed to Israel and to the individual, in the latter, "Holy, holy, holy, is the Lord of hosts; the whole earth is full of His glory" is directed to the world at large, a proclamation to creation that God alone whose glory fills the whole earth is to be worshipped. And by the very declaration itself He is glorified before the whole world, the Name is sanctified. The angels sanctify the Name in heaven—that, indeed, is their function. Israel sanctify the Name on earth—[165] that is their function, and they have other ways, besides uttering the declaration, of performing it. The worship of idols is a denial that "the whole earth is full of His glory;" hence the destruction of idols is sanctification of the Name. The Holy One blessed be He thus explains His grace toward Israel: "They and their ancestors have shown Me favoritism for they destroyed all the idols in the world and sanctified My name in the world;"[166] and particularly is His grace shown them for the sake of Abraham who, "destroyed all the idols in the market-place, and in the world, and sanctified My name in the world."[167]

When the people of Israel declare that God alone is to be worshipped, and the Nations of the World attempt to force them to worship idols, God is sanctified through martyrdom. Heroic men and women who choose death at the hands of their persecutors rather than renounce God testify by renouncing life instead that there can be no other God in the world. It is with this final demonstration of loyalty that the term *Ḳiddush Hashem* has largely been associated in the popular mind, since, after the fall of pagan Rome, Christian Rome likewise continually

[165] The angels do not say *Shirah* above until Israel says it below—"Additions," p. 47.

[166] "Additions," p. 41—וקידשו שמי בעולם.

[167] "Additions," p. 47. The story of Abraham and the idols is given on p. 27 and repeated and enlarged in "Additions," pp. 47–8

forced upon Israel the tragic role of martyr-witness. The first martyr in Jewish history had well-nigh been the first Jew, Abraham, who "offered himself unto death for the glory of Heaven in Ur of the Chaldees" and who would have been burnt alive had God not saved him by a miracle.[168] A popular tale reflecting the martyrdom of the Jews in the pagan world of Greece and Rome is the story, referred to above, of Miriam, daughter of Tanḥum, and her seven sons. Offered life on condition of bowing to the idol, the sons refuse and meet death proclaiming their belief in God. The youngest son, a child upon whom the cruel emperor took pity, even refused to simulate idol-worship and pick up a ring in front of the idol, and was thereupon killed. And the mother, who had encouraged them in their resistance, when her sons were gone, exclaimed, "My sons, happy are you that you did the will of your Father in heaven, for you were in this world only to sanctify His great name through yourselves!" Whereupon she went up to the roof and jumped down and died.[169] The Rabbis extol in the strongest terms death for the glory of Heaven or for the sanctification of the Name.[170]

Between *Malkut Shamayim* and *Ḳiddush Hashem*, there is great similarity, as we have noticed, yet they must be distinguished from one another. At times, they seem to blend into one another, as when the martyr accepts the sovereignty of God by uttering "Hear, O Israel," and then by martyrdom again affirms that God's glory alone fills the earth, giving his life as proof.

The Name can be sanctified by Israel on every occasion when they come in contact with the Gentile world. When the superior ethics of the Torah are practiced by the Jew in his relations with the Gentile, the latter cannot but realize both the divine source of the moral commands and Israel's loyalty to their Author. This can be deduced from a passage in Seder Eliahu which at first sight is somewhat ambiguous.[171] The passage begins with a description of *Ḳiddush Hashem* as exemplified

[168] Page 27. [169] Pp. 151–153.
[170] Pp. 37, 27—לכבוד שמים.
[171] P. 140.

by the learned in their practice of Torah, and then continues: "The Torah was given only to sanctify His great name, as it says '. . . Thou art My servant, Israel, in whom I will be glorified' (Is. 49:3). From this the learned inferred (lit. 'from this they taught'—מיכן אמרו): One should avoid taking anything illegitimately from an Israelite and from a Gentile and even from any man in the marketplace. For he that steals from a Gentile in the end will steal from an Israelite; and he that robs a Gentile in the end will rob an Israelite; he that swears falsely (נשבע) to a Gentile in the end will swear falsely to an Israelite; he that lies to a Gentile in the end will lie to an Israelite; he that sheds the blood of a Gentile in the end will shed the blood of an Israelite. And the Torah has been given only to sanctify His great name—'And I will work a sign among them, and I will send such as escape of them unto the nations' (Is. 66:19). At the conclusion of the thought, what does it say? 'And they shall declare My glory among the nations.' " (*ibid*).

What conception of *Ḳiddush Hashem* does this passage contain? At first glance, it seems to teach a rather tribal kind of ethics—one should refrain from wronging a Gentile lest the habit become established in one and lead to the wronging of an Israelite. Friedmann declares that the two statements—the one concerning *Ḳiddush Hashem* and the other just referred to as "tribal ethics"—are not related to each other.[172] But if this is the case why are the two ideas connected by the phrase מיכן אמרו—"From this the scholars inferred"? And why does the passage close with another statement about *Ḳiddush Hashem* supported by a verse from the Bible? Our problem is solved, however, if we regard this section as dealing with one social relationship in which two ethical incentives figure. The Gentile is not to be wronged, one reason given being the tribal motive, and the other reason the higher one of *Ḳiddush Hashem*. The whole passage is thus a discussion of *Ḳiddush Hashem*, interrupted by what may well be an interpolation. It begins by describing how the scholars either sanctify or desecrate the name of God. Then there follows the statement that the Torah

[172] P. 140, note 4.

was given in order to sanctify the Name; from this statement the scholars infer that "one should avoid taking anything illegitimately from an Israelite and from a Gentile and even from any man in the market-place." The ethics of the Torah, brought home to the Gentile through the way in which the Israelite behaves toward him, sanctify the Name. (Elsewhere, too, the Rabbis say that robbing a Gentile is a graver sin than robbing an Israelite because of *Ḥillul Hashem*).[173] A new motive is then added parenthetically which we have designated as tribal ethics. At the close, the passage once more reverts to the main subject of *Ḳiddush Hashem*, repeating the original statement "The Torah has been given only to sanctify His great name," a repetition made necessary because the trend of thought had been interrupted. But now the biblical verses used in support explain how it is that the Torah sanctifies the Name. Israel, practicing Torah, has been deliberately dispersed by God that, by their behavior toward their neighbors, "they shall declare My glory."

As we have seen above, Abraham, as the first Jew, was the first to sanctify the Name, according to the Rabbis. He sanctifies the Name not only by destroying idols and by his readiness for martyrdom, but also in his behavior toward the Gentiles of his day. When the king of Sodom went to greet Abraham, he expected Abraham to take the booty won in battle. But Abraham said, " 'Fool, do I need silver and gold . . . they are worthless to me . . .' On that occasion Abraham sanctified the name of God."[174]

The Name is sanctified when Torah is prized by men; the Name is profaned when Torah is cheapened among men. The learned are responsible in either case. When they deal honestly

[173] Tos. Baba Kama, Chapter 10, quoted by Friedmann, l. c.

[174] P. 128. There is a hint also, on p. 104, that Joseph when he appeared before Pharaoh, and foretold the seven years of plenty and the seven years of famine, sanctified the name of God. It was thus that the Egyptians came to know Him. "The Holy One blessed be He gives wisdom, understanding, knowledge, and discernment only to sanctify His great Name;" Gen. 49:23 and 24, the verses in Jacob's blessing concerning Joseph are the proof-texts of this statement. The Targum and Rashi take these verses from Genesis to refer to Joseph's gift of prophecy.

in their transactions in the market-place and in traffic with their fellow men people say, " 'Happy is so-and-so who studied Torah! Woe to my father who did not teach me Torah. So-and-so studied Torah; see how beautiful are his deeds, how lovely his ways. By the Temple service! let us study Torah and teach our sons Torah.' And thus the name of Heaven is sanctified through him (i. e. through the learned man)."[175] But when a scholar deals dishonestly with men, people say, " 'Woe to so-and-so that he studied Torah! Happy be my father that he did not teach me Torah! So-and-so who studied Torah, see how bad are his deeds, how corrupt his ways. By the Temple service, we shall not study Torah, we shall not teach our sons Torah!' And thus through him the name of Heaven is profaned."[176] The scholars must be extremely careful lest their teaching cause the Name to be profaned. "They have taught in the Mishnah: Ye learned, be ye careful with your words lest ye teach one thing that is not according to the Torah, and ye become guilty of (the) death (penalty) to Heaven. And also the pupils that come after you will teach in your name something that is not according to the Torah, and they will become guilty of (the) death (penalty) to Heaven. Thus, God forbid, the name of Heaven will be profaned."[177]

The Name is sanctified through the infallible operation in this world of God's justice. Shall we wonder that wicked tyrants, cruel to Israel as well as godless, have flourished even as have the worthy? God brought it all about—Abraham, in reward for Shem who prophesied for four hundred years; the Greek empire and Alexander, in reward for Japheth who covered his father's nakedness; the Persian empire in reward for Cyrus, who wept and grieved at the destruction of the Temple; Sennacherib, the wicked, and his empire, in reward for Asher who was righteous; Nebuchadnezzar, in reward for Merodach who honored God; Haman, in reward for Agag's fears. (Each of these is the descendant of the person whose deeds constituted the "merit" by virtue of which his progeny was exalted.) "All this,

[175] Page 140.
[176] Ibid.
[177] P. 12.

in order to sanctify His great name."[178] Were God to show favoritism even to Israel there would be profanation of the Name. The Quality of Justice, personified, argues before God, that, since Israel swear falsely in the market-place, gossip evilly of their friends and covet their neighbors' wives, should God show them favoritism (or rather grace משוא פנים), "will there not be in this *a profanation of the Name*?"[179] " 'The great God, the mighty and the awful' (Deut. 10:17) 'the great' ...; 'the mighty' for Thou art mighty in calling to account all who transgress; 'and the awful'—for all fear Thy judgment, which is a true judgment: If Thou wilt show favoritism to Israel will there not be a profanation of the Name in this thing?"[180] God finally convinces the Quality of Justice that in His treatment of Israel, He is indeed just.

There are no passages in Seder Eliahu indicating how the prevalence of God's love sanctifies the Name. This may be merely an accidental omission, or else because justice with its sternness and exactness always is more strikingly a manifestation of God, and acknowledged by the common run of men as such.

VII

The Worship of Strange Gods (Idol-Worship)

The affirmation that God alone rules and is to be worshipped —in the acceptance of *Malkut Shamayim* or through sanctifying the Name—is made necessary by the prevalence of idolatry and other forms of impure worship. Under Rome, the Rabbis witnessed the worship of the emperor and under Persia that of fire. But the most widespread of all was the worship of idols. When the term "strange worship" occurs in Seder Eliahu it

[178] Pp. 114–115. The plagues mentioned in Leviticus are in punishment for definite sins. "Blessed be the Omnipresent, blessed be He, who sanctifies His great name in the open forever!"—p. 77.

[179] "Additions," p. 37, and note 9, p. 37. On the personification of מדהדין see below in chapter on God's justice.

[180] "Additions," page 40. The argument is continued on ("Additions") page 41. For an analysis of the ideas in these passages see below in chapter on God's justice.

usually refers to idolatry; indeed, the latter is spoken of as the rival of God, although, to be sure, merely because it led astray the people of Israel in the days of the First Temple.[181]

The Rabbis present, in a number of passages, arguments proving how absurd is idol-worship. Abraham's glory lies in his discovery that idols are vanity, a discovery which turns him to the worship of the true God;[182] and the stories told of him abound in these arguments. Each person who comes to buy an idol from Abraham wishes to have one suited especially for himself, the strong man wants a mighty god, the poor woman a weak, poor god.[183] Of what low intelligence these idol-worshippers are can be gauged by their accepting Abraham's statement that the idol who happens to be at the top of the pile is the strong god and the one at the bottom the weak god.[184] But they are convinced of the idols' futility when Abraham points out that they are greater than the idols since the latter were made only yesterday with his father's mallet.[185] After Abraham tests the idols by offering them food and drink as propitiation "and there was not one among them that took (any thing)," he describes their utter helplessness by reciting Ps. 115:5–8, and then he breaks all of them and casts the pieces into the fire.[186] Thus, the beginnings of Judaism, according to the Rabbis, consisted in the conviction that idolatry was the worship of futilities. When God revealed to Abraham, as the latter was pursuing the kings at Dan, that in that very place Israel would revert to idol-worship, "his strength left him" since he felt his whole purpose defeated.[187]

The grave sin of the commonwealth of the First Temple was idolatry. Its enormity was so great that God, when he exiled Israel at that time, almost intended never to restore them back to their place.[188] The valley described by Ezekiel

[181] Page 148—עבודה זרה.

[182] "Additions," pages 47–9; similar story, though fragmentary, page 27.

[183] Ibid.

[184] Ibid. [185] Ibid.

[186] "Additions," page 48.

[187] Page 28.

[188] Page 148.

as being full of bones was the scene of God's punishment for the sin of idolatry.[189] The idol-worshipping kings—Jereboam, Ahab, Ahaz and Manasseh, the last going so far as to place an idol of four faces in the Temple itself—[190] have no portion in the World to Come, for by their betrayal of God they committed the unforgivable sin.[191] No matter how fit otherwise for the highest religious office, "he who worships idols from youth to old age, even though he be fit to be High Priest, has no portion in the World to Come."[192]

No less false than the worship of idols is the worship of man. And again it is Abraham who demonstrates how irrational such worship is. After Abraham had destroyed the idols, Nimrod finds him and says, "Do you not know that I am the lord of all things! The sun and the moon, the stars and the constellations and mankind, (all) go forth at my command." Abraham, being given wisdom by God, thereupon asks Nimrod to command the sun to rise in the west the next day and set in the east; and to tell what is in Abraham's heart. Nimrod cannot do this, of course, he is but mortal: "Just as you could not save your father so cannot you be saved (from death)."[193]

In a parallel passage, Nimrod makes no claim to divinity but asserts that his god is fire.[194] This parallel was no doubt written by one who lived under Persian rule in Babylon, whilst the other passage has in mind perhaps the worship of the Roman emperors.[195] Still another passage contains a debate between a Persian priest, who attempts to prove from the Torah that fire is god, and one of the authors of Seder Eliahu who meets every argument: "You say that fire is not God; why then does it say in your Torah, 'Fire shall be kept burning on the altar continually (Lev. 6:6)?' I answered, 'My son, when our ancestors stood on Mt. Sinai to accept the Torah upon themselves, they

[189] Page 24.
[190] Page 188.
[191] Page 16.
[192] Ibid.
[193] "Additions," page 48.
[194] Page 27.
[195] See Chapter I, pp. 9–10.

saw neither the form of a man nor the form of any creature nor the form of any soul that God created upon the face of the earth, as it says, 'Take ye therefore good heed unto yourselves—for ye saw no manner of form on the day' etc. (Deut. 4:15) . . . and you say that fire is god. It is only as a rod, however, that is given for use upon mankind on earth. Let me give you a parable: A king took a whip and hung it in his palace. And he said to his sons and servants and members of his household, 'With this I shall smite you, with this I shall scourge you, with this I shall slay you' in order that they should return and repent . . . Therefore it says, 'Fire shall be kept burning upon the altar continually' . . . You might answer me and say that it is written, 'For the Lord thy God is a devouring fire' (Deut. 4:24). But it is a parable: The sons and servants and members of the household of a king were not acting properly. He said to them, 'I am a lurking bear to you, I am a lion to you, I am the angel of death to you, because of your ways.' Therefore it says, 'For the Lord thy God is a devouring fire.' "[196]

Sun-worship was another form of idolatry. The Rabbis felt that the sun though so far removed, yet was defiled by being thus worshipped. " 'Which is as a bridegroom coming out of his chamber (Ps. 19:6)'—just as a bridegroom enters pure and goes out defiled, so the wheel of the sun goes out pure and returns defiled." Were it not that God forces the sun to go out, he would not go forth to shine, so great is his aversion to being worshipped.[197]

God alone rules and is to be worshipped: the worship of idols and of man is stupid as well as wrong; of fire, unwarranted and wrong; of the sun, defiling to the sun and wrong. For God is One and His glory fills the whole earth.

[196] Page 6. Under fairly primitive conditions and in huddled towns, fire must have been a frequent and dreadful catastrophe.

[197] Page 11. See Friedmann's note No. 48.

CHAPTER IV

CREATION

I

The Conception of Nature

God created the world and "all is His and the work of His hands."[1] He created the entire world but for His glory.[2] This should not be taken to mean that nature with its order and seasons, by reason of its very orderliness and rhythm and law, proclaims the glory of its Creator. Such an idea belongs rather to philosophy than to rabbinic theology, as indeed do all the strictly teleological proofs of the existence of God.[3] We shall find, in this chapter, that nature proclaims His glory, according to the Rabbis, in quite another way. Heaven and earth, the sun and the moon, insects and beasts—all respond to, and are affected by, the four fundamental aspects of God's activity: His justice, love, Torah and His selection of Israel. When the Rabbis say that God created the world but for His glory, they mean that nothing in creation has an independent purpose or exists in and for itself, but that all things in nature have been created and carry on with reference to the four points of reference. To attribute to the Rabbis, therefore, a conception of nature which should include beliefs in a fixed physical order and in natural law is entirely to misunderstand rabbinic theology.

One of the most baffling problems rabbinic theology presents to the modern student—how to distinguish firm popular

[1] Pages 115, 90, 172.

[2] Page 185, "Additions, p." 20.

[3] In Chapter III of the Kuzari, Yehudah Halevy finds support for the argument that God designed the world not so much from the usefulness to man of the sun and moon, as from the remarkable construction of the ant and the bee. In rabbinic theology, on the other hand, the relation of nature to man is much more emphasized, as will be seen shortly.

beliefs from what is just poetic or imaginative fancy—comes to the fore in any consideration of the rabbinic conception of nature. Seder Eliahu, beyond any doubt, attributes to objects and phenomena in nature emotions, activities, even acts of will we today associate only with human beings.[4] The question remains, however, whether the Rabbis intended all these homilies to be taken for statements of sober fact, or whether they were merely indulging in poetic flights, or whether they elaborated popular beliefs into luxurious, imaginative productions with no clear line between the two. That "heaven and earth, sun, moon, stars and constellations early and late do the will of their Creator"[5] was a firm conviction with them we can safely assume. A religious attitude toward the world we expect should include the general belief that nature manifests God's will no less than man. Similarly we may understand the statement: "The heavens were created first and they are worthy to declare the praise of Him who spake and the world came into being,"[6] though possibly here the author may have had in mind actual speech.

But when the qualities of personality—of consciousness, emotion, deliberate action—are attributed to natural phenomena with more and more concreteness, are we to assume these to be expressions of belief or products of poetic fancy? The sun, knowing that he will be defiled by pagans worshipping him, is forced to his task, according to the Seder.[7] The jubilees, that is, the cycles of fifty years of time, love God.[8] The light enjoyed by the world during the first three days of creation, then hidden by God, rejoiced thereat, and consoled itself for being withheld from the righteous in this world.[9] When the angels seek God in order to say *Shirah* before Him, they ask the sea if it saw Him. The sea answers, "From the day when He made me dry

[4] Similarly in other rabbinic sources and in cognate literature. Comp. Ginzberg, Legends of the Jews, Vol. V, p. 34, note 100, and p. 40, note 112.

[5] Page 195.

[6] Page 9.

[7] Page 11.

[8] Page 37.

[9] "Additions," page 34.

land and caused His children to pass through me I have not seen Him again." Mount Sinai answers in similar vein when approached by the angels; and Zion, too, declares she has not seen God since He destroyed His Temple and withdrew His *Shekinah*. The passage closes with the appearance of God, who returns from wreaking vengeance upon Edom.[10] In the World to Come, at the time of judgment, "the earth will open its mouth like a man and will speak to God and say to Him, 'Master of the world, so-and-so has committed a sin in this and this place, and so-and-so has robbed so-and-so in that and that place; and so-and-so has sworn falsely by Thy name in this and this place.' "[11] Gehenna will also open its mouth and plead with God to fill it with the sinners among Israel;[12] it will open its mouth to enable the idolators to come forth and see Israel's bliss.[13] God will call heaven and earth, and the sun and the moon to account: "When you saw My *Shekinah* withdrawn and My house destroyed, and My sons exiled among the Nations of the World, why did you not beg mercy for them?"[14] The sun and the moon are guilty of countenancing idolatry: "And not only that, but the kings of east and west came and put their crowns on their heads and bowed down to you and you did not say, 'We are potsherds like unto an earthen potsherd, bow not down to us.' "[15]

A moment's consideration of these passages will convince us that they cannot be brought under modern categories of thought, under the hard and fast divisions of belief, fact, and products of the imagination. In one passage the sun appears as an involuntary and protesting object of worship; in another, as acquiescing at being placed in the role of a god. Surely, then, these statements cannot be taken as positive beliefs. A deeper

[10] "Additions," page 29.

[11] "Additions," page 32.

[12] Ibid.

[13] "Additions," page 35.

[14] "Additions," page 30. Thus, also, the stars and the constellations (as well as the throne of glory and the Patriarchs and the ministering angels) are called to account for not begging mercy for Israel when they were being exiled—"Additions," page 31.

[15] "Additions," page 30.

examination of the quotations shows us that, with one exception, they are associated with one or another of the four points of reference.[16] This examination is made below in some detail.[17] For the present, we need notice that the sea, Mt. Sinai and Zion are given speech in a passage concerning God's justice; the earth and Gehenna likewise are so endowed in one also concerning His justice; heaven and earth, the sun, moon and constellations are given the attribute of culpability in passages concerning Israel. We should conclude, therefore, that the Rabbis accented not anthropomorphism in nature, but the four fundamental concepts. The former is incidental to the latter; the elaborate stories in which anthropomorphism in nature figures are "poetic truths," inspired by the four points of reference.

The category into which we might place these homilies on nature eludes the modern student. Apparently the Rabbis accepted the principle of anthropomorphism in nature, for otherwise the dramatic stories built upon it would be to them, also, only figments of the imagination. And to the Rabbis these stories were not sheer imaginative fancies: They are the vehicles for the four points of references which were certainly felt, experienced, believed in. On the other hand, by that very token, the principle of anthropomorphism in nature is made subordinate, almost incidental, to the four points of reference. Further proof that it was taken not too seriously are the contradictory stories to which it gave rise, as obvious to the Rabbis as to us. Perhaps the safest conclusion is this: Anthropomorphism in nature as a general principle was a sort of incidental belief; particular instances of this principle were not matters of belief, but were employed largely as background for the four fundamental concepts.

While it is true that nature proclaims God's glory mainly through the manner in which it responds to the four points of reference, His power can also be glimpsed in the very acts of creation themselves. "A king built a palace for himself . . . and he brought a scroll and ink; and sketched a room by itself, and

[16] That exception is the passage concerning the sun as an object of idolatry. It has been dealt with under "Idolatry."

[17] Below, pages 83–88.

a garret by itself, and a toilet by itself, and, after all this, built his palace. But in the creation of heaven and earth, they were created at one time, for it says, 'When I call unto them, they stand together' (Is. 48:13)."[18] "God stood and created the whole world from one end to the other, as it says, 'I have made the earth and created man upon it' (Is. 45:12)."[19] God has made His world on so grand a scale that man is too puny to endeavor even to explore it: "The learned have said that the revolution of the sun is a distance of five hundred years (i. e., were men to walk it). Come and see whence he goes out and whither he enters, or whether his voice is heard in his going or coming, or whether he is seen by anybody in his entering or going out."[20] It is this grandness of scale—the world so vast that it is unexplorable—which accounts for man's present inability to find objects in nature the Bible tells us do exist: "Just as the revolution of the sun is a distance of five hundred years so the tree of life is five hundred years distant."[21]

We must not suppose that the rabbinic conception of nature was entirely limited by their theology. There are the beginnings, as well, of pure scientific observation, halting perhaps, but none the less clear. But we must not expect to find in these beginnings agreement with the latest findings of the trained naturalist. R. Eliezer interprets Exodus 8:2 as referring to the peculiar call of the frog—which thus exhibits "intelligence"—signalling to the birds that they may come without fear and drink of the water of the canals and swamps.[22] In comment on the plague of lice that fell on Egypt, the Rabbis enumerate fourteen species of lice,[23] surely a tribute to their powers of observation. The

[18] Page 160.

[19] Page 21.

[20] Page 10. I accept what seems to me the far better variant found in the Venice edition. See Friedmann, note 32.

[21] Ibid.

[22] Page 41. A play on דעה. It is interesting to note that in this connection R. Eliezer derides R. 'Aḳiba's attempt at Haggadah, telling him to remain in his field of ritual law. Does R. Eliezer, the naturalist, resent 'Aḳiba's far-fetched haggadic interpretation?

[23] Ibid.

heaven, no less than objects on earth, receives their scrutiny, although, to be sure, the following passage cannot be a lesson in astronomy today: "The learned said: The entire world is between the Great Bear and the Scorpion . . . I said: All the creatures of the world dwell underneath one star. They replied: Give us proof of that. I replied: . . . My masters, let two men stand in *Ereẓ Yisra'el* and fix upon one star above their heads, whether at sunrise or sunset, in the first of the month or the fifteenth, and then let them go and stand in the great city of Rome, will not he who stands in *Ereẓ Yisra'el* (be under the same star) as he who stands in the great city of Rome? Thus you learn that all the creatures of the world dwell under one star."[24]

Observation of natural phenomena, in some instances, led to religious conclusions which, had they been fully developed, would have constituted theological arguments. Had the Rabbis persisted in their examination of nature, they might have developed a philosophy as well as a theology, or perhaps the former might have crowded out the latter. As it is, Seder Eliahu presents but two passages where the argument from design is adumbrated. The individuality of every created thing is proof, to them, of the constant activity of the Creator: "Come and see how many kinds of cattle there are in the world and how many kinds of beasts in the world, and how many kinds of fish in the sea—is the voice of one like that of the other, or is the appearance of one like that of the other, or is the intelligence (דעתו) of one like that of the other, or is the taste of one like that of the other? Neither in voice nor appearance nor intelligence nor taste is one similar to the other. Our learned have taught in the Mishnah (San. 4:5): The greatness of the King of the kings of kings, the Holy One blessed be He is seen from this: Man makes many coins with one stamp, and they all look the same. And the King of the kings of kings, the Holy One blessed be He, has stamped all mankind with the stamp of Adam, yet no one looks like his fellow. Therefore it says, 'How great are Thy works, O Lord, Thy thoughts are very deep' (Ps.

[24] Page 9.

92:6)."[25] Thus, the individuality displayed by the apparently infinite number of created forms argues only a divine design. We find design also in the beautiful arrangement of the stars: "What is the nature of the Pleiades which are seven stars in the firmament, all close to one another? Scripture taught *Derek Ereẓ* to the generations so that one should not ask, 'Why is not the firmament thick with stars?' Parable: A king had a brick of gold—Had he put it on his head, would it have looked well on him? It would not have looked well. What did he do in his wisdom and understanding? He took therefrom half-a-coin's weight and made a necklace of gold and hung it on his neck; and that was an improvement. So the Holy One blessed be He, may His great name be blessed forever and ever, created stars in the firmament and gave each one a place to itself."[26] Beauty in nature is thus also evidence of a divine design.

Among the ancients both magic and astrology were in high repute. But the Rabbis declared that anything smaller than a lentil could not be created by magic.[27] This statement occurs in connection with the biblical account wherein Pharaoh calls in his magicians to duplicate the feats of Moses and Aaron. Since the biblical account could not be gainsaid, apparently the Rabbis at least endeavored to exclude the possibility of magic in those situations where leeway was given them. The impression is left that not only were they averse to magic but tended also to deny its efficacy.[28]

The single passage on astrology in Seder Eliahu is given in the name of Rabbi Eliezer, the son of Parta. He declares that "if an eclipse of the sun occurs in the middle of the month, the fish will increase and multiply in the sea, and the fruit will begin to grow again upon the trees. And if an eclipse of the

[25] Page 10.

[26] Page 9. On the conception of דרך ארץ, see below, Vol. II.

[27] Page 41.

[28] Magic, they said, was taught man by the fallen angels, Uzzah and Uzi and 'Aza'el "who went down to the earth and desired the daughters of men and caused them to sin and taught them magic"—"Additions," page 49. The origin of magic is sin, an explanation which indicated that the Rabbis were averse to magic. That they tended to deny its efficacy, or at least to limit it, is proved by the passage above.

moon occurs in the middle of *Mar-Ḥeshvan*, sword and famine will come upon the world, and much distress will come anew, and evil decrees."[29] An eclipse of the sun is an ill omen for the Nations of the World and an eclipse of the moon, an ill omen for Israel; if the eclipse is in the west, an ill omen for those that dwell in the west, etc. "If the eclipse occurs on its entering (upon the horizon), retribution is slow in coming; if on its leaving, retribution is hastening to come. And some say of these things the opposite." "And when Israel does the will of the Omnipresent they need have no fear, for it says, 'Thus saith the Lord: Learn not the way of the nations, and be not dismayed at the signs of heaven; for the nations are dismayed at them' (Jer. 10:2)—the nations are dismayed, but they (Israel) should not be dismayed."[30] Astrology, it appears, was not taken seriously by the Rabbis. Opposite interpretations were given freely to unusual phenomena. Still more significant is the fact that they did not consider "the signs of heaven" as omens for Israel when Israel does the will of God. Israel's actions determine its fate, not stellar phenomena: the latter, then, do not portend with the infallibility associated with a thorough-going belief in astrology.

We have discussed in this section the rabbinic conception of nature. The Rabbis attribute anthropomorphism to natural objects only as background to the four points of reference. They do not possess a belief in the fixed order of nature or in inexorable natural laws. God's power is glimpsed in the very acts of creation themselves, His world being created on so large a scale as to make impossible man's exploring it. There are the beginnings of an objective kind of observation of nature quite independent of theology. In a few instances, this examination of nature led to religious conclusions, approaching theological arguments. Finally, as to the ancient substitutes for science, astrology and magic, the former did not greatly concern the Rabbis, and the latter they sought to rule out.

[29] "Additions," page 11.
[30] "Additions," page 10.

II

Nature and the Four Points of Reference

The Rabbis manifested a certain interest in nature, as we have seen, gathering facts from observation of it and finding beauty in its forms. But obviously this type of interest was comparatively slight. They accented much more heavily the four points of reference, even interpreting from this point of view passages in the Bible inspired by nature's grandeur. Daniel (2:21) utters the praises of God: ". . . He changeth the times and the seasons . . . He knoweth what is in the darkness, and the light dwelleth with Him." Seder Eliahu finds in these phrases references to God's justice and to Israel: " 'He changeth the time' —this refers to the time of Sodom; 'and the seasons'—refers to the time of Jerusalem . . . 'He knoweth what is in the darkness'—the measure of punishment for the wicked in Gehenna; 'and the light dwelleth with Him'—the reward of the righteous in Paradise."[31] Plainly, a shift from the biblical interest in nature is revealed here. We are prepared, therefore, to find that, in the view of the Rabbis, nature is subservient to the fundamental concepts of their theology. Indeed, we do find that the great majority of rabbinic comments on nature occur in connection with the four points of reference.

God loves man, and His loving-kindness toward him can be observed in the very structure and nature of the universe. It is He "from whom go forth brightness and light to the world; and who causes rain to fall and grass to grow."[32] He made the earth a dwelling place for man, and the spread of heaven is likened to a tent above him.[33] "The heavens declare the glory of God," (Ps. 19:1–2)—Why? Because heaven and earth, the first creations of God, sustain His creatures. "For the entire world—man and beast and the fowl of the heaven—obtain their sustenance only through the activity of heaven and earth: For six months they cause fruit to grow in the winter; for six months they cause fruit to grow and ripen in the summer, and this is

[31] Pp. 84–85.
[32] Page 8.
[33] Page 161.

the sustenance of all the creatures He created in the world." Only because of what they do for God's creatures are they worthy to declare His glory.[34] It is probably for this reason, too, that the Rabbis say that heaven and earth together are among the five possessions (קנינים) God has made especially his own, together with Israel, Abraham, Torah and the Temple.[35]

What is man's relation to the rest of creation? "And with His wisdom and understanding He created His world and established it, and after that He created Adam and caused him to rule (over the world) before him."[36] When Adam sinned, God supplied his progeny with the possibilities for wresting a livelihood from nature. One of the authors of Seder Eliahu has a discussion with a scoffer, who claims relief from the Torah since discernment and knowledge were not granted him. "I said to him, 'What is thy work?' He answered, 'I am a fisherman.' I said to him, 'My son, who told you to take flax and make it into nets and then throw them into the sea that you may bring up fish from the sea?' He answered, 'My master, in that respect discernment and knowledge were given me from Heaven.' "[37] Emphasizing as they do God's love for man, the Rabbis believe that the rest of creation, animals and fish, are here for man's sake, to serve him, to enable him to live; and that God supplies him with the knowledge wherewith to use all things for his purpose.

That nature centers around man is implied in another passage having as its theme God's loving-kindness toward him. Our author was seized by the Persians, and a magus offered him his release providing he could answer a question put to him. "He said, 'Why has God created loathsome insects and creeping things?' I answered: 'God is a judge; God is holy, righteous, gracious and true forever and ever; and telleth the latter end from the beginning, and from the beginning that which has not yet happened, knoweth what has happened and what will happen, and hopes for good and not for bad, and is

[34] Page 9.
[35] "Additions," page 20.
[36] Page 3.
[37] Page 196.

rich and findeth joy in His portion. With His wisdom He created His world and established it, and after that He created man and brought him into the world. He created him only that he might serve Him with a whole heart and that He might find satisfaction in him and in his progeny after him to the end of all generations. And when he became fruitful and multiplied —this one worshipped the sun and the moon and that one worshipped stocks and stones, and every day they were deserving of complete destruction. When He considered again all the works of His hands, He said, 'These have life and the others have life; these have souls and the others have souls; these eat and drink and the others eat and drink—let them be regarded as the cattle and beasts and other insects and creeping things that God created upon the face of the earth.' Thereupon He is resigned and does not destroy them. Thus you learn that insects and creeping things were created as an aid to men on earth.' "[38] Again, therefore, we have nature viewed and interpreted from the standpoint of God's loving-kindness: insects and creeping things have the purpose of reminding God, as it were, to forgive man's transgressions.

The Rabbis took this love of God for man literally—all things and creatures exist for man, even woman exists for man's sake. ". . . For all the good things and comforting things that Thou hast told Israel, Thou hast told them with wisdom . . . For it says, 'And the Lord God said: It is not good for man to be alone,' etc. (Gen. 2:18)—'a helpmeet for him'—a helpmeet to cause him to stand on his feet, and a helpmeet to give light to his eyes." Woman does four things for man: She makes his food (from the grain she grinds, etc., and finally hands him bread), and his clothing (from the flax); brings him children for the world; and keeps him sexually pure.[39]

[38] Page 5–6. Friedmann, note 21, explains this selection as being an answer to the dualism of the Persians, who regard insects, etc. as being created by the god of evil. Comp. Ginzberg, Legends, V, p. 60, note 191, where other references of this kind are made to rabbinic literature, likewise relating the existence of noxious animals with a special mission, generally not like here of God's love but of His justice.

[39] Page 51.

God's love for man is reciprocated by the righteous in their love toward Him. The Rabbis projected their love for God into the very essence of life, into time itself. Time loves God. "Therefore do the *'alamot* (עלמות) love Thee" (Song of Songs 1:3) the Rabbis say refers to the jubilees, the fifty year cycles, *'olamot*.[40]

God's justice is also reflected in nature. We must remember, however, that with the Rabbis, natural phenomena include those mentioned in the biblical story of creation. Before the sun and the moon were created on the fourth day, the world was lighted by a special light described as God's light—"In Thy light do we see light" (Ps. 36:10.)[41] This light was hidden by God and reserved by Him for the righteous in the World to Come. "Why did God hide it? Because the Nations of the World will in the future provoke Him. He said, 'Those wicked (men) will not have the merit to use this light; but let them use the light of the sun and the moon, for these in the future will be destroyed, and these (i. e. the wicked) will in the future be destroyed.' "[42] The light rejoiced thereat. "The light of the righteous rejoiceth" (Prov. 13:9)—and said, "Even though I have been withheld from the righteous Israelites in this world, I long only for Thy light that Thou wilt bring upon me."[43]

When the final reward will be given to the righteous, the whole world of nature will be changed, not only the celestial lights. God will destroy the whole earth, and will make anew the heaven and the earth.[44] The earth will be the witness against the wicked, opening its mouth like a man and speaking to God, for no mortal sin can possibly be hidden from it.[45] Gehenna, too, will open its mouth and demand that it be filled with the sinners among Israel.[46] Gehenna and Paradise (גן עדן) are part of "nature" for they have their distinct place in Creation, the

[40] Page 37.
[41] "Additions," page 33.
[42] Ibid, page 34.
[43] Ibid.
[44] Ibid, page 31.
[45] Ibid, page 32.
[46] Ibid.

former having been created after the latter,[47] and both being among the six things created before the Cherubim.[48]

Torah, abstract as it may appear to us, the Rabbis, perhaps for that very reason, find more effectively incorporated in nature than even God's love and justice. When God created the world, "He consulted only the Torah."[49] It was one of the six things that were created before the Cherubim, indeed being the first mentioned in that list.[50] The first letter with which the Torah begins, ב, was the one God used in creating the world.[51] Once created, the world is still largely determined by Torah; it is central in the whole scheme of history: "For the entire existence of the world is to be six thousand years—two thousand years of chaos, two thousand years of Torah, two thousand years of the period of the Messiah."[52] Because Torah has been given only to man, other living things are secondary, incidental to man. "Why does it not say, 'And He drove out the cattle . . . the beasts . . . the birds?' I call to witness heaven and earth that since cattle, beasts and birds do not circumcize nor study Bible or Mishnah, therefore Scripture has included them in man, saying, 'And He drove out the man' (Gen. 3:24)."[53]

Israel, too, affects the constitution of nature. *Shekinah* bids Jacob look up to heaven "and see the twelve stars and constellations in the firmament—twelve hours the day, twelve hours the night—as against the twelve tribes that I will give you."[54] The course of nature is interfered with in behalf of Israel—the sun stands still in heaven—not only, as the Bible tells us, once in Joshua's time, but in the time of Moses as well, when Moses did battle with Amalek: " 'Day unto day uttereth speech' (Ps. 19:3) . . . This refers to the day of Moses that

[47] Page 3.

[48] Page 160. The six things created "before" are: Torah, Gehenna, Paradise, the throne of glory, the name of the Messiah, and the Temple.

[49] Page 160. [50] Ibid.

[51] Page 164.

[52] Page 6. Note how in contrast to Torah, the previous existence of the world is described as "chaos." The period of Torah begins with Abraham.

[53] Page 164. In man's downfall they were included and will be included in his restoration as well—Friedmann No. 60.

[54] Page 29.

announced the day of Joshua . . . And thou canst not say since the Holy One blessed be He slew Sichon and Og who will tell this to all men, for the sun (tells it) which stood still for Moses."[55] In the World to Come, God will bring heaven and earth, the sun and the moon, the stars and the constellations to judgment on account of Israel, saying to them, "When you saw My *Shekinah* withdrawn and My house (the Temple) destroyed and My sons exiled among the Nations of the World, why did you not beg mercy for them?"[56] Israel's land has a special quality of holiness, and was "separated" by God for that reason; the Temple area in Jerusalem is most holy.[57] The Temple was also one of the six things God created before the Cherubim.[58] He "stood therein and created the whole world from one end to the other."[59]

We have done little else in this section than enumerate the passages with nature references in Seder Eliahu and group them under the four points of reference. All of such passages have been given here, and the great majority have been found to deal with the fundamental concepts. It is obvious, therefore, that the major interest of the Rabbis was not in nature itself. We have indeed noticed above that the Rabbis were to some extent occupied with the facts of nature, perhaps even for their own sake, but only to a slight extent. By and large, the Rabbis saw in nature, too, the four fundamental concepts, which, in their sight, affected its constitution and phenomena.

III

Angels and Spirits

Every homily in Seder Eliahu that speaks of angels is an exposition of a concept, no matter how detailed the angelology may be. In no case does there appear to be a description or even any mention of angels in and for themselves. Where they play

[55] Page 10. [56] "Additions," p. 30.

[57] Page 173. [58] Page 160.

[59] P. 21. Rabbinic sources in which Israel is regarded as the purpose of creation are cited by Ginzberg, op. cit., V, pp. 67–8. Cf. *idem* for further analysis of the idea.

any role at all it seems to be in support either of one of the points of reference, apparently in the majority of cases, or else of other concepts we have already discussed. Before drawing our conclusions from this thesis, we shall first attempt to establish it.

In God's throne of glory, created before the Cherubim,[60] is projected His love for the entire world. The *Ḥayyot* in the throne consisted of the likenesses of man, lion, ox and eagle.[61] "Give . . . I took My reward (said God) . . . the reward of the face of man which is in the Chariot (מרכבה) for all the sons of men that are on the earth; the reward of the face of the lion which is in the Chariot for all the beasts that are on the earth; the reward of the face of the ox which is in the Chariot for all the cattle that are on the earth; the reward of the face of the eagle which is in the Chariot for all the birds which are on the earth."[62] God's regard for all His creatures on earth prompts an intimacy with them as it were, impossible even for the angels, the Cherubim and *Ofannim*, to whom, as Friedmann observes, God offers this explanation above as to why the *Ḥayyot* were placed in the throne of glory and not they.[63] "For when God created the world, He put them (i. e. *Ofannim* and Cherubim) outside (the throne of glory). And they cried and wept greatly, saying, 'Master of the universe, why didst Thou take us out from that condition of perfect bliss?' "[64] God's answer to that reveals that His creatures on earth, not only man, are nearer and more precious to Him than even the angels. Apparently jealous of God's love for man, the ministering angels, when Adam was created, exclaimed "Master of the universe, 'What is man that Thou art mindful of him . . .?' (Ps. 8:5–9)."[65] When they thus "conspired against the Holy One blessed be He,"

[60] P. 160.

[61] P. 161.

[62] Ibid. I left the opening sentence of this homily untranslated. "... תנו שכרן לחיות—the text is very corrupt" (L.G.). But the idea is still to be discerned in the remainder of the passage here translated.

[63] Ibid.—Friedmann's note No. 37.

[64] Page 161. This is a variant of the haggadah given in Ginzberg's Legends, I, p. 15. Comp. V, p. 18, notes 52–53.

[65] Page 162.

His reply was that since man was one of the four classes of beings in the Chariot his permanence in this world was assured.[66]

As in the passage just cited, the ministering angels, with their complaints against man, often act as the foil to God's loving-kindness toward him, bringing the latter into stronger relief. The angels object to God's rescuing Abraham from the fiery furnace because man is unworthy: Once before when God went so far as to make a canopy for Adam in the Garden of Eden and sat with him there, "in the end he transgressed your commandments." To which God replies: "What shall I do to flesh and blood (i. e. man) who dwells in an unclean place, and in whom the Evil *Yeẓer* holds sway, when you who dwell in an abode of purity and in whom the Evil *Yeẓer* does not hold sway —what did some of you do, Uzzah and Uzi and 'Aza'el, who went down to earth and desired the daughters of men and caused them to sin, and taught them magic . . .? And this one (Abraham) sanctified My name in the world."[67] The angels, then, make it necessary for God to be the pleader of man's virtues.

Qualities associated with God's love figure in the conduct and governance of the heavenly court. Charity is a quality attributed by Scripture to the throne of glory, according to the Rabbis' interpretation of Ps. 97:2;[68] and peace, which God promotes among men, He also causes to reign among His 496,000 myriads of angels.[69] These, therefore, are additional instances of our general proposition that the background of angelology brings out the more prominently, in concrete and striking fashion, God's active love for mankind and the world.

Similarly, against the background of angelology, God's justice is seen more vividly. The reward of the righteous in the World to Come is to consist of the halo which will render them radiant. This reward the Rabbis find implied in Judges 5:31: " 'But they that love Him shall be as the sun when he goeth forth in his might.' This is not said concerning the ministering

[66] Ibid.

[67] "Additions," page 49.

[68] Page 170.

[69] Pages 156, 84.

angels."[70] In Paradise, God will be surrounded by the righteous, "and Gabriel will take two thrones, one for God and one for David," the angel being the servitor of the righteous as well as of God.[71] Bliss ineffable is the portion of the angels, who are near *Shekinah*: "And they (i. e. the angels) were as though eating and drinking . . . and rejoiced greatly . . . If those standing outside and seeing *Shekinah* inside were as though they were eating and drinking and were satisfied and rejoiced greatly, all the more those who enter into His throne of glory."[72] Now we have noticed above[73] that nearness to *Shekinah* is the destined reward of the righteous, who are likened in that respect to angels. The angels, therefore, in these passages, supply the background against which is depicted the reward of the righteous, a background itself rich with dramatic elements, as when they cry out in anguish over their exclusion from the immediate proximity of *Shekinah*.[74]

The behavior of the angels who came to visit Abraham is, according to one view, a reward for Abraham's righteousness: "All who say that the ministering angels did not eat when at Abraham's say naught; but because of that righteous man's righteousness and because of the trouble he took, the Holy One blessed be He opened their mouths and they ate."[75] This passage will bear further scrutiny, but it is clear, at any rate, that our author was at pains to indicate that although eating was an exceptional act with angels, yet this exception was made as reward for Abraham's goodness.

Angels are the instruments of God's justice in punishment as in reward. Every day angels of destruction descend from God's presence to destroy the entire world; it is only the merit

[70] Page 193.

[71] "Additions," p. 32.

[72] P. 161. "Those who enter into the throne of glory" are the *Ḥayyot*.

[73] Above, p. 55.

[74] P. 161. Cited above, p. 89.

[75] P. 59. On p. 60 occurs the rather careful expression that the angel "found pleasure" in Gideon's bread (נהנה ממנו), and did not in Manoah's; and similarly another homily in Abraham's case, p. 59. See Ginzberg, Legends, V, p. 236, note 143, who states, "The old view was that angels may sometimes partake of food, and that they subsist on manna." See also here, below, p. 99f.

of those who are to be found in the houses of prayer and study which daily stands between the world and its destruction.[76] Ten ministering angels were appointed for the punishment of Nebuchadnezzer.[77] Again, as we have found before, angelology is employed to lend dramatic emphasis, as background, to God's justice. The Rabbis see in the sixty-third chapter of Isaiah a divine drama enacted: Angels, prepared to chant the praises of God, and finding Him not, seek Him at the sea, at Sinai, at Zion. They find Him coming from Edom and see that His garments are red as scarlet. "Who is this that cometh from Edom? . . . Wherefore is Thine apparel red?" (Is. 63:1–2) God answers that He is come forth after punishing Edom.[78] Thus, the presence of the angels, their search and the dialogue that ensues are the setting in which is placed longed-for vengeance upon the enemies and oppressors of Israel.

The angel who is particularly the instrument of God's punitive justice is the Angel of Death. Because of mankind's propensity for sin, he acts as a necessary moral purgative for the world. "Were it not for the Angel of Death what would we not have done against our Father in heaven! Go, learn from the first ten generations, to whom God vouchsafed from that bliss which is reserved for the World to Come, yet they were about to destroy the entire world!"[79] In David's day, the Angel of Death "descended from the high heaven and slew Gad, the prophet, and four sons of David and the elders" and many more in Israel all because of Israel's sins which David saw "marshalled up to the firmament."[80] David, too, was punished: "Since David saw the sword of the Angel of Death—from that time onward —trembling and chills seized him, and he never more possessed strength."[81] In the World to Come, however, the world of perfection, when sin will be no more, there will no longer be any necessity for the Angel of Death, and he will be removed.[82]

[76] P. 182.
[77] P. 24.
[78] "Additions," p. 29.
[79] P. 81.
[80] P. 39. [81] Ibid.
[82] P. 81.

The Rabbis permit themselves to gloat over his removal, assigning him to Gehenna, which God "widened and deepened for the Angel of Death that it might accommodate his full height."[83] Their inconsistency in designating punishment to the Angel of Death when he only performed his unavoidable mission may be explained on the ground that he personified in their imagination all the evils overwhelming man, even Death itself.

Angels are sometimes employed in the interests of justice, other than in a punitive setting. "I the Lord . . . give every man according to his ways . . ." (Jer. 17:10) and Ps. 18:26–7 are the textual grounds for the statement that to every man is given an angel who deals with him as is the man's character —pious, tricky, or average.[84] In one passage of the book an angel plays the part of justifying God in the fate that overtook a teacher and his two hundred pupils. He tells our author that their death was merited, and that it was brought about for a definite sin.[85]

The Rabbis seem to observe two principles in their use of angelology as background in connection with Torah.[86] In homilies wherein the main interest is God and Torah, angels figure hardly at all; in those which center on man and Torah, angels are strong either in number or emphasis. To give first an instance of the latter: A certain woman, we are told, sees one of the learned at the head of the students "like a general (i. e. leading them in discussion) and Gabriel (the angel) was standing at his right hand."[87] The story concerns the redemption of this woman when she apprehends the transcendent worth of Torah, and the appearance of the angel Gabriel helps her to realize

[83] P. 160. He is here identified with the Evil *Yeẓer*. See below in chapter on motives.

[84] P. 176. See Ginzberg, op. cit. V, middle of p. 76, who regards such an explanation of the guardian angels as highly rationalized, but says that in Jewish sources this rationalization appears quite early.

[85] Pp. 100–1.

[86] This discussion on angelology in connection with Torah is based on the texts as Friedmann has rendered them. A much simpler treatment of the subject follows immediately below, based on a different rendering of the text.

[87] "Additions," p. 39.

its transcendence. On the other hand, the Torah's claim to exalted worth rests on its divine origin; therefore, in statements dealing primarily with Torah's relation to God, and wherein other factors if present are secondary, angelology, being apt to blur the fact of its single and divine authorship, is consciously made faint. Thus, in the course of a homily wherein the angels are shown to be subordinate to the righteous, the Rabbis say: "When the Holy One blessed be He revealed Himself on Mount Sinai to give the Torah to His people, He revealed Himself with only one (angel) and of the 248 angels that are of His presence;" the angel here appearing, apparently, in the role of servitor of God.[88] While the state of the text here is corrupt, it would seem that the Rabbis wish to emphasize that only one of the 248 angels of His presence was with God when He revealed the Torah.[89] Now, in another place, Seder Eliahu describes the same event differently, employing the same figures to give an opposite impression: "When the Holy One blessed be He revealed Himself to give the Torah to His children, He did so with 248 (myraids of angels—Friedmann note No. 4) of His presence . . . And when He came and rested on Mount Sinai (it was) with angels appointed for each and every Israelite, who took (i. e. the angel) him back twelve miles and then brought him forward again . . ."[90] Again the text is somewhat doubtful, but if Friedmann's rendering is correct, the multitude of angels was needed, apparently, not for God's sake but for Israel's, and the awful grandeur of the Torah revealed catastrophically by God is emphasized by the angels' service to every Israelite. In still another place, the text clearly states that angels were present with God on Sinai: "When I revealed Myself to give them the Torah on Mount Sinai the ministering angels also were revealed with Me and they (also)

[88] Page 193. See below, here, note 92.

[89] Friedmann, ibid, note No. 3, hints that this angel was the מלאך הפנים, the special servitor of God. The majesty of God, we may imagine, requires at least a minimum of retinue.

[90] P. 119. The text reads: "with 248 of His presence (שלפניו) and 248 myriads of His presence. The Venice edition says: "242 myriads of His presence."

wished them well."[91] The whole tenor of this passage is to indicate that the angels were not jealous of Israel on that occasion, and tends to bring out the desirability and worth of Torah.

The discussion thus far on angelology and Torah is based on the texts as Friedmann renders them. We cannot shut our eyes, however, to the possibility, which is almost a probability, that between the two passages in which the number 248 occurs there was originally complete agreement. It is more than possible that in both cases the text declared that 248 myriads of angels of His presence were revealed with God on Mt. Sinai.[92] This is the more likely because the third passage which mentions no numbers at all also states that the ministering angels were revealed on that occasion together with God. If we can take this line of departure, our problem of angelogy in connection with Torah is greatly simplified. We need attribute no particular principles to the Rabbis beyond the one that angelology tends merely to enhance the transcendent worth of Torah. In the first passage on Torah cited, this point has already been made. And in the other three passages, all of them dealing with the revelation on Sinai, the vast importance of Torah, its cosmic and eternal significance, is vividly emphasized by the dramatic spectacle of God and His retinue on earth, afforded only once in the world's history, and then only when the Torah is given.

By employing angelology, rabbinic theology also makes vivid the conception that God's special concern is with His chosen people, Israel, and that thus Israel occupies a unique position in the world's economy. The very throne of glory, in which all beings on earth are represented, is affected by Israel's history. Israel's greatest sin, the worship of the golden calf, causes a change in the constitution of the throne of glory: "When Israel sinned with the golden calf, He brought the cherub and substituted it for the face of the ox."[93] That God's special con-

[91] P. 186. On p. 154 it would seem that the angels were jealous of Israel because the Torah was given the latter, again emphasizing the worth of Torah.

[92] "On p. 193 read: לא נגלה אלא לאחד [ואחד] במאתים ומ"ח וכו', the number רמ"ח corresponding to the רמ"ח אברים. Comp. p. 190 (top). In ed. Venice אחד ואחד is found, but is wrongly placed." (L.G.)

[93] Page 161. The Rabbis were, of course, aware of the differences in the

cern is with Israel is brought out by the part played by the angels in protecting Israel and in rescuing them miraculously from death. When the Egyptians threw the children of the Israelites into the river, the angels went and stood ankle-deep in the water, and caught the children and placed them on the rocks in which God had provided breasts to suckle them.[94] God tells the angels, moreover, that for this very purpose they were created—direct evidence, if we needed any, of the role assigned in rabbinic theology to the angels in connection with Israel.[95] Angels are God's auxiliaries in protecting the learned who engage in the Torah: "Every one of the learned (ת"ח) who engages every day continually in Torah in order to increase the glory of Heaven has no need of sword or spear or long spear, nor indeed for anything as protection for him, for the Holy One blessed be He protects him, and the ministering angels stand round about him with swords in the hands of all of them and protect him."[96]

As with the three concepts discussed above, so for the concept of Israel, as may have been noticed, angelology forms a dramatic background. Angels furnish the occasions for demonstrating God's concern and love for Israel. A touching example is the following: "The Holy One blessed be He wanted to go with them (into exile). The ministering angels (thereupon) gathered around Him to pacify and comfort Him. They said to Him, 'Thou hast after all seventy peoples in the world, and we here are without end and without number.' " But God regards their comfort as worse than vain. " 'This comforting is contemning to me. But go ye down from My presence and see My people, the house of Israel, how they walk in exile with burdens upon their shoulders.' With anxious haste they descended from His presence and took off the burdens from their

description of the *Ḥayyot* in the first and in the tenth chapters of Ezekiel; and in this way they reconcile the two versions.

[94] Page 43. Rabbinic theology abounds in literalizations of what in the Bible are purely poetic passages. This story literalizes "And He made him to suck honey out of the crag" (Deut. 32:13); and there are innumerable other examples of this tendency in Seder Eliahu.

[95] Ibid.

[96] Page 19.

shoulders."[97] Here again, as before, the angels are given the task of serving Israel, a role in which angelology emphasizes Israel's supreme importance not only among nations, but in the world in general. The Rabbis regard Israel's exile as a cosmic catastrophe, against which everything in the universe should have protested. They express this idea when they depict God, at the judgment hour, rebuking the angels, as well as natural phenomena, for their silence when that tragedy occurred: "And so (will He act) with the ministering angels. He will call Metatron and say to him 'I have called your name like Mine'—as it says '. . . for My name is in him' (Exod. 23:21)—'When you (speaking to the angels) saw My *Shekinah* withdrawn and My house destroyed and My children exiled, why did you not beg mercy for them?' He will judge them and put them to one side."[98] The same rebuke is also administered to the throne of judgment.[99] On that occasion—at the hour of judgment—Israel will come into their reward. This reward is only adumbrated, suggested, but is made to appear the more desirable by a device in which angelology is employed. Israel's bliss is to be so great that the very witnessing of it by their enemies constitutes the latter's punishment. "Gabriel will say to the Holy One blessed be He, 'Master of the universe, let all the idolators come and see the bliss of Israel.' "[100]

We have considered by now all the passages on angels in Seder Eliahu which occur in connection with the four points of reference. One activity, however, the angels do engage in which cannot be subsumed under any of the four fundamental concepts. "Two rows of angels standing before Him sanctify His great name. From the rising of the sun until the setting of the sun, they say 'Holy, holy, holy;' from the setting of the sun until the rising of the sun, they say, 'Blessed be the glory

[97] Pages 188–189. God's telling the angels that their comfort is contemning to Him is based on Is. 22:4, with a play here upon the verbs אוץ and נאץ.

[98] "Additions" page 31. This passage has been referred to above, page 77.

[99] Ibid.

[100] "Additions," page 35. These "Additions," as has been remarked above, page 46, are more pictorial in angelology and anthropomorphisms than the rest of the Seder.

of God from His place.' "[101] The number of angels thus engaged is stated in three places to be 496,000 myriads,[102] and in another place as being 999,000 myriads.[103] It is these declarations of the angels that apparently constitute their song to God—*Shirah*.[104] Now this activity of the angels, the *Shirah* whereby they sanctify God's name in heaven is, we have seen above, used in exposition of the concept *Ḳiddush Hashem*, which alone gives it meaning.[105] We have not found, therefore, any activity or mention of angels in this Seder that is given in and for itself. Possibly the story of the fallen angels referred to above,[106] who succumbed to lust and had concourse with the daughters of men and taught men magic, might at first thought be regarded as an exception to this rule. But this story, too, only proves the rule: It is employed for the purpose of showing God to be the pleader of man's virtues, and in demonstration of his love for man.

What conclusions can we draw from the fact that has been established, namely, that the Rabbis employ angelology only in the exposition of a concept? First, that angelology, like anthropomorphisms and the attribution of personality to natural phenomena, is absorbed by—dissolved into, so to speak—the points of reference or other concepts. The four points of reference and *Ḳiddush Hashem* overshadow angelology in rabbinic experience and engulf it, so that, in a certain perspective, it can no longer be distinguished as an entity in itself. We must conclude, then, once more, that the primary interest of the Rabbis was in the concepts. These concepts are the main values they experienced in the world; angelology and other popular beliefs they used only to give these concepts richer coloring and dramatic vividness and prominence.

101 Page 163.

102 Page 84 and page 156, and page 34.

103 Page 193.

104 "Additions," page 28. Even this *Shirah* is utilized to show God's preference for Israel; the angels say it above only *after* Israel says it below—"Additions," p. 47.

105 See above, pages 64–65.

106 Above, page 90.

Our second conclusion is that the rabbinic conception of monotheism is pure. Since there is no occasion in rabbinic theology when angels act otherwise than in the service of a concept—since, that is, they never appear to possess life or being in and for themselves—there remains only One spiritual Being, to whom all the concepts have reference. The Rabbis state in so many words this conclusion we have drawn regarding the position of angels as means only. The very meaning of מלאך is "messenger:" In comment on "Behold I send an angel before thee . . ." (Exod. 23:20), there is uttered the prayer, "May it be Thy will, O my Father in heaven, that Thou never put us into the hand of a messenger—שליח."[107] Here by the employment of שליח instead of מלאך it is almost as if they wish to emphasize the meaning of "angel." And again the subordinate position of angels is defined, when, in telling of the host of angels who were about God, the Rabbis say, "They were servants of His."[108] Yet, despite these statements, the activity of the angels, their remonstrances to God, the very presence of *Ḥayyot*, Cherubim and *Ofannim*, the mention of angels by individual names such as Gabriel and Metatron might lead one to believe that angels had, in the rabbinic mind, an independent existence. From the perspective of the four points of reference and the concept of *Ḳiddush Hashem*, however, we have been able to see that the angels are merely employed as background and have no independent existence.

The popular belief in angels, while teeming with concrete figures, was by no means a fixed and dogmatic affair. Concreteness was necessary if angelology was to supply force and vigor to the concepts it serves. On the other hand, differences of opinion in angelology are not infrequent, thus allowing both for special emphasis upon one of the points of reference and room for individual predilections among the Rabbis. We quoted above the midrash in which our author takes issue with those who say that the angels did not eat of Abraham's repast.[109] Now it is clear that our author wished to emphasize that God

[107] Page 119.
[108] Page 193—הן משרתין אתו.
[109] Above, page 91.

rewards the righteous. But those with whom our author disagrees were at liberty, apparently, to apply a principle of their own, that of removing the grosser anthropomorphisms from spiritual conceptions, a principle we have noticed in operation above,[110] and which we shall meet again. The very constitution of angels is thus a moot question, surely demonstrating that we are not dealing with a matter that has the faintest tinge of dogmatism about it. The number of the ministering angels who sanctify God's name is also, as we have seen, not a matter of agreement even among our own authors. Variously given as 496,000 myriads[111] and 999,000 myriads,"[112] they are also put down as being "without end and without number."[113] We can conclude again, therefore, that details of angelology were by no means fixed.

But if the concepts which angelology serves are to become thereby more vivid, angelology must also possess concreteness. Giving them definite numerical strength supplies this concreteness; and this is achieved also by a definite place in the order of creation, some knowledge of their constitution, their function, and by even singling out individual angels by name. The throne of glory was created before the Cherubim,[114] then the Cherubim and *Ofannim* and then, apparently the *Ḥayyot.*[115] The ministering angels were created before the world, apparently after the Cherubim and *Ofannim.*[116] The angels dwell in an abode of purity and are not swayed by the Evil *Yeẓer.*[117] As to the function of the angels, we must remember that the Rabbis were obliged to take the characterizations found in the Bible, particularly in Ezekiel, Chapters 1 and 10. Cherubim and *Ofannim* play but a small role, whereas the Rabbis assign much greater

[110] Above, page 46.

[111] Pages 84 and 156.

[112] Page 193. Friedmann, note No. 1, has an ingenious explanation which tries to reconcile the numerical differences.

[113] Page 189. On page 160, the numbers are given as: 2,000 myriads of Cherubim, 2,000 myriads of *Ofannim*, 2,000 myriads of ministering angels.

[114] Page 160.

[115] Page 161.

[116] Page 160.

[117] "Additions," page 49.

prominence to the ministering angels. It is they, in fact, who are the subjects of most of the homilies quoted in this section. The term "angels of destruction" is also used, thus designating a function among certain angels other than that of saying *Shirah* and of acting on particular behests of God.[118] The Angel of Death, nameless here, is also designated by his function.[119] Individual angels mentioned are Metatron, who is, it seems, the chief of the angels, God saying to him, "I have called your name like Mine;"[120] Gabriel, who appears as the protagonist of Israel,[121] as the servitor who takes two thrones, one for God and one for David, in the World to Come,[122] and as the angel who, standing at the right of the scholar, brought home to the sinful woman the transcendant importance of Torah[123]—thus seeming to have a dual capacity in which both Israel and Torah figure; and Uzzah, Uzi and 'Aza'el, the fallen angels.[124] In such wise is angelology given concreteness.

IV

Two Chronologies of World-Order

In a small section of Seder Eliahu, there is an obvious attempt to give a definite chronology and order not only to human history but also to the history of the cosmos. The Rabbis looked upon the world as finite in time, more, as fixed in time. The world is an *ordered* world; and this applies to man's history as well as to nature—indeed, the two are integrated into one world-order. This would seem to be a natural consequence of their belief that God governs the world, and that His governance is unfailingly, unceasingly exercised:

118 Page 182.
119 Page 160, etc.
120 "Additions," page 31.
121 "Additions," page 35.
122 "Additions," page 32.
123 "Additions," page 39.
124 "Additions," page 49. Note that names of angels are found *only* in "Additions," but not in the Seder proper. See above, p. 97, note 100.

(a) "The Holy One blessed be He created His world in two "stages" (שיטות): 2,000 myriads of Cherubim, two thousand myriads of *Ofannim*, two thousand myriads of ministering angels, and the throne of glory above them all, and the Sapphire above that . . ."[125] If the creation of the angels is one stage, the second stage is nowhere mentioned. Were it not that the term שיטה is used as "stage" in some of the homilies that follow, we might be inclined to suspect that here it is employed somehow to describe the numerical character of the angels created —*two* שיטות referring to *two* thousand myriads Cherubim, *two* thousand myriads *Ofannim*, *two* thousand myriads angels.[126] We shall return to this matter later.

(b) After mentioning that from the time the world was created until the flood there elapsed 1656 years; and then God's sorrow and the manner of His mourning and the angel's resentment of man, there occurs this statement:

"From the Deluge and until the generation of Manasseh there was one stage (or period—שיטה)."[127] A parable regarding the generation of Manasseh is then given, but the text appears to be corrupt so that little meaning can be gleaned from it. No explanation is to be found here as to why this is one period, nor the principle governing such an organization of history.

(c) Following the parable is this statement: "From the generation of Manasseh and until the last Temple was built there was one stage (שיטה). Thus there elapsed 3,408 years (since creation). And since the last Temple was built until it was destroyed 420 years elapsed. And since it was destroyed until the present 900 years have elapsed." Then there follows a prayer in which God is described as longing for Israel's return to Him so that the Messiah may come.[128] Again, no principle is to be discovered in the light of which we can account for the organization into just *these* periods.

[125] Page 160. The word "order" as used in this discussion is equivalent to the term "schema."

[126] Elsewhere, as we have seen above, the number of angels is given as much greater.

[127] Page 162.

[128] Page 163.

We are not concerned now with the chronology, but with the apparent desire to find an *order* in history. It is barely possible that שיטות in (a) refer to the numerical character of the spiritual beings created, especially as the term is not explained in (b) and (c). If this is the case, we may regard the term only in (a) as authentic and in (b) and (c) as later interpolations by an editor who misunderstood the term and simply composed the formulae—"From the Deluge . . . to Manasseh there was one stage" and "From . . . Manasseh until the last Temple was built there was one stage"—to link the homilies telling of the creation of the spiritual beings, the flood, the generation of Manasseh and of God's longing for Israel's return and the Messiah. That part of the chronology here was a later interpolation is the belief of Friedmann.[129] If we are satisfied with this explanation, then the so-called division of history into stages disappears.

But even if we regard the formulae in (b) and (c) also as authentic,[130] we cannot attach too much weight to them. There is no discernible principle underlying them; the homilies which they introduce do not explain them further. Moreover, they occur only in this small section, between the pages 160–163, and are never again referred to in the entire Seder. At best, therefore, we are forced to the conclusion that this attempt to find an order in history is confined to one of our authors only; it is by no means characteristic of the Seder as a whole, and should not be imposed upon the other homilies in it.

One more chronological passage giving an order to the world is isolated in an early chapter of the Seder. And here not only is the chronology definite but the stages as well, the latter being governed by expressly stated principles: "For the entire exis-

[129] See Chapter I, p. 4.

[130] "I read ש ב ע שיטות: 1) Creation of כרובים, etc.; 2) מיצירת העולם—מבול; 3) מבול—מנשה; 4) מנשה—בנין בית שני; 5) בנין בית—חרבן; 6) חרבן—ימות המשיח; 7) ימות המש'—עוה"ב" (L.G.).

Bacher in his Terminologie II, p. 300 (Hebrew translation by A. Z. Rabinowitz), does not raise the question at all, but accepts the text, with Friedmann, as being: וברא את עולמו שתי שטות. He also accepts Friedmann's interpretation of שיטה as "period," but does state, however, that the second period is nowhere mentioned and that it may only be inferred.

tence of this world is to be 6,000 years—2,000 years of chaos, 2,000 years of Torah, 2,000 years of the period of the Messiah. Because our sins have multiplied, a period of servitude has encroached upon the 2,000 years of the period of the Messiah and has lessened the latter by more than 700 years."[131] Now this passage, separated from those we considered above by many chapters, one of many homilies with varied themes on Ps. 139:16, cannot be looked upon as supplementary merely to that other order which divided the world into stages from Creation to the Flood, to Manasseh, to the building of the Second Temple. It is a distinct order in itself, much more precisely stated than the one above and with understandable principles. We have, then, two separate attempts at defining the world-order, if we accept the first one considered, as valid.

Friedmann, in his Introduction, takes pains to include as many homilies and events as possible within the framework of these two outlines of the world-order.[132] In the first place, he combines the two outlines, not a difficult achievement because both deal with the same "historical" material. The two thousand years of chaos end and the period of Torah begins in Abraham's day.[133] It is surprising, certainly, that so important a division should not be named a stage (שיטה), if the two descriptions of the world-order supplement each other, which Friedmann implies they do. To leave no unexplained terms in his outline of the world-order, he identifies the two שיטות (stages) in (a) as referring to the creation of the Chariot and to the creation of the world, a gratuitous assumption. Finally, he groups all the homilies in the Seder having the remotest connection with traditional historical events under one or the other stages, and then he dubs the whole "the world-order according as Elijah taught it."[134] There is absolutely nothing intrinsically in any of the homilies he has gathered up to justify

[131] Page 6. Friedmann claims that the phrase "and has lessened the latter by more than 700 years" is a later interpolation. See Chapter I, p. 4.

[132] Introduction to Seder Eliahu, pages 106–110.

[133] Friedmann quotes Rashi on 'Abodah Zarah 9a, where our homily is found in the Talmud.

[134] Introduction to Seder Eliahu, page 106.

the view that they are meant to be included in the outline provided by the שיטות. He has imposed a fragmentary and doubtful outline of a world-order contained in a very small section of the Seder, and never referred to again, upon the entire Seder itself.

While the Rabbis believed that the world does possess an order, as can be seen clearly from at least one of the midrashim cited above, their theology does not allow itself to be organized on such a basis.[135] Their world outlook was dominated by integrally related concepts, such as the four points of reference, *Ḳiddush Hashem*, *Malkut Shamayim* and other concepts we have yet to discuss. These concepts determine their interpretation of history and of the Bible. In the latter, the Rabbis sought, even in the non-historical portions and often on the slightest textual support, for verification and exemplification of the concepts. A single verse in the Bible, as is the case with Ps. 139:16 cited above, is frequently the source of several interpretations dealing with as many concepts. Thus, both the form in which rabbinic theology is couched and its content, as well, prevent it from being cast into a consistent and unanimously agreed upon presentation of a world order. The homiletical form in which the theology is expressed does not lend itself to an orderly presentation of historical sequence. And the variety and number of the concepts also stand in the way. To classify historical events, the fewer the concepts employed the more readily are the purpose and sequence of history apparent; and here the multitude of concepts makes such a treatment well-nigh impossible. Moreover, we have seen that the Rabbis differed in the stress they laid on different occasions upon the concepts themselves. Hence, whenever we do find in rabbinic theology an outline of a world-order we ought to consider it, not as applying to the entire theology and as being a consensus of opinion, but as limited to the homily involved and to the author who uttered it.

[135] Even works amounting to sheer chronologies are not put into the framework of a world order, perhaps for the reason given here shortly. See Seder 'Olam Rabba in Texts, Documents, and Extracts, ed. by Ad. Neubauer, Vol. II, Oxford, 1895.

We have reached the conclusion in this chapter that the Rabbis attribute personality to nature and employ angelology only to make the four points of reference more vivid. Anthropomorphism in nature and angelology are thus both absorbed by the points of reference. When we discussed *Ḳiddush Hashem* and *Malkut Shamayim* in the previous chapter, we found that these, too, can be understood only in terms of the points of reference. Yet the latter do not absorb the former: *Ḳiddush Hashem* and *Malkut Shamayim* not only are not absorbed, but their character is even more clearly defined, by the points of reference. Why should the application of the points of reference to these concepts have just the opposite effect from the same application to anthropomorphism in nature and to angelology?

Ḳiddush Hashem and *Malkut Shamayim* are concepts; anthropomorphism and angelology are not. The former are abstract generalizations while the latter belong to the realm of facts, wrong facts perhaps from the modern point of view, but facts in the rabbinic purview of things. *Ḳiddush Hashem* and *Malkut Shamayim* are generalizations culled from the experiences and feelings of the Rabbis that God alone reigns in the world. These generalizations may be based on what we would accept as facts or on what only the Rabbis accepted as facts—such as that the angels proclaim God's glory and kingship in heaven—or rather, to be fair, on a kind of category of "facts" possessed by the Rabbis so different in its earmarks from our own that we cannot apply either the tests of belief or of fact to it. These generalizations may also be illumined by other generalizations, other concepts, are, indeed, inextricably integrated with them, as when *Ḳiddush Hashem* is expressed in terms of God's justice, or Torah or Israel. We shall see later that what may at first sight appear merely as facts such as Israel, Torah, the righteous, the Nations of the World are, upon analysis, concepts or abstract generalizations.

Now the rabbinic outlook upon the world, rabbinic theology, is, as we have said above, composed of integrally related concepts. The facts the Rabbis found in history or in nature elucidate or verify or vivify these concepts. Angels are among such facts. As "facts" they have some kind of existence in the rabbinic mind, though as we have seen, they are by no means in the same category as historical facts like the exodus from Egypt, for example. Rabbinic theology is not, however, an exposition of facts but an array of concepts. A fact, therefore, may serve several concepts or all of them, that is, may be absorbed into various concepts on different occasions. What applies to angelology applies to anthropomorphism in nature. The latter, as is the case with anthropomorphism in general, appears to serve only the four points of reference.

CHAPTER V

GOD'S LOVING-KINDNESS[1]

I

The Organic Unity of the Four Points of Reference

Immediately as we approach the four points of reference we become aware of their organic unity. The fundamental concepts were not evolved by an individual who philosophized about them, nor are they the product of an intellectual effort at systematizing existing beliefs. Hence, they do not possess the stiff, stone-like quality, the crystalline hardness of outline so characteristic of philosophic conclusions and rationalistic classifications. The fundamental concepts "are the vantage points from which the Rabbis—and the people as well—regarded the world"; that is, the world became intelligible to them, they reacted toward it in all the multifarious details of practical living, by means of these concepts. Their mental outlook thus partakes of the nature of a physical organism, the analogy, indeed, being so apt just because of the inter-relation of mental outlook and physical organism. The fundamental concepts, then, are parts of a living, active mental organism. To cut through and extract one of the concepts cleanly is impossible: the others are frequently intertwined with it. We cannot conceive of the nature of God's love unless we grasp the way in which it affects God's justice;[2] prayer, by means of which, through God's love, we are allowed to communicate with Him, is affected by Torah

[1] מידה של חסד—For the larger aspects of God's loving-kindness, this seems to me more adequate than the term מידה של רחמים. Both are found in apposition to each other on p. 183. מידה של רחמים has, however, become associated with God's mercy in judgment, whereas מידה של חסד seems free of any specific connotation.

[2] Below, pp. 209–211.

and Israel;[3] in short, no fundamental concept is found in complete isolation from the others. As a matter of fact, the concepts display a marked tendency to go in pairs, God's love and justice often interlacing with one another, as we might expect, but so also do Torah and Israel. Yet this tendency never precludes the possibility of an entirely different combination or even of a combination of three or else of all four concepts.

The complexity of rabbinic theology, as we have described it, however, is literally more apparent than real. Rabbinic theology assumes a complex aspect to us because we are dissecting it in order to realize its coherence and its fine articulation. We are attempting to extricate individual concepts out of a mental organism which functioned always as a *whole* organism. This organic quality is never present in any system produced by ratiocination, and is immediately lost whenever a living organism is subjected to analysis. And so rabbinic theology loses its most distinctive quality by our very attempt to understand it. But if once we recognize, at least, that it *had* organic unity, we can sense how to the Rabbis their theology was a spontaneous, natural and unpremeditated reaction to life—as spontaneous and unpremeditated as life itself. To be sure, it was their belief in God that gave unity to their theologic concepts, but neither the belief nor the unity is purely intellectual. The organic unity of their theology is the inevitable result of answering to all of life's stimuli with the vital faith in God and the characteristic conception of Him evolved by their history.

II

The Personalness of God—Providence

God loves mankind. More concrete anthropomorphisms cluster around this than about the other three points of reference, for this concept above the others must needs draw upon God's personalness. The appellation "Father in heaven," which we have discussed above,[4] expresses in a name this conviction that

[3] Below, pp. 159–160, and the references cited there.

[4] See above, p. 49 and p. 57.

God's interest in man is so intense as to be described only in personal terms. The relation of God to man is, however, not paternal alone; this is but one of the modes in which the Rabbis apprehended a whole gamut of tender personal relationships. At times God's love for man is the same as that which the husband has for his wife. When God sent Adam away from the Garden of Eden, it was as though He were parting with His mate: " 'So He drove out (ויגרש) the man' (Gen. 3:24)—from which we learn that the Holy One blessed be He gave him a divorce as (is done) with a woman."[5]

The closest of kin cannot love a man more dearly than does God. This theological conclusion the Rabbis draw from the Jewish laws of mourning: "A man should not weep, lament, sorrow and groan over his dead more than the measure set by the learned: Three days for weeping and lamentation, seven days of mourning, thirty in which the cutting of hair and bathing are forbidden, and for other matters. Thence onward, he that injures himself forfeits his own life. For it says 'Weep ye not for the dead' (Jer. 22:10)—You cannot have more compassion upon him than I."[6] God mourned over the generation of the Deluge, who were destroyed for their sins, observing Himself, as though He were close of kin, the law of mourning: "When He brought the Deluge upon them, He ceased studying Bible and Mishnah and from doing any work."[7] That period "was in the category of mourning before Him," and Noah and his sons were prohibited from cohabitation—which is forbidden during the period of mourning—all the time they were in the ark.[8] Particularly is God's compassion aroused toward those who have no other protectors, toward the poor, the unfortunate, toward young orphans and widows whether rich or poor, and toward unhappy Israel "in all the places of their habitation."[9]

In rabbinic theology, the personal quality of God's love for man finds more poignant expression than in the Bible. The very

[5] P. 3—A play on the word גרש.

[6] P. 18—Apparently they did not yet have the year of mourning.

[7] P. 162.

[8] Ibid.

[9] P. 143. See Friedmann, note No. 5.

passage in Genesis (3:18–19) that states with harshness the conditions of Adam's life after the Fall is so interpreted by the Rabbis as to become a message of comfort and sympathy: " 'Thorns also and thistles shall it bring forth to thee' (Gen. 3:18). When the Holy One blessed be He said this to Adam, his limbs trembled. So He said to him, 'Since thy limbs trembled at that, thou shalt eat bread,' as it says 'In the sweat of thy face shalt thou eat bread' (Gen. 3:19)."[10] Even the decree of death pronounced upon Adam was mitigated, transformed indeed to a promise of everlasting life: " 'For dust thou art and unto dust wilt thou return' (Gen. 3:19). It does not say, 'Unto dust wilt thou go' but 'unto dust wilt thou *return*' (i. e., thou wilt return to the earth)—in which is contained a hint in the Torah for the resurrection of the dead."[11] So certain are the Rabbis of God's eternal love and goodness that they cannot believe that it was through God's deliberate will that Adam sinned and fell. They are even willing to grant that 'the hand of the Potter trembled' rather than admit that He ordained man's evil: "It was the (original) intention of the Holy One blessed be He not to give speech to any animal; and as soon as He gave speech to the serpent, he (i. e., the serpent) corrupted the entire world."[12] Thus, in dealing with that greatest of all theological problems, the problem of evil, the Rabbis, by acknowledging that God's intention would have fulfilled His love but that God's action, instead, made room for evil, would seem to sac-

[10] P. 164.

[11] Ibid.

[12] P. 190. "It is a favorite topic with the Haggadah to show the justice and wisdom of God in the course of history or in the acts of nature. People might find fault with God for not having given speech to the animal world—He permitted an exception in enabling the serpent to speak, and the evil brought upon the world by his speech is the best justification for God's limiting speech to man"—(L.G.). In this homily we have, therefore, another example of anthropomorphism in nature which emphasizes God's justice. The philosophical implication to which we alluded, however, while not to be stressed, of course, is still present. God also regretted that He created the Evil *Yeẓer*—p. 62. Comp. below, p. 119. See, also, below, p. 202, where the point is made that the Rabbis would not take up the philosophical implications these questions arouse, for then they would have to deal with concepts not part of the organic complex.

rifice His omniscience to His love. Such philosophic speculation, of course, is not strictly the province of the Rabbis, although, as we shall see in the chapter on Justice, the ethical attitude of the individual who experiences evil is of deep moment to them.[13] With the fundamental crystallizations of moral and religious experience the Rabbis were always far more concerned than with the adjustment of the logical difficulties to which these sometimes give rise. One such fundamental crystallization of religious experience is the concept of God's everlasting, tender, personal love for man. In rabbinic theology, it is more strongly stressed, more individualized, and more widely conceived than in the Bible.

Because the Rabbis do not take for granted the necessities, much less the comforts, of man's existence, they see God's protecting love and providence everywhere. God is the source of peace—"Peace belongs to the Holy One blessed be He."[14] It is God alone who makes peace among all His creatures,[15] among the angels as among men.[16] If the seventy nations of the world, divided by language and interests, are at peace with one another it is because "He intends and promotes peace amongst the seventy tongues in the world, and also intends and promotes peace amongst all His creatures that He created."[17]

God's watchful providence the Rabbis discern in the ordinary conditions that make man's existence possible. One of God's chief concerns is to supply food to His creatures, an act which is designated as charity (צדקה) on the part of God: "Since the world was created down to the present hour . . . one-third of the day I do charity and provide for and feed and sustain all the world and all that I have created in the world."[18] As we have noted in the previous chapter, the Rabbis find in nature and its ordinary phenomena assurance of God's love and providence: He made the earth a dwelling-place for man; He gives light to the world, and causes rain to fall and grass to grow; His first

[13] Below, pp. 196ff.

[14] P. 84. [15] P. 84.

[16] P. 156; p. 84.

[17] P. 156.

[18] Pp. 130, 162, 62 (twice), and 90. See above, full quotation, on p. 38.

creations, heaven and earth, sustain with their produce all the creatures of the world.[19] Man has been given dominion over the rest of creation, which has been created to serve him, to enable him to live; and man has been given by God wisdom and understanding so that he may use all things to his purpose.[20] The Rabbis took pains to teach the people to recognize that the skill which they employed in order to obtain their livelihood was really a gift from God who took this means to provide for His creatures. One of our authors met with a man "who knew Bible but no Mishnah" and who begged to be enlightened: "My master, why does it say 'He giveth bread to all flesh' (Ps. 136:25) and 'He giveth bread to the cattle' (Ps. 147:9)? Does not man provide for himself?" I answered: "Is it not the way of the world (דרך ארץ) for a man to do it with his own hand and for the Holy One blessed be He to bless his handiwork? . . . Lest we should think that God will do it without man working for it himself, Scripture teaches 'in all that thou doest' (Deut. 14:29)." Neither pupil nor teacher, however, was thoroughly satisfied with this explanation. The pupil demurred, and the Rabbi after expressing his hope that his Father who is in heaven will give him the wisdom to answer, went on: "Go, learn from this halfwit passing by in the market-place! When wisdom, understanding, knowledge and discernment are withheld from him, can he provide for himself for even a moment? So, indeed, are men. Were wisdom, understanding, knowledge and discernment taken away from them, they would be of no more account than the cattle or beasts or birds and all the other souls the Holy One blessed be He created upon the face of the earth. I call heaven and earth to testify for me that the Holy One blessed be He sits and apportions with His hand food for all who enter the world and for all His creatures in the world, both man and cattle, and creeping things and fowl of the heaven."[21]

The belief in God's providence sustained the Rabbis and those whom they led. It made them feel at home in the world, that "dwelling-place for man."

[19] Above, p. 83.
[20] See above, p. 84.
[21] P. 70.

III

"The LORD, God, Merciful and Gracious"

God's loving-kindness the Rabbis associated with the tetragrammaton. That term symbolized for them the thirteen distinct qualities (מידות) of God, each of them an aspect of His goodness, which they discovered in Exodus 34:6,7. "It says 'I will make all My goodness pass before thee, and will proclaim the name of the Lord (the tetragrammaton)[22] before thee' (Exod. 33:19)—that refers to the thirteen qualities (of God): 'The Lord, the Lord, God, merciful and gracious, long-suffering, and abundant in goodness and truth; keeping mercy unto the thousandth generation, forgiving iniquity and transgression and sin; and that will by no means clear the guilty; visiting the iniquity of the fathers upon the children, and upon the children's children, unto the third and unto the fourth generation' (Exod. 34:6,7) . . . And it says, 'And the Lord descended in the cloud, and stood with him there, and proclaimed the name of the Lord. And the Lord passed by before him, and proclaimed . . .' (Exod. 34:5,6). When Moses saw that it was the quality of loving-kindness (מידה של חסד) and that it was the quality of mercy (מידה של רחמים), he wrapped himself around and stood in prayer before the Holy One blessed be He."[23] To the Rabbis, who recognized with the same facility as do the modern critics, how the tetragrammaton stands out in this passage, its use is determined by the context. In 33:19 God says that He will come to pass His goodness before Moses, and will proclaim, then, the name of Lord; again in 34:5, God appears as Lord; in 34:6, He speaks as Lord; hence, what He proclaims of Himself must be the description of His goodness, and this, in 33:19, He has made synonymous with Lord. What the Rabbis attributed to Moses, they believed themselves: They saw in the tetragrammaton "the quality of loving-kindness and the quality of mercy"

[22] The Jewish Publication Society's translation of the Bible translates the tetragrammaton as "The Lord," capitalized; hence, in this book, which avails itself of the J. P. S. translation wherever possible, the term is employed similarly.

[23] P. 183.

which they further analyzed into thirteen aspects on the basis of Exod. 34:6,7.[24] We shall return later to the fact that this goodness of God has largely to do with His forgiveness.

It is surprising, no doubt, to find that among the thirteen qualities of God's goodness is listed "visiting the iniquity of the fathers upon the children, and upon the children's children, unto the third and unto the fourth generation." But this, too, the Rabbis wish to interpret as demonstrating not the unforgiving anger of God but rather His everlasting mercy: "David stood in prayer before the Holy One blessed be He. He said before Him: Lord of the universe, if Thou hadst not written for us 'unto the third and fourth generations' no man would be living on the face of the earth and the whole world would have been destroyed (for man's sins); but what didst Thou do in Thy wisdom and understanding? Thou hast written for us 'unto the third and fourth generations' . . . until the end of all generations . . . Why? Because Thou art merciful, Thou art gracious, Thou art long-suffering, Thou art חסיד (dealing with loving-kindness);" and the passage concludes with a fervent declaration that God judges and rewards each man according to his deserts.[25] Man is so sinful that he deserves immediate destruction, and only God's promise to visit his sins upon later generations renders the existence of his progeny inevitable. The idea in this passage is perhaps more clever than ethically profound; but the warmth with which it is uttered, and the sublime convictions with which it is surrounded express the real intention of the Rabbis. They cannot brook that any statement in the Bible, the basis of their theology, should do aught but reveal God's mercy, kindness, graciousness. Once more we notice that the rabbinic conception of God's love is larger, as well as suffused with more emotion, than the biblical.

With all that has been said regarding the thirteen qualities, each an aspect of God's loving-kindness, we must nonetheless realize that they do not have the importance of a dogmatic formulation. The important core is not the number nor even

[24] Comp. Ginzberg, Students, Scholars and Saints, p. 103, and Ginzberg's Legends, V, p. 4, note 6.

[25] Pp. 98–9. See text; also see below, here, p. 145.

the specific aspects but rather the sheer conviction itself that God is absolutely kind and good. A selection in Seder Eliahu depicts God as uttering these words: "I ask from you only that just as I investigated within Myself and found eleven qualities—so I but ask from you eleven qualities. And they are: 'He that walketh uprightly, and worketh righteousness' etc. (Ps. 15:2ff)."[26] Of the number "eleven" there can be no doubt since it tallies with the number of virtues required of man in the psalm quoted; hence, neither "eleven" nor "thirteen" possess undue significance. Significant only is the fundamental concept itself, the belief in God's loving-kindness.

God's love, as we learned, is expressed in personal terms. We have evidence from the natural world that God loves and cares for man, for He provides him and all His creatures with food and sustenance. How is God's love manifested in the moral sphere? The Rabbis, in affirming that God's loving-kindness is manifest in the moral sphere, have now to draw even more heavily upon the personalness of God. God is affected by the actions and motives of man. And because He is thus affected by man's actions, His love is mirrored in His reactions which, of course, can be described only in personal terms. Any religious outlook that views man's actions as important must in some way or another include a belief in the personalness of God.

God, knowing all, even that which has not yet happened, watching with anxious love the doings of man, is moved in various ways in accordance with the good or evil of man's deeds. Out of His love toward man, He is patient with him, long-suffering, forgiving. When Moses asked in what way God judges His creatures, He answered, "With forbearance."[27] Forbearance and forgiveness are the two most prominent aspects of God's love, for the reason, no doubt, that erring man stands most in need of them. Above we remarked how God's goodness, symbolized in the tetragrammaton, is stated in terms of the thirteen *midot* which are largely concerned with God's forbearance and forgiveness.[28] We have observed, also, how, His omniscience

[26] P. 65; compare b. Makkot, end.

[27] P. 144—בא‎ריכות אפים.

[28] Above, pp. 114–115.

aiding His forgiveness, God foresaw that Adam's progeny would provoke Him and therefore decided "to cause their early sins to pass away" lest "the world should not stand;"[29] how God created insects and creeping things that He might be reminded, as it were, to forgive man's transgressions;[30] and how God, as the pleader of man's virtues to the angels, even finds grounds to excuse man's sinfulness.[31] Soon we shall see how repentance, among the deepest of man's religious experiences, is made possible only because of this capacity of God's for forgiveness.

But God is not like an indulgent father who weakly passes over the waywardness of his children and does not allow it to disturb his own peace of mind. God's love for man is too profound for that. He grieves and is sorely distressed over the sins of man: "Go, learn from the way of the world (דרך ארץ):[32] A man until he marries and has children is contented, and has no sorrow and grief in his heart, and finds satisfaction within his home; but when he marries and has children and his family increases and multiplies, and his children do not conduct themselves properly, he becomes ill at ease, he has sorrow and grief in his heart and finds no satisfaction within his home. Thus have we done to Him that gives light to our eyes: Until He created man on the earth, He was content; but since He created man on the earth we have angered Him, like children who make their father's mind uneasy by their ways and their deeds; there entered, so to speak, sorrow and grief in his heart and He finds no satisfaction with the entire world."[33]

And, finally, when God rewards or punishes every man according to his merits, even then He is affected by the very destiny He has ordained for man: "Because Thou wantest good (for man), and wantest not evil: Thou wantest good to pay it with joy (on Thy part); Thou art not anxious to pay evil, and then only with sighing (i. e. reluctantly)."[34] Aye, when

[29] Above, p. 36.
[30] Above, p. 85.
[31] Above, p. 90.
[32] This term is analyzed below in Vol. II.
[33] P. 185.
[34] Pp. 98–9.

at the last, He visits His judgment, even then He exercises it in mercy. And the judgment itself when meted out to the wicked, moves him to the profoundest sorrow: "In every generation the Holy One blessed be He strikes His two hands (in grief) and puts them over His heart. Then He puts them on His arms and weeps over them, whether in secret or in the open. Why does He weep in secret? Because it is undignified for the lion to weep before a jackal . . . or for the owner before his hired laborer . . . The Holy One blessed be He, who has divided His world into two divisions, the righteous and the wicked, (weeps with the wicked)."[35]

In this section we have considered the manner in which the personalness of God renders possible the projection of His love in the moral sphere. God is affected by man's behavior. He is long-suffering and forgiving; He is distressed over man's sinfulness; He longs to reward man and grieves when He must punish him.

IV

Repentance, Atonement and Reconciliation

Repentance, according to Seder Eliahu, is equally as important as the Torah.[36] It is greater than prayer: For all the prayers that Moses our master uttered, God did not hearken to him to allow him to enter *Ereẓ Yisra'el*; but Rahab, the harlot, was received in repentance.[37] It is greater than charity, "(even though) charity involves an expenditure of money and repentance does not involve an expenditure of money."[38] There is an implication in these contrasts of the essentially inward nature of repentance, religiously more important than the

[35] P. 87. Friedmann (note No. 38) explains that the proof-text, Jeremiah 8:23, "Oh that my head were waters . . . that I might weep day and night את חללי בת עמי" is taken by the Rabbis to refer to God, and that את is understood by them to mean "with." God weeps with the wicked who have died. The anthropomorphism involved here has been discussed in a previous chapter.

[36] "Additions," p. 37.

[37] Ibid.

[38] Ibid, pp. 37–8—Friedmann so explains the passage, in note No. 15.

attitudes that externalize themselves in spoken prayer or in the giving of charity. Although in the end, repentance may involve both prayer and charity, as well as other manifestations of a change of heart, the chief value is this change of heart, the decided and decisive inner alteration of character.

The term for repentance in rabbinic theology is תשובה, "return," a return to God. The figure is not that of a man who has lost his way, wandered among by-paths, and then seeks to return to the right road; but of a man who has left his Father, travelled a long distance, and then determines to go back and be reunited with Him. Thus, the Rabbis in telling of the virtue of repentance, quote from Hosea: "I will heal their backsliding, I will love them freely" (Hos. 14:5).[39] Conscious of having forfeited God's love, the individual longs for a complete reconciliation with Him. Only the personalness of God can induce or resolve such a state of mind: Only when one senses a close personal supervision on the part of God, a kindly, loving solicitude that takes account of every thought and deed, can one experience that start of conscience culminating in the acute longing to be at peace with Him and never resting till the all-embracing love is felt once more. However we may account for this state of mind, to the Rabbis it becomes of itself an evidence of God's love for "I (God) have created repentance for them."[40]

The need for repentance exists because there was a flaw in the creation of man: he is sometimes swayed by innate tendencies for evil which the Rabbis personify as the Evil *Yeẓer*. God, say the Rabbis, regretted that He created the Evil *Yeẓer*.[41] Obviously, then, the Rabbis are not blind to the problem of how God's omniscience is to be squared with His justice or His love. They seem to concede, as above,[42] a loss to His omniscience rather than to His love, but they do not follow up the avenue of philosophic speculation thus opened. Instead of speculating about the nature of God, which is the way of philosophy, rabbinic

[39] Ibid, p. 38, p. 40.

[40] "Additions," p. 37.

[41] P. 62. The conception of the Evil *Yeẓer* will be dealt with in the chapter on motives.

[42] Above, p. 111. See Prof. Ginzberg's remarks there, in note 12.

theology from the same starting point goes back to man with a message of comfort. "At that moment (i. e., when God regretted that He made the Evil *Yeẓer*), a door of mercy was opened to the rebellious among Israel (פושעי ישראל), and (to allow them) to say to Him, 'Master of the universe, it is revealed and known before Thee that the Evil *Yeẓer* incites us. In Thy great mercy, receive us in complete repentance before Thee.' "[43] The flaw in man, created by God, only serves to supply the wicked with a legitimate excuse when they turn to God in repentance.

How were the wicked made aware of the saving power vested in repentance? Through the historic instance of King David, who sinned grievously yet was received in repentance. The Rabbis declare that David sinned deliberately in order to provide for God an example of sin and subsequent repentance so that He might "acquit the wicked in the World to Come. Thou wilt say to them, 'Just as David, king of Israel, who committed a grievous thing before Me, when he repented, I received him in repentance, so you, if you have repented I will receive you.' And whence do we know that David spoke thus? For it says, 'Against Thee, Thee only, have I sinned and done that which is evil in Thy sight' (Ps. 51:6)"[44] The proof-text—לך לבדך חטאתי—ought perhaps be rendered, "For Thy sake only have I sinned."

The figure used to describe God's welcome to those who seek His forgiveness and love—can the Rabbis do otherwise than employ images and figures in this expression of God's personalness?—is the outstretched hand of God: ". . . The Holy One blessed be He whose hands are stretched forth to receive the one who repents (עושה תשובה)."[45] " 'Come now, and let us reason together, saith the Lord' (Is. 1:18)—of whom did Isaiah say this verse? He said it only of repentant sinners (בעלי תשובה). For the hands of the Holy One blessed be He are stretched forth to receive those that repent, and He says, 'When will they repent that I may receive them in complete repentance before Me?' For it says, 'And they had the hands of a man

[43] P. 62.
[44] P. 7.
[45] P. 93.

under their wings' (Ezek. 1:8)—to teach us that the Holy One blessed be He sits on His throne of glory and His hands are stretched forth under the wings of the *Ḥayyot* to those that repent, and He says 'When will Israel repent (completely before Me)?' "[46] The same figure of the outstretched hand of God is also derived from another verse: " 'My beloved (i. e., God) put in his hand by the hole of the door, and my heart was moved for him' (Song of Songs 5:4)—of whom did Solomon say this verse? He said it only of the *Keneset Yisra'el* (the church of Israel). She said to Him, 'Master of the universe, were it not for Thy mercy and Thy many kindnesses, for Thou hast compassion upon me and Thy hands are stretched forth under the wings of the *Ḥayyot* and Thou receivest me in complete repentance, I would not have the strength to stand before the quality of Justice (מידת הדין).' "[47]

Repentance will cause God to forgive all sins no matter how many or how grave. "My Father that is in heaven, may Thy great name be blessed forever and ever, and mayest Thou have satisfaction from Israel Thy servants in all their places of habitation: For thou hast said, 'I will receive their sinners (פושעיהן) in repentance; so that even though a man pile up an hundred transgressions, one above the other, I have mercy and receive him in repentance.' For even if a man stand and blaspheme the Above, and he retract and repent, the Holy One blessed be He forgives all."[48] Those who are completely wicked amongst Israel, provided only they repent in sorrow at their death, are equally with the righteous destined for the World to Come;[49] indeed, he that repents before his death "is like the righteous of the world with respect to everything."[50]

Once you repent, you must try to expunge the memory of the sin from your consciousness. "If a man committed a sin this year, when the Day of Atonement comes, he is forgiven; next year do not recall it overmuch, for thus have the learned

[46] "Additions," p. 37.
[47] "Additions," p. 40.
[48] P. 121; with a few minor textual changes also on p. 189.
[49] P. 117.
[50] P. 16.

taught: 'Better an hundred flatterers (or hypocrites) than one who is brazen-faced.' "[51] Though the last phrase, the analogy with human relationships, is a bit confusing, the paramount idea in the midrash is clear enough: Reconciliation with God should mean to man that he should regard the past as closed, that he should let bygones be bygones. This principle of the complete oblivion of sin in repentance is, however, not just a device to safeguard man's mental health. It is a theological doctrine: God, too, puts the sin out of mind. "When a man has had a quarrel with his friend, were he to go to his friend all alone his friend would not be reconciled. Only after he gathers many men (to go with) him, only then is his friend reconciled. And even after the reconciliation there is some rancor left in his heart. But I (God) am not so: If a man commits a transgression before Me, and he sorrows and repents, I am moved to pity, and accept him in repentance; and since I accept him in repentance, I do not remember even a portion of his sins."[52] Here we are given all the conditions for true reconciliation—man, repenting, should endeavor to forget his transgression and God, also, will refuse to remember it. For repentance itself has the power to heal the soul of the tendency to sinfulness: "Go tell Israel there is no better way for you than repentance, for it heals Israel of all their iniquities. For it says, 'I will heal their backsliding, I will love them freely' (Hos. 14:5)."[53]

We have now to consider what *Teshubah* means when used in a sense somewhat different from repentance over specific deeds or thoughts. In a few passages in Seder Eliahu "doing *Teshubah*" is a term employed with reference to persons who are not described as having been guilty of misdeeds. As reward for having been at one time God-fearing, Jehu is promised that he would have four generations sitting on the throne of Israel: "And Jehoahaz his son came—had he done *Teshubah*, he would be in the category of the righteous to whom good befalls; had he not done *Teshubah*, he would be in the category of the wicked

[51] P. 106.

[52] P. 18. The homily ends with a warning to those who keep on repeating the transgression and do not repent.

[53] "Additions," p. 40, p. 38.

to whom good befalls. And Joash the son Jehoahaz came after him—had he done *Teshubah*, he would be . . . the righteous to whom good befalls; had he not done *Teshubah*, he would be . . . the wicked to whom good befalls," etc.[54] Similarly, four generations of poor men are accounted for on the supposition that the great-grandfather did evil, and in every case the formula is applied to his descendants: "Had he done *Teshubah*, he would be in the category of the righteous to whom evil befalls; had he not done *Teshubah*, he would be in the category of the wicked to whom evil befalls."[55] Now in both quotations "doing *Teshubah*" constitutes righteousness, and not doing it wickedness; in both quotations, moreover, we are given no inkling that the righteous man who "did *Teshubah*" was before this change of heart a wicked man or that he had even committed any specific transgression which might be expunged by repentance. Taking all the circumstances into account, the word *Teshubah*, therefore, as used here may have two possible meanings. First, there is a sense in which it may be taken here also to mean repentance over past wrong-doing—not, to be sure, over wrong-doing on the part of the individual who repents, but over the wrongs committed by his forbear. For in both instances, that of the kings and that of the poor men, the founder of the line did evil; and it is possible that the Rabbis looked on all four generations as links in one chain, as a sort of corporate personality extended in time. Hence, when one of the descendents proved to be a righteous man, the Rabbis may have thought of him as repenting for the sins of his ancestor.[56] Second, *Teshubah* may denote

[54] P. 184. What may be the last fragment of this passage referring to the last king, Zechariah, is on p. 88.

[55] P. 181. The aspect of divine justice in this and the preceding quotation is dealt with below, on pp. 183, 204.

[56] Professor Ginzberg holds that "in this passage עשה תשובה is used because of its contrast to קלקל מעשיו in reference to Jehu; and the tacit assumption is that the son followed in the footsteps of the father. In the second place, the son of the wicked is supposed to have been first a sinner like his father, hence עשה תשובה." He refers specifically to the passage on p. 184, but the same reasoning would apply also to the one on p. 181.

It seems to me, however, that this reasoning may hold true of the son who immediately follows the ancestor definitely designated as wicked, but not

in these quotations something analogous to repentance but with different connotations, particularly if we bear in mind that "doing *Teshubah*" is tantamount to righteousness. It may mean in these midrashim that the son, remembering his father's ways, strives to live on a higher level than that established by his predecessor or ancestor. *Teshubah* would then be equivalent in some sense to our term "the higher life," and the "doing of *Teshubah*" to a conscious struggle to live "the good life." This conception of *Teshubah* appears to be the more likely of the two; we have another passage in Seder Eliahu which is best explained by assuming it. When Israel was about to enter the Promised Land, "Joshua came and said to them, 'Sanctify yourselves; for tomorrow the Lord will do wonders among you' (Josh. 3:5). And it says, 'Prepare you victuals' (*ibid* 1:11)[57]—did they have victuals there? Were they not only eaters of manna which they would collect every morning, and put away until evening, and which in the evening would disappear from their hand? Why, then, does Scripture say 'Prepare you victuals?' But thus did he (Joshua) say unto them: Do *Teshubah* in order that ye may enter the land and eat of the grain of the land. For it says, 'And the manna ceased on the morrow' (Josh. 5:12)."[58] The Rabbis take "sanctify yourselves" as throwing light on "prepare you victuals," and conclude that both were injunctions to "do *Teshubah*." Thus the latter in this case is

of the succeeding generations. The third and fourth generations followed men who either had repented and were thus righteous, or else who did not repent, and thus were wicked. The statement that "the son of the wicked is supposed to have been first a sinner like his father" does not fit the first of these two alternatives.

[57] Also a statement of Joshua's.

[58] P. 101. "This is very likely based upon the haggadah that till their entrance into the Holy Land they were not punished for נסתרות, and hence the admonition at the moment of entering it to repent. Comp. Sanhed. 43b–44a." —(L.G.).

Again, in this instance, it appears to me, however, that *Teshubah* refers to "the good life" rather than specifically to repentance over the sins of the past. Granted that the haggadah in Sanhedrin is the basis for ours here, it cannot be merely a question of repentance for hidden sins of the past, because they were not punished for them. It refers, therefore, to an attitude toward the future. Finally, note the way ועושה תשובה is employed on p. 1, "Additions."

not sheer repentance over sins of the past but the striving to lead a holy life. In other words, Joshua by urging upon them *Teshubah* adjures them to lead a higher life than had been their custom in the wilderness, to live on a higher level.

Do the Rabbis include Gentiles within the scope of repentance? "He said it only of the *Keneset Yisra'el*" we have read in a preceding paragraph.[59] The organic unity of the four fundamental concepts, discussed above, justifies this statement. God's love and justice and Torah and Israel are interwoven in one living pattern; hence, rabbinic theology might well have taught that to merit God's love one ought to believe in God's justice, to observe Torah and to be identified with Israel. There are Rabbis, who do indeed, together with R. Eliezer, the author of the homily cited above, teach this doctrine. But there are others who exalt God's love above the rest of the concepts on some occasions. This different emphasis on different occasions upon one or another of the fundamental concepts we have found to be a striking feature of rabbinic theology, and in this instance it made for a breadth of vision almost unparalleled among other religions. Zechariah was the last of the kings of Jehu's line: "Had he 'done *Teshubah*' he would be in the category of the righteous to whom evil befalls; had he not 'done *Teshubah*,' he would be in the category of the wicked to whom evil befalls. And this rule applies to all the races of the earth, whether among Israel or among the nations."[60] Those who uttered this principle envisioned God's love as embracing all humanity, the least of whom by striving to lead a higher or better life could gain righteousness and be reconciled with God.

Repentance was not altogether left to the individual's own moods but was consciously stimulated by various religious institutions and symbols. Incorporated as it was in the institution of the Ten Days of Repentance, the Rabbis also taught the people to be sensitive to other reminders of the need for repentance. Both in repentance as institutionalized and in most of the other reminders we have perforce to notice the organic

[59] Above, p. 121.

[60] P. 88; the same expression occurs on p. 184.

unity of the four fundamental concepts, specifically, how the factors of Israel and Torah enter into the call for repentance. God gave Israel the ten days between *Rosh Hashanah* and *Yom Kippur* in order that if Israel repent He will receive them in complete repentance before Him.[61] But why was the number "ten" chosen? "As against the ten tests by which Abraham our father was tested . . . and as against the ten commandments that Israel received at Sinai."[62] The last of the ten days, *Yom Kippur*, on which day particularly the fate of "the men of the middle class" is decided,[63] was instituted in the wilderness because Israel did evil but repented in secret; "therefore was His compassion moved and He gave them the Day of Atonement (as a day) of pardon, for them and their children and their children's children until the end of all generations."[64] We see in all these homilies how the institution of repentance was associated with the early history of Israel. Two symbols enjoined by Torah, the *tefillin* and *ẓiẓit*, also become in rabbinic theology reminders of the need for repentance: Referring to the man who gathered sticks on the Sabbath, God said to Moses, "On a week day with *tefillin* on his head and *tefillin* on his arm, he would see and repent of his deeds; now without *tefillin* this man profaned the Sabbath." God thereupon instructed Moses to explain to Israel regarding *ẓiẓit*, "which they are to wear on holy days and sabbaths (also)."[65]

[61] "Additions," p. 38. [62] Ibid.

[63] P. 20. See Friedmann, note No. 29. The statement refers to the "moral mediocrities" (Moore) whose repentance during the ten days weighs them to the side of merit.

[64] P. 86. The proof-texts are Exodus 33:8–10; hence, the sin referred to must have been the worship of the golden calf. "Israel decreed a fast-day, a day of privation, on the last day (of the second forty days that Moses was on Mt. Sinai) . . . On that occasion the compassion of the Holy One blessed be He was moved . . . and He said to them: My sons, I swear by My great name that this weeping shall be unto you a weeping of joy, and that this day shall be unto you a day of forgiveness and atonement and pardon—to you and your children and your children's children until the end of all generations" pp. 180–1.

[65] P. 132. I take חוזר במעשיו to mean "repent," but Professor Ginzberg takes it to be the same as פשפש במעשיו or בודק במעשיו and thus it would mean "scrutinize his actions." See below, note 67.

Man's own experience ought to suggest to him the need for repentance. David profited by his experience: the revolt against him caused him to repent.[66] Three occasions ought to bring home to every man the same message of the need for repentance—when he attends to his natural wants, when he is being bled, and when he stands over his dead: "When he attends to his natural wants, he is being told: See, thy way is like that of the animal; when being bled . . .: See, thou art only flesh and blood; when he stands over the dead, . . .: See whither goest thou. And yet he does not repent but sits and multiplies additional sins."[67]

The organic unity of the four concepts is again evident in the *means* taken to reconcile oneself to God. Though repentance consists primarily in a change of heart or else in a determination to lead a higher life, it is expected that some kind of action be taken, even when there is no occasion to correct specific transgressions, which will assure reconciliation with God. One such effective means of reconciliation is, of course, prayer. "The Holy One blessed be He seeks from Israel only repentance and words, as it says, 'Take with you words and return unto the Lord' (Hos. 14:3)."[68] The same biblical verse is used as authority for another means of reconciliation, Torah: "My children, (says God), come and penetrate into the words of the Torah; and see what I have written for you (in order) to forgive your transgressions and to take away your iniquities and to cause your sins to pass away from before My countenance. Now come against Me with the words of the Torah like a man who converses with his neighbor in rivalry (במלחמה). For it says, 'Return, O Israel, unto the Lord thy God . . . Take with you words . . . Ashur shall not save us; we will not ride upon horses . . .' (Hos. 14:2–5)."[69] God's close friendship with man,

[66] P. 94.

[67] P. 176. "Repent" here is חוזר. "דברים is a euphemism for חטאים."—(L. G.).

[68] "Additions," p. 38.

[69] P. 189. "Words" are contrasted with "horses" which is a symbol of war in the proof-text, from which the Rabbis draw the conclusion that in Torah discussions there is an element of rivalry with God who gave the Torah. For a similar idea see the interpretation of Lam. 2:19 on p. 89.

the Rabbis declare, is strengthened by the very interest generated in warm discussion of Torah. A metaphor frequently indulged in by the Rabbis likens Torah to water: Just as water purifies everything (ritually), so the words of Torah are a source of purification to Israel wherever they dwell, purifying the rebellious of Israel, when they repent, even from idol-worship.[70] When repentance is accompanied by a study of Torah all adverse decrees are annulled: "A man who committed many transgressions and concerning whom death was decreed unto four generations . . . and he returned and repented and studied the Torah, the Prophets and the Writings and studied Mishnah, Midrash, Halakot and Agadot and studied with the learned—even though an hundred decrees were made concerning him, the Holy One blessed be He removes them from him."[71] This passage is introduced by a biblical text (I Sam. 2:8) that is understood by the Rabbis to refer "to the righteous in the days of the Messiah and the World to Come"; hence it is in the World to Come that the punishments decreed were to be meted out, but are instead removed from him. The same text and the same introductory statement begin a very similar passage wherein God's love for the repentant sinners who have studied Torah is put in terms of endearment that are very vivid: God's grief is so great over their death that He cannot find comfort until "He raises them out of the dust . . . and places them between His knees, fondling them and embracing them and kissing them and bringing them to the life of the World to Come."[72] In both passages the means of repentance are Torah.

Sheer identification with Israel is also a means of reconciliation with God. God will tell the righteous in the World to Come how He has rewarded each generation for the measure of Torah they have accomplished; "but I (God) do not remember the sins of Israel, nor do they come to mind. As it says, 'Remember ye not the former things' (Is. 43:18)."[73] Prayer, Israel and

[70] P. 105.

[71] P. 22.

[72] P. 21; see above, p. 39.

[73] P. 4, similarly on p. 52.

especially Torah can, therefore, be the means of reconciliation with God.

A means of reconciliation discussed by the Rabbis which deserves separate treatment is sacrificial atonement. They endow the prosaic biblical account of the sacrifices with noble ethical values, again by linking the atoning sacrifices with repentance, Torah and good deeds, and Israel—in short, by removing the sacrifices from the sphere of Temple ritual into the sphere of personal ethics. To be sure, they are at one with the prophets—quoting them—in denouncing the substitution of sacrificial formalism for repentance, mercy and good deeds: "When Israel were in their own land (במדינה), what was said regarding them? 'Thus saith the Lord of hosts, the God of Israel: add your burnt-offerings unto your sacrifices and eat flesh' (Jer. 7:21); and it says, 'For I desire mercy, and not sacrifice' (Hos. 6:6)."[74] They couched their own words of denunciation in the guise of a prophetic message: "And thus did the Holy One blessed be He say unto Jeremiah: Go and say unto Israel: How long will ye keep on saying unsightly and unseemly things? And ye say of Me, 'He dealt far too harshly with our ancestors and with us, and with all our ways.' Go, proclaim these words towards the north and say: 'Return, thou backsliding Israel,' etc. (Jer. 3:12)."[75]

Nevertheless, the Rabbis, unlike the prophets, at the same time that they negated the belief that the sacrifices in themselves were a means of propitiating God, did find them symbols of great ethical importance. They felt that something of man's essential being was associated with the sacrifices, that these were not necessarily empty, formal gestures: "And some say: From the place that the earth was taken from which Adam was made, (from the same earth) was also built the altar."[76]

[74] P. 38.

[75] Ibid. See Friedmann, note No. 60. I have rendered טמנים דברין מכוערין in accordance with Prof. Ginzberg's suggestion, who called my attention also to a similar use of the term—ויטמנו דברי תורה בפיך (on p 37). He further suggested that in our passage here the reading may have been originally מטיחים דברין וכו'.

[76] P. 173.

To obtain a clear notion of the implications of this attitude toward sacrifices, it will be necessary to analyze at some length the homilies on sacrifices in Seder Eliahu.

Scripture, say the Rabbis, gives preference to the meal-offering and the guilt-offering over the burnt-offering and the sin-offering. This is derived from the presence of the conjunctive ו with which the laws of the former are introduced in Leviticus but not those of the latter.[77] What matters here, of course, is not the manner of derivation from the text but the structure of interpretation built upon it. First, the Rabbis take the occasion to deny that sin-offerings and burnt-offerings have any propitiatory power in themselves: The law of the sin-offering is deliberately thus written "in order that a man should not say, 'I will go and commit a sin and then bring a sin-offering and I will be atoned thereby.' For the learned have taught in the Mishnah: He that says, 'I will sin and repent, sin again and again repent' is not given the opportunity to repent (Yoma 8:9)."[78] Likewise, the law of the burnt-offering is deliberately thus written, "in order that a man should not say to himself 'I may go in unsightly ways and do unsightly things; then I shall bring a burnt-offering, which is entirely to be burnt, and bring it upon the altar. Will not (God then) favor me?' "[79] The Rabbis recognized that a burnt-offering especially lends itself to the erroneous belief of propitiatory sacrifice.

What should a man do that he may be reconciled with God? We have learned that there must be repentance in his heart, and that the means of reconciliation are Torah and good deeds. These conditions the Rabbis find implied in the meal-offering, which, being of small expense, cannot engender the error that it propitiates God: "But let him engage in good deeds and the study of Torah, and let him bring a meal-offering only amounting to a selah or an assar, and let him bring it upon the altar, and I (God) will turn in mercy toward him and receive him in repentance."[80] For both meal-offerings (Leviticus 2:5 and

[77] P. 38.
[78] Ibid.
[79] Ibid.
[80] Ibid.

ibid 2:9) were prepared with oil, a symbol to the Rabbis of Torah and good deeds: "A man should not say, 'I shall go in unsightly ways and do unsightly things and then bring a meal-offering because of the love I bear the Omnipresent (מקום).' God says to him (by means of the ritual of oil mingled with the meal-offering), 'My son, why did you not mingle your deeds with words of Torah?' For 'oil' refers to Torah, and 'oil' refers to good deeds (Song of Songs 1:3)."[81] There is hardly any need to remark on the large emphasis placed on Torah as a means of reconciliation; "good deeds", we shall learn later, are intimately related to Torah.[82]

We can observe that the Rabbis took into account two circumstances when endowing the offerings with ethical symbolism: They drew their lessons from inexpensive as opposed to expensive sacrifices and from sacrifices consumed in large part by the owner as opposed to those either wholly burnt or largely consumed by the priests. The less expensive was preferred by Scripture, according to the Rabbis, because negatively, it helped to destroy the idea of sacrificial propitiation. Another example may be in place because a different support is found in Scripture: "And wherefore is 'offering' mentioned in the case of the ram and not in the case of the bullock (Lev. 1:13 and *ibid* 1:9)? So that a man should not say 'I may go and do unsightly things . . .' "[83] Positively, the Rabbis taught, as we have seen, that repentance, Torah and good deeds were the lessons contained in the symbolism: "But a man should engage in good deeds and the study of Torah, and bring a ram . . . and I (God) shall receive him in repentance."[84] Even when the element of repentance and means of reconciliation (Torah) were necessarily absent as with a peace-offering, the sacrifice was still reinterpreted, or, better, interpreted away: "Why does it say 'And this is the law of the sacrifice of the peace-offering (with a ו)'? (Lev. 7:11) Thus did God say unto Israel: My sons, do good deeds, and bring peace offerings which go entirely

[81] P. 37.
[82] Below, Vol. II.
[83] P. 36.
[84] Ibid.

to those who offer them, and only the blood and certain designated parts are devoted to the altar; and, behold, I will rejoice with such men eternally."[85]

The rabbinic interpretation of the guilt-offering follows the same general trend we have thus far described. It is one of the preferred sacrifices, and to the Rabbis it symbolizes the call to repentance, deep humility and a sense of sin. " 'And this is the law of the guilt-offering (with a ו) (Lev. 7:1)'—thus did the Holy One blessed be He say to Israel: My sons, I am He who said unto you, 'My desire is only the humbled man (בדכה *not* ברכה), and the man that is without transgression. (But) I have (now) retracted My words: Even though a man pile up an hundred transgressions, one above the other, and then he returns and repents, and humbles himself, and regards himself as if he were half-innocent and half-guilty, and regards himself as though bound daily to bring the guilt-offering given when in doubt as to the commission of a sinful act (אשם תלוי), I will turn toward him in mercy and receive him in repentance; and I will give him sons, males of stature, and sons who engage in Torah and keep the *mizwot*, and the words of My Torah will be hidden in his mouth (i. e., will always be on his lips).' "[86] The passage concludes with an interpretation of Isaiah 53:10 sufficiently corrupt textually to have misled Friedmann into thinking it a polemic against Christianity.[87]

[85] P. 38.

[86] P. 38—ויטמנו דברי תורתי בפיו.

"I do not think that the text is correct: אין חפצי אלא ברכה is impossible, according to my opinion. Read בדכא=בדכה, a play on Is. 53:10—וה' חפץ דכאו—which verse is later explained haggadically: God desires the humbling of the sinner, etc.; but also as: God finds pleasure in the humble, i. e., the pious. The correct reading as suggested by me is found in Menorat Ha-Maor by Al-Nakawa, ed. Enelow, III, 12, where this passage is quoted from Wayyiḳra Rabba." (L. G.).

"The daily guilt-offering is an allusion to Mishnah Kerit. VI, 3." (L.G.).

[87] See Friedmann's note No. 58 on p. 38. The text reads כך אמר להן הקב"ה לישראל אל תשימוני כחולה זה שאינו לא מן החיים ולא מן המתים. אלא ישפיל אדם עצמו ויתחיל ויאמר וכו'. "But the words אל . . . המתים give absolutely no sense if they allude to Jesus who certainly was a מת to the Jews; and, besides, 'Do not consider Me like Jesus' would be a blasphemy in the mouth of the Jew. It is evident that the phrase כחולה וכו' describes the attitude of

Finally, there was also a communal means of reconciliation with God—a communal sacrifice offered twice daily, one sheep in the morning and another at twilight, on behalf of Israel. In common with the other sacrifices, this, too, is reinterpreted and made the subject of symbolism, but of a different sort than that discussed thus far, since no personal repentance is involved. The symbolism hinges on the verse in Leviticus referring to the sacrifice: "*Ẓafonah* before the Lord" (1:11) which is interpreted as "hidden" or "treasured" with God. "On the day that Abraham our father bound Isaac his son upon the altar, God ordained two sheep (for the Temple service) . . . And all this wherefore? For at the time that Israel bring the daily sacrifice, and read this verse '*Ẓafonah* before the Lord,' God recalls the binding of Isaac, the son of Abraham. I call to witness heaven and earth that whether Gentile or Israelite, whether man or woman, whether man-servant or maid-servant read this verse . . . God (at that time) recalls the binding of Isaac, the son of Abraham."[88] The symbolism in the sacrifice God intended, as it were, more as a reminder to Himself rather than to Israel, unlike that of the other sacrifices. Thereby He recalls the unquestioning obedience of Abraham and the self-abnegation of Isaac, and thus becomes reconciled to their descendants and to Gentiles also. The Merit of the Fathers is conceived as interceding for the children, a suggestion, at least, of the corporate unity of Israel throughout time. In the interpretation of this sacrifice the Rabbis carry their attitude toward all sacrificial offerings to its logical conclusion: The actual offering of the sacrifice, always incidental to the symbolism, is here so far lost sight of that the mere reading of the biblical verse enjoining it is also sufficient to reconcile one with God. That Gentiles as well as Israelites can be reconciled with God we

the man who wavers between sin and virtue like the sick man who wavers between life and death. But the word תשימוני cannot be correct: תשימו עצמכם perhaps? Of course, it is also possible that the lack of faith in God is described in the phrase. In all events, there is no allusion to Christianity in the passage." (L. G.).

[88] P. 36. The same verse is similarly interpreted to refer to the remembered deeds of the Patriarchs, and of Moses, Joshua, etc.—(ibid).

have seen to be not foreign to rabbinic thought, although the means described here, association with the Patriarchs, argues Gentiles in close sympathy with Israel. This matter will be discussed in a later chapter.[89]

The sacrificial offerings are, because of the symbolic meanings given them in Seder Eliahu, a means of reconciliation with God. These symbolic meanings have the effect, negatively, of denying that the sacrifices have any propitiatory efficacy, and positively, of pointing to the things really desired by God. The latter consist of repentance, sometimes together with the attendant moods of humility and the sense of sin, Torah and good deeds, and in one case, association with the Patriarchs of Israel.

There is still one other means of communal reconciliation with God described, but not stressed, in Seder Eliahu—vicarious atonement. Vicarious atonement, in rabbinic theology, is the doctrine that an *individual* Israelite atones through the sufferings visited upon his person for the sins of *all* Israel. Of the two references to this doctrine in our text, one does little else than mention it: "The House of Israel, (may) I be their atonement in all the places of their habitation" is an expression of the love felt by one of our authors for his people.[90] The other reference gives us a case of vicarious atonement: "And if you have seen anyone of Israel who has upon him one of the four varieties of plagues, he is an altar of atonement for Israel in all the places of their habitation; if you have seen anyone of Israel who has upon him one plague of those mentioned (in the Torah), he is the scapegoat for Israel in all the places of their habitation."[91] Now it is a strange doctrine that teaches that the sins of all Israel are atoned for, that all Israel is thus reconciled with God, through the sufferings of one Israelite; it is doubly strange

[89] Below, in chapter on Nations of the World.

[90] P. 163; also on p. 25, there occurs the phrase ". . . Israel, may I be their atonement," and similarly on pp. 105, 159 and p. 141.

[91] P. 25. The parallel to the first part of this statement found in b. Berakot 5b ends with the phrase "they are an altar of atonement;" but Rabbinowicz in דקדוקי סופרים offers a variant from Nachmonides which adds "for all Israel."

when we recall that sacrificial offerings of the Temple ritual the Rabbis all but interpret away. We can explain vicarious atonement only on the ground that the Rabbis felt and taught the sense of corporate responsibility for all Israel. Incidentally, in the case of the man stricken by a plague, it is likely that the Rabbis argued that he deserved punishment but that the extreme torture meted out to him was not in proportion to his deserts, and hence constituted "an altar of atonement for all Israel." At any rate, the whole doctrine is, as has been said, little stressed in Seder Eliahu.[92]

The organic unity of the four fundamental concepts is apparent, we have observed, in the reminders of repentance and in the means of reconciliation—aside from vicarious atonement—both of which involve Torah and Israel. It is again evident in the power assigned to repentance, when the principle of divine justice is brought into play. Repentance brings with it its reward, either immediate or remote; unrepenting, the sinner frequently draws upon himself swift punishment. Repentance has the power to cause men to reign in the world (as was the case with David); to bind "ornaments on their heads;" to cure the sick; to save men from trouble and sorrow; and to save them from the judgment of Gehenna.[93] Repentance removes the plagues mentioned in Leviticus, sent, the Rabbis say, as punishment for sins—the plagues on the body, for speaking falsely or acting insolently towards family or teachers or any man;[94] the plague on clothes, for being fond of taking things illegitimately (גזל);[95] the plague on houses, for lying to a poor man who asked for a loan of wheat or barley or dates, declaring

[92] Related to the idea we have discussed is the midrash which states that when the children of the learned die in youth it is to atone for the sins of the learned (p. 191). Any notion of human sacrifice is harsh to us, although it has been made the central theme of Christianity. But we should notice that here it comes as an *explanation* of a fact observed frequently in ancient times—the appalling mortality in children. Again, in vicarious atonement proper, the plague is made the subject of an explanation. The matter will be taken up again in the chapter on justice.

[93] P. 91. For the explanation of "ornaments" see Friedmann, ibid, note No. 31.

[94] Pp. 76–77. [95] P. 77.

that these are not in the house;[96] and the plague of gonorrhea, upon men[97] and women[98] who fail to adhere to prescribed sex ritual. In all these cases, repentance has the power to heal the affliction. It will also bring material prosperity, the Rabbis applying to repentance Hosea 14:8, "They that dwell under His shadow shall again make corn grow and shall blossom as the vine;"[99] whilst Joshua, according to the Rabbis, held out to Israel that only after repentance they may "enter the land and eat of the fruit of the land."[100] On the other hand, it brings, as well, spiritual reward: Because Habakkuk repented of having spoken "superfluous words," God showed him all His qualities by which He rules the world even as He did unto Moses;[101] and because Rahab repented—her name the Rabbis say was given her for being "*rehabah*, wide, in merit"—"there went forth from her seven kings and eight prophets."[102]

When the wicked do not repent of their deeds, their guilt brings them death; it is concerning these men that the Rabbis quote, "Have I any pleasure at all that the wicked should die," etc. (Ezek. 18:23).[103] Nabal the Carmelite was such a man, and God slew him only after he was given ten days in which to repent, corresponding to the Ten Days of Repentance God gave Israel, and he refused to repent.[104] He who, unrepenting, persists in his wickedness is even uprooted from the World to Come: He "who has committed a transgression and then again and then a third time and did not return and repent—weep ye for him for he is uprooted from the world, 'For he shall return no more, nor see his native country' (Jer. 22:10)."[105] But the

[96] P. 77. The ethical aspect of these cases is discussed in the chapter on justice, below, p. 178.

[97] P. 78. [98] P. 79.

[99] "Additions," p. 40. [100] P. 101.

[101] P. 194. See Friedmann, note No. 6. Ginzberg holds that Friedmann puts the idea of repentance into the text without warrant. "The text says only that Habakkuk received a complete answer upon his many questions. On the phrase דברים יתירין comp. p. 111, line 7 from below." (L.G.).

[102] "Additions," p. 37. Above, p. 132 the reward of male children who engage in Torah and *mizwot* is promised him who brings the guilt-offering.

[103] P. 189.

[104] P. 109. [105] P. 18.

completely wicked of Israel who repent, grieving before death over their deeds, are destined even as the righteous for the World to Come,[106] God's love being particularly manifest to those who repented and studied Torah.[107] The halo, reserved for the righteous in the World to Come, is not given to the unrepentant wicked: "Some are given darkness of countenance as that of a pot . . . This is true only if he did not repent, but if he repented and died he is like the righteous of the world with respect to everything."[108] Sometimes, a single experience can move the wicked to complete repentance, and this leads to an act which alone destines them for the World to Come. In the story of the harlot and one of the learned, referred to above,[109] the repentant harlot cures the man of his love for her and for all women, whereupon, "a *Bat-Ḳol* went forth and said, 'Such and such (the woman) and so-and-so (the man) are destined for the life of the World to Come.' "[110]

In all these homilies depicting the reward of those who repent and the punishment of those who do not, we recognize how organically God's justice is integrated with repentance which itself is possible only because of God's love for man. It is a further exemplification of the underlying organic unity of the four points of reference.

V

Prayer and Contemplation

God "hears prayer immediately,"[111] since He is "merciful and gracious, full of great compassion."[112] In this aspect of God's love, the Rabbis must again draw on God's personalness. Man's prayer reaches God who hears it immediately. The sense of the near presence of God to whom they speak is always felt by

[106] P. 117.

[107] P. 21. Modifications of this view that the wicked of Israel do not inherit the World to Come will be found on the chapter on the World to Come.

[108] P. 16. The contradiction to several homilies immediately above is obvious. But see preceding note.

[109] Above, p. 93.

[110] "Additions," p. 39–40.

[111] P. 113.

[112] Ibid.

those engaged in prayer: "When Israel meets with trouble, they shall all stand, in one band, before Me and they shall say before Me the order of (prayers) for forgiveness."[113]

When man prays, the mood or frame of mind which accompanies or colors his prayer is all-important. He ought to realize, first, that he prays not because God needs his homage but for his own sake. God does not need man's worship of Him. With the myriads of angels who daily chant His praise, "did He need to come to flesh and blood, who eats and excretes like an animal, that he should worship Him?"[114] The mood required in prayer, far from being the same as when one converses with his fellow, should be that of complete self-abasement. When Hezekiah appeared to pray in the mood of a man talking with his fellow, God rebuked him through Isaiah: "When a man speaks before one who is flesh and blood but greater than he is, his body and limbs tremble; he that speaks before the King of the kings of kings, blessed be He, it is all the more proper that he should speak with terror and fear and with trembling and with trepidation."[115]

The rabbinic conception of prayer will become more clear as we analyze the contents of the prayers found in this text and as we become cognizant of the things prayed for or of the states of mind the prayers express. Some of the prayers are obviously spontaneous expressions of individual Rabbis; others have been put into the mouths of historical characters; and some prayers have either found their way into the liturgy or else have been taken from it. Without entering into the problem presented by the last group of prayers, we may, for the present, safely consider all the prayers as the expressions—whether borrowed or not—of the religious outlook of the individual authors of our text. We have all the more right to make this assumption because none of the prayers about to be cited or described are marked as quotations from the liturgy, surely an indication that the "borrowed" prayers had been thoroughly assimilated into both their outlook and its expression in prayer. Moreover, the smoothness and naturalness with which all the prayers are integrated

[113] "Additions," p. 42.

[114] P. 193.

[115] P. 46.

with the text, be it introduction, comment or exhortation, must convince any reader of the absolute harmony of text and prayer and argues for the same integration in the minds of the authors. No doubt it was this fact that helped to convince Friedmann that the parallels to the prayers in our text found in the liturgy were taken from Seder Eliahu.[116] At all events, we are justified in regarding all the prayers in the book as expressive of the outlook of our authors. Later, when we shall deal with the references to prescribed prayers in Seder Eliahu, we shall again take up those prayers that are also to be found in the liturgy.

That category of prayer which is petition has the character of petition alone by which it may be distinguished; the things prayed for may range all the way from rain or material prosperity to better fortune for Israel, moral rectitude or knowledge of Torah. Certain men by praying for rain can cause it to fall;[117] and others who neither because of their own deeds nor because of their fathers' deeds can have any hope (referring to the dictum in Exodus stating that the sins of the fathers descend upon the children), but "who stand and bless (Me) and ask for grace and pray much before Me" will have their sustenance doubled.[118] The prayer of Jabez in I Chronicles 4:10 is at one time interpreted as a prayer for material and family well-being: " 'Oh that Thou wouldst bless me indeed'—with sons and daughters; 'and enlarge my border'—with (family) increase; 'and that Thou wouldst work deliverance from evil' (מֵרָעָה)—the life which Thou givest me, (may it be such) that I will not experience either sickness of head or of eyes or of stomach, 'that it may not pain me.' "[119] We shall notice soon that the same verse is interpreted as a prayer for knowledge of Torah. Similarly, while the first half of Psalms 71:9 is also taken to be a plea for strength in Torah, the second half is given the following interpretation: " 'When my strength faileth forsake me not'—Master of the

[116] Friedmann's Introduction, p. 78.
[117] P. 92.
[118] P. 183.
[119] P. 31.

universe, do not make my teeth blunt (i. e. give me pain) concerning my sons and daughters."[120]

Pleas for forgiveness, we have seen above, accompanied and expressed the mood of repentance. God seeks from Israel repentance and words.[121] The legitimate excuse of the rebellious in Israel is, as has been observed, found in the prayer: "Master of the universe, it is revealed and known before Thee that the Evil *Yeẓer* incites us. In Thy great mercy, receive us in complete repentance before Thee."[122]

Ethical rectitude, freedom from sin, and strength to overcome temptation are also subjects of petition to God. "One should pray for himself, his wife, his children and members of his household that none of them come to sin or to (do) an unsightly thing."[123] A story is told of a priest (in the exile of Babylon) who had ten children, six boys and four girls, and who "feared Heaven in secret (היה ירא שמים בסתר):" Every day "he would pray and prostrate himself and beg and plead, licking the dust with his tongue, that none of them (i. e. his children) should come to transgress or to (do) an unsightly thing."[124] Sometimes the subjective effect of such prayer is patent as in the story of the virgin whom R. Joḥanan found in the synagogue. She was standing in prayer and saying, "Gehenna, I am stronger than you (טובה ממך): if I should consent that ten men come to me, and eat and drink with me and then do a lewd thing, they and I would enter you; but I am stronger than you, for I bend my *Yeẓer* and save myself from you."[125]

Torah, Israel and the appeal to God's justice, three of the points of reference, figure largely in petitions to God. God's love for man, the fourth point of reference, is implicit in all

[120] "Additions," p. 43. Friedmann rightly explains that they understood "strength" in the verse in the same sense as it is used in Gen. 49:3, that is, "children." The passage refers to children who die young.

[121] Ibid. p. 38.

[122] P. 62; see above, p. 120. Friedmann, in his Introduction, p. 81, points out the similarity of this prayer to that of R. Jannai found in b. Ber. 17a.

[123] P. 115. The term for "pray" here and elsewhere is בקש רחמים. The use of the term is apparently limited to prayers of petition.

[124] P. 90. Here, too, "plead" is the translation of מבקש רחמים.

[125] "Additions," p. 22.

petitions, whatever be their content, since it is the conviction of the Rabbis that God is nigh to men and hears their prayers. Jabez's prayer in I Chronicles 4:10, referred to above,[126] is given a different interpretation, this time with Torah as the subject. He prays that God bless him "with the learning of Torah;" and enlarge his border, "with the learned." He prays that he forget not his learning; that he be given friends like himself (מְרֵעָה); and that the Evil *Yeẓer* pain him not lest he be prevented from study.[127] And, again, the first half of Psalms 71:9 is interpreted as David's prayer for Torah in his old age: " 'Cast me not off in the time of old age'—Master of the universe, do not cause my hand to become lax (i. e., to lose my energy) in the Torah and in the *miẓwoth*."[128] Now it is to be noted, as a matter not without significance, that in the Bible the prayer in Psalms, as well as that in I Chronicles, is solely for material well-being but that the Rabbis interpret both to refer to Torah.

Petitions in behalf of Israel are seldom found dissociated from Torah or the appeal to God's justice. "May it be Thy will, my Father who art in heaven, that Thou never deliver us into the hands of an agent,"[129] a prayer which puts implicit faith in God's mercy, has reference to Israel alone. But in the other petitions with Israel as theme there enter as factors both Torah and God's justice. When Israel sinned with the golden calf, Moses, according to the Rabbis, appealed to the justice of God. Standing in prayer before Him, he said: "Master of the universe, Thou art righteous and kind, and all Thy works are in faithfulness! For the sake of three thousand who served (the idol) with a whole heart shall six hundred thousand die—and those who are twenty years old and below, and those who are eighteen and fifteen and two and one . . .?"[130] One of our authors, concerned for the individuals in Israel, calls for prayer wherein Torah and justice as one should intervene: "Pray for the heads of families (בעלי בתים) in Israel because of the *Derek Ereẓ* they

[126] Above, p. 139.
[127] P. 31.
[128] "Additions," p. 43.
[129] P. 119. [130] P. 17.

possess; all the more, if words of Torah are in them! Pray for those that engage in the work of the community for the sake of heaven, whom the Holy One blessed be He gives the reward of *Derek Ereẓ* in this world whilst the principal remains for them in the World to Come!"[131] In a prayer welling out of love for Israel, filled with woe and pain, once more a plea for justice to his people based on what they do for Torah is wrung from our author: "Our Father who is in heaven, look upon our affliction and plead our cause, and may our shame rise before Thee always! Recall how many heads of families there are in Israel who possess nothing, yet engage in Torah every day continually! Recall how many poor and needy there are in Israel whose skin the Nations of the World pull from their backs, yet they engage in Torah every day continually! Recall how many blind there are in Israel who have no food and yet give money that their children may study Torah! Recall how many little lads there are in Israel 'who know not their right from their left hand,' yet engage in Torah every day continually! Recall how many old men and women there are in Israel who come early in the morning and in the evening to the synagogue and house of study, and desire and long for and look eagerly to Thy help every day continually! My Father who is in heaven, Thou art righteous, Thou art kind, and all Thy works are in faithfulness, have mercy upon Thy children . . .!"[132] (Somewhat farther in the book the same prayer is enlarged and supplied with biblical texts, no doubt the work of a later author.)[133] These prayers in which Israel, Torah and the appeal to God's justice actually form a single theme are, of course, examples of the organic unity of the fundamental concepts.

We are accustomed to regard prayer as a plea to God in behalf of oneself. Yet if prayer be thought of as an expression

[131] P. 103. Again the word "pray" is the translation of בקשו רחמים.

[132] P. 110. Friedmann, in his Introd. p. 81, calls attention to the phrase "look upon our affliction and plead our cause," which is found also in the daily *'Amidah*.

[133] P. 112. In this prayer, it is argued that Torah depends on Israel: "If, God forbid, Israel should disappear from the world, Thy Torah would disappear also."

of feeling, it may also be uttered in behalf of someone else about whom we are deeply concerned. Nay, one who can pray for someone or for the community and does not, shows himself to be callous to others and is therefore guilty of sin: "He that has the power to pray for his fellow and for the community and does not do so is called a sinner."[134] Above we have read that one ought to pray for the members of his household that they should be kept from sin; we have observed that our author called for prayer in behalf of those who possess *Derek Ereẓ*; and we have also reason to believe that prayers in behalf of the community, that is, of all Israel were common.

God both hears and answers prayer. He makes the rain to fall, if petitioned to by one who has learned and loves the Torah.[135] He doubles the sustenance of those who, though neither their deeds nor their fathers' deeds give them hope, yet pray much and ask for grace.[136] In the two interpretations of Jabez's prayer, for material well-being and for Torah, God granted his request: the former concludes, (Jabez) "found contentment in his old age;"[137] and the latter, "The Holy One blessed be He gave him that which he requested."[138] God hearkened to Moses' plea for justice for all the six hundred thousand of Israel and became reconciled with them.[139] When troubles come upon Israel, they have only to stand in one band before God and say the prayers of forgiveness revealed by Him to Moses, and He will answer them.[140] Communal prayer for communal welfare imposes, it would seem, the condition that all pray, if the prayer is to be answered. Not only that, but it is required that the lesser ones be first in prayer: When Israel was at the Red Sea, God did not respond until the Israelites lifted up their voice (Exod. 14:10); "thus thou dost learn that the Holy One blessed be He does not respond to the great until the lesser ones have first prayed."[141] The contradiction between the last homily and the first in this paragraph is the result of different emphasis

[134] P. 87. [135] P. 92.
[136] P. 183. [137] P. 31.
[138] Ibid. [139] P. 17.
[140] "Additions," p. 42.
[141] P. 44.

upon two points of reference—in the last homily Israel is emphasized, and in the first, Torah. It is a principle to which attention has already been directed.[142]

Thus far we have discussed that form of prayer which is petition. God both hears and answers prayer. Petitions may be, should be, offered God in behalf of one's fellows and of the community, as well as for one's own needs. The things prayed for or the themes of the prayers are: rain, material well-being, children, family-welfare, forgiveness of sin, moral rectitude, Torah, the welfare of Israel and justice. The last three—Torah, Israel's welfare and the appeal to God's justice—often constitute a single theme in prayer, as we might expect because of the organic unity underlying the three concepts.

When we turn from petitions to praises of God, we find a somewhat similar range of themes. Prayers in praise of God on occasion simply extol His power or greatness; but they may also rise from a mood of deep thankfulness for some specific gift conceived as coming from God or from gratitude for the love or justice the Rabbis felt God exhibits in ordering the world. It is in this category of prayer which is praise of God that practically all the parallels to the liturgy are to be found. This is perhaps to be explained on the ground that prayers of praise bulk so large in the liturgy as a whole.

A prayer extolling God's power and greatness in general is the following: "Blessed be the Lord God, God of Israel, the Dweller among the Cherubim. Thou art God alone over all the kingdoms of the earth; Thou hast made the heaven and the heavens above them with understanding." Israel, according to the Rabbis, said this prayer after Moses placed before them the laws.[143] Phrases in the *Ḳedushah*, taken from the Bible, may

[142] God answers not only direct prayers but the doubts of the righteous as to their fitness. When Abraham died, Isaac said, "Woe unto me! Perhaps there are no good deeds in me such as there were in father; what will the Holy One blessed be He do unto me?" Thereupon God's mercy was moved and He spoke unto him at that time—p. 129.

[143] Pp. 122–123. Friedmann, in his Introd. p. 81, states that this prayer was probably recited in the time of the author after the reading of the Torah. He also calls attention to the similarity of the phrases in the prayer of the liturgy "Thou art the Lord our God . . . Thou hast made the heavens and

also be regarded as general prayers of praise. These the angels as well as Israel recite, saying, from the rising of the sun until its setting, "Holy, holy, holy" (Is. 6:3); and from the setting of the sun until its rising, "Blessed be the glory of the Lord from His place" (Ezek. 3:12).[144]

Thanksgiving or prayers of gratitude for specific gifts or for qualities of God in evidence in the world naturally are no more limited as to theme than are the petition-prayers. If the things we pray for because we desire them cannot be limited or fixed, neither can those things be fixed which we have received, and for which, therefore, we thank God. Children, the subject of petition, may also be a theme for gratitude. "When a man marries a woman and has one son or two sons from her, he should bless and praise and exalt and sanctify and magnify the name of Him who spoke and the world came into being, the Holy One blessed be He."[145] Forgiveness and justice, for which we appeal to God, we thank Him for when we are conscious of having received them. "David stood in prayer before the Holy One blessed be He. He said before Him: Lord of the universe, if Thou hadst not written for us . . . Thou art merciful . . . (dealing with loving-kindness).[146] Thou art righteous and dost judge the sons of men according to their ways, and payest to every man according to his deeds—'measure for measure'. . . "[147] Forgiveness is also the theme of the following prayer, though the note of Israel, too, is struck: "My Father who is in heaven, may Thy great name be blessed forever and ever, and mayest Thou have satisfaction from Thy servants Israel in all their places of habitation: For Thou hast said, 'I will receive their sinners in repentance' . . ."[148] Israel is in these prayers of praise associated with other concepts, just as it was

the earth," etc. (Singer Prayer Book, American edition, p. 10). See Friedmann ibid, for further remarks. Incidentally, the biblical name of God appearing here seems to strengthen his contention.

[144] P. 193. See above, p. 65, where other references are given.

[145] P. 31.

[146] The full text up to this point is found above, p. 115.

[147] Pp. 98–9. The term "measure for measure" is explained in the next chapter.

[148] P. 121. The full text is given above, p. 121.

in prayers of petition, except that now God's love is an occasion of gratitude as His justice was a matter for appeal. That God forgives Israel's sins is the theme at the end of this prayer, most of which is found in the liturgy: "Blessed be He who spake, and the world came into being; blessed be He who speaketh and doeth, blessed be He who decreeth and performeth; blessed be He who was the Maker of the world in the beginning. Blessed be He who remembereth the first things, and passeth by the latter things."[149] The "first things" referred to here is the acceptance of the Torah, and "the latter things," the worship of the golden calf. God's love for Israel, His constant protection from adversary and enemy, is recounted in another homily which closes with a prayer of thanksgiving very similar to one in the liturgy: "From now on, if we and our sons and daughters were to stand (and pray), and we had a mouth as the sea, and our tongues were as the multitude of its waves, and our lips were as the wide-extended firmament, we could not thank Him (enough), saying before Him, 'O Lord our God' . . ."[150]

Humility is also expressed in prayers of praise. It is a note struck by David at the end of a prayer in which he extols God for having given the Torah to Israel: "My Father that is in heaven, may Thy great name be blessed . . . and mayest Thou find satisfaction from Israel . . . for having raised us, exalted us, sanctified us and praised us, and for having bound us with the crown of the words of the Torah; the Torah I have done, I have done only from Thine; the deeds of loving-kindness I have done, I have done only from Thine; and as reward of the little Torah I have done before Thee, Thou hast given me this world, the days of the Messiah and the World to Come."[151] There is even an injunction to utter a prayer that should express one's

[149] P. 179. The last clause only is not found in our prayer book; the rest of the prayer is on p. 19 of Singer's P. B. (American edition). Friedmann, Introd., p. 81, declares that ours is the original text, being composed of expressions from Yer. Ber. 11d, and gathered into a prayer.

[150] P. 163. It is, of course, similar to part of נשמת, Singer's P. B., p. 183. Friedmann, Introd. p. 81, cannot decide whether it was first in the liturgy or in our text.

[151] P. 89. Very similar is David's prayer on p. 157. It concludes, however, "The deeds we have done are not proper before Thee."

humility before God's greatness, and this prayer is paralleled by one in the liturgy: Let a man fear Heaven (in secret?) acknowledge the truth and speak the truth in his heart. Let him rise early every day and say, "Master of all worlds! Not because of our righteous acts do we lay out our supplications before Thee, etc."[152]

In the prayers of praise and thanksgiving in Seder Eliahu the themes, then, are: The power, glory and greatness of God; thanksgiving for children, and for forgiveness and just dealing, and for His kindness in giving Israel the Torah, and for His protection and love for Israel. In addition, the attitude of humility is evoked by the realization of God's greatness and beneficence, an attitude reminiscent of the petition-prayers for ethical rectitude. Prayers of praise and thanksgiving have,

[152] P. 118. This quotation, ending with 'וגו presupposes we know how it is to be continued. Friedmann, note No. 28, declares that it is the prayer found in our liturgy (Singer P. B. p. 8), and ends with מקדש שמך ברבים. In his Introduction, p. 80, he proves that the remainder of the prayer as found in the prayer-book abounds with expressions common to the Seder Eliahu. He also calls attention to the fact that the prayer is in the Siddur of R. Amram and in the order of prayers of Maimonides, and that the author of Shibbale Halleḳet claims that it was composed in a period of persecution.

Mann, Changes in the Divine Service, (Hebrew Union College Annual, Vol. IV, pp. 302–10 and pp. 250–1) following the hint contained in the Shibbale Halleḳet declares that the prayer was composed c. 450, when the Persians persecuted the Jews in Babylon; hence, he seeks to establish both the date and provenance of the Seder on this basis. The word בסתר, "in secret" by means of which Mann tries to prove that at that time the *Shem'a* in the prayer as found in the liturgy was said at home, privately—that word happens to be omitted from our text though it is present in the prayer of the liturgy. Granted, however, that the omission represents merely a textual error, as Friedmann seems inclined to believe, the theory is too heavy to be based on so slight a foundation. The word בסתר is found elsewhere, and in those places can in no wise be connected with persecutions. See the homily quoted above, p. 140 where exactly the same expression ירא שמים בסתר is employed, and can in no conceivable way be associated with persecutions. See also its use in Seder Eliahu, p. 84, which indicates how the term is truly employed there and elsewhere in the Seder.

"Many of the medieval authorities give the Yerushalmi as the source for this prayer (comp. Ratner אהבת ציון Berak. 199–200); and the Babylonian origin of this prayer is therefore excluded"—(L. G.).

therefore, one theme characteristic of themselves—the glory, power and greatness of God. All other themes, with the possible exception of humility, they have in common with petition-prayers, always bearing in mind, of course, the primary difference in mood between the two types of prayer. It is the difference in mood, rather than any specially characteristic theme, that, by and large, distinguishes the prayer of praise and thanksgiving from the prayer of petition.

We ought also to remember that the four prayers that have parallels in the liturgy are in no way to be distinguished, either in theme or style, from the remainder of the prayers considered. Thanksgiving for God's kindness to Israel, the extolling of God's greatness, and humility—the notes struck in these prayers—are struck in the other prayers of praise, as well.

Now the prescribed prayers, many of which are referred to in Seder Eliahu, conform, both as to theme and mood, to the two types of prayer we have studied. As to mood, they include prayers of petition and of praise; and they are also characterized by the same variety of themes. We exclude, however, from the category of prayer the three paragraphs of the *Shem'a*, not primarily because they are excerpts from the Bible, but because they are excerpts which do not conform either in theme or mood to what we have seen to be the characteristics of the prayer-types. Its three paragraphs contain instruction, admonition, exhortation and commandments, themes outside the purview of prayer. This does not hold true of the first verse of the *Shem'a*,[153] and of the Trishagion and the prayers for forgiveness, also taken from the Bible, which fully conform to prayer types, and are so regarded in this discussion. It is wrong to bulk together all excerpts from the Bible in the liturgy, and to conclude that all of them are not prayers simply because they are contained in the Torah.

A prescribed prayer of petition emphasized by our text is the prayer for forgiveness. "When troubles come upon Israel, they shall all stand before Me in one band and they shall say

[153] See above, p. 60 where this verse of the *Shem'a* is shown to be the declaration of His one-ness, or rather only-ness, and is the affirmation by which the *Malkut Shamayim* is accepted.

before Me the prayers for forgiveness (סדרי סליחה)."[154] These prayers were revealed directly to Moses by God, who "went down from His thick dark clouds like the leader of prayers (ש״ץ) who is wrapped in his *talit* and reads the prayers."[155] The form in which this prayer is couched—a declaration of God's mercy and goodness (Exod. 34:6–7)—may be that of a prayer of praise with God's forgiveness as theme, but the mood required is one of petition. Other prescribed prayers of petition mentioned are: גאולה, at the end of which is a plea for Israel's redemption;[156] the eighteen benedictions, which contain some prayers of petition—for wisdom, health, return of Israel, etc.;[157] and the seven benedictions of the *'Amidah* on the Sabbath,[158] wherein the benediction of the *ḳedushat ha-yom* contains a petition.[159]

Prescribed prayers of praise are by far in the majority, as has been observed. Mentioned in our text are the Trishagion—"Holy, holy, holy,"[160] and "Blessed be the glory of God"[161] from the *Ḳedushah*; and the *Shem'a*, which is no doubt referred to in the statement, "But Israel . . . proclaim My oneness twice every day continually" (corrected after Ginzberg),[162] and

[154] "Additions," p. 42.

[155] Ibid. עובר לפני התיבה. The prayer referred to, then, is "The LORD God, merciful and gracious . . ." (Exod. 34:6–7).

[156] P. 113. "The גאולה in its original form is not a prayer for redemption but one of praise of God for the redemption of Israel from Egypt! Compare Ginzberg, Geonica II, 89." (L. G.).

[157] P. 172. The term used is תפילה, prayer; also so referred to on p. 113. Other references are on pp. 13, 15, and elsewhere.

[158] P. 172.

[159] There are, of course, benedictions in these *'Amidot* that contain general laudations of God.

[160] P. 193. See above, p. 65. [161] Ibid.

[162] "Additions," p. 37. Professor Ginzberg declares Friedmann's reading to be incorrect. The phrase used, he says, is that of the *Ḳedushah* of שבת—המיחדים שמו . . . פעמים בכל יום; and instead of ומקדישין in our text, suggests ומיחדין. "In all events, it refers to the *Shem'a*. By the way, Friedmann did not notice that the text he offers is impossible since after משכימין ממטותיהן the phrase פעמים בכל יום is hardly intelligent!"—(L. G.). Comp. Ginzberg, Genizah Studies I, p. 119.

On p. 36, "Additions," the reading קדשו . . . פעמים is doubtful. See Friedmann, note No. 19.

which is also designated by name frequently.[163] These prayers are general declarations of God's glory, oneness, and kingship. There is also a reference to the people in the synagogue on *Sukkot* responding to a prayer of the leader by "Hallelujah;"[164] and another of people in the synagogue responding "Amen," "and blessing the Holy One blessed be He by 'Amen.'"[165] Again, when one is called to the Torah, he occasions the blessing of God by the public, apparently by the response, "Blessed be the Lord," etc.[166] The blessing "Bless ye the Lord who is to be blessed" occurs later in a story of an orphan whose father in Gehenna was doomed to eternal punishment until the boy was able to say this prayer; and Professor Ginzberg has shown that it refers to ברכו in the יוצר prayer, uttered by the boy as leader in prayer.[167] It is likely, also, that the קדיש, which is a prayer largely of general praise and laudation of God though containing a petition as well, is referred to in the homilies, "If a man has studied Torah . . . he should bless . . . and sanctify the name of Him who spake . . . and, it is not necessary to say, if one has studied Halakot,"[168] and "the Agadot, through which they sanctify His great name."[169] There are also prescribed prayers of gratitude and praise not recited in the synagogue at all. Among these are the benedictions after waking and eating and drinking. They give man preeminence over the beasts for he, unlike them, does not take the daily gifts from God for granted: "Why, a man eats and says grace, drinks and says a benediction, sleeps and says a blessing and awakes and says a blessing—how can he be compared to a beast that cannot distinguish anything?"[170] Specifically mentioned are the number of blessings over the seven species of food, one before and the

[163] Pp. 140, 13, 15 and elsewhere.

[164] P. 65—Referring probably to הלל.

[165] P. 52.

[166] P. 99. See Friedmann in note, end of p. 25 of "Additions," in which he shows that this may have been taken to refer to קדיש יתום.

[167] "Additions," p. 23. See Ginzberg, Genizah Studies, Vol. I, pp. 235–6. See also Friedmann's note No. 52 on passage in text.

[168] P. 31.

[169] P. 11.

[170] "Additions," p. 43.

one after eating, the one blessing over other species, and the number in the grace after meals, "three and the blessing 'who art good and dispensest good' making (in all) four."[171]

We have not permitted ourselves to make an inquiry into all the prayers of the prescribed liturgy, as being outside the range of our study.[172] It will be noticed, too, that some of the prescribed prayers are not completely either prayers of praise or of petition, sections of petition being interspersed with sections of praise. But the principle is the same as in those prayers that are not prescribed: The mood is either that of petition or praise and thanksgiving, and the themes range in variety from health and material goods to moral values.

How, then, do the prescribed prayers differ from those not prescribed? Precisely in the implications and consequences of their being prescribed. They are prescribed by authority; and in Seder Eliahu two instances are given illustrating the sources of this authority. Above we have read that God Himself revealed to Moses the prayers of forgiveness; the words of the Bible, then, directly revealed by God, are the source of this prayer. The following homily explains the source of other prescribed prayers: "One time as I was travelling, a man met me and came to me with a heretical argument (בדרך מינות). He knew Bible but not Mishnah. He said to me 'The Bible was given us at Sinai; the Mishnah was not given us at Sinai.' And I said to him, 'My son, were not Bible and Mishnah both given by God (מפי הגבורה)? Parable: A king had two servants and he loved them dearly and gave to one a measure of wheat and to the other a measure of wheat, to one a bundle of flax and to the other a bundle of flax. What did the clever one do? He took the flax and wove it into a cover, and took the wheat and ground it into fine flour. He sifted it and ground and kneaded and baked, and placed it on the table and spread the cover over it and left it until the king should come. After a while the king came home and said: My sons, bring me what I gave you. One brought bread of fine flour on the table with the cover spread over it,

[171] P. 172.

[172] Not all of the prayers mentioned in the preceding paragraph are, strictly speaking, prescribed by rabbinic authority.

and the other brought the wheat in a basket and the bundle of flax upon it . . .' I said, 'My son, if I find you in the midst of the Mishnah of the learned (that is, acting upon it), your words will be false?' He answered, 'Yes.' I then said to him, 'My son, when you lead in prayer on the Sabbath, how many (benedictions) do you say?' He answered, 'Seven.' 'And on the other days of the week?' 'The entire *Tefillah*' . . . 'And on the seven species (of food), how many benedictions do you recite?' 'Two: a benediction before and a benediction after, eating.' 'And on the other species?' 'One benediction.' 'And in the grace after meals?' 'Three and the טוב ומטיב ("who art good and dispensest good") making (in all) four.' I said to him, 'My son and do we have these from Mt. Sinai, and are these not but from the Mishnah of the learned? But when the Holy One blessed be He gave the Torah to Israel, He gave it to them only as wheat from which to make fine flour, and as flax from which to make a garment.' " Several hermeneutic rules, which really constitute the application of the parable, conclude the homily.[173] The source of the prayers mentioned here is the Mishnah of the Rabbis, which derives its authority from, and as the homily says is an elaboration of, the Bible. The prescribed prayers are, then, authorized and commanded by supreme religious authority.

Not only are the prayers commanded by supreme authority, but all the details concerning these prayers are prescribed, as well. There are seven benedictions in the *'Amidah* of the Sabbath and eighteen on week-days; there are two benedictions on the seven species, one before eating and one after eating, and one benediction on the other species; there are four benedictions in the grace after meals.[174] The order of the prayers is also prescribed as we can see from these instances and from another example in the Seder, namely, that the *Tefillah* must immediately follow after נאולה.[175] In fine, the prescribed prayers take on much of the character of ritualistic commandments, were associated, indeed, with "other *mizwot*."[176]

[173] Pp. 171–2.
[174] Ibid.
[175] P. 113.
[176] P. 15.

As commandments, they constitute a claim upon the justice of God when they are performed, or rather when they are recited. Those who recite the prescribed prayers can count on being rewarded by God. "Even though a man possess neither Bible nor Mishnah but does come early in the morning and in the evening to the synagogue and house of study and recites the *Ḳeri'at Shem'a* for My great name's sake, and prays the *Tefillah* for My great name's sake, his reward is deposited with Me—provided only that he guard himself from sin."[177] Even the wicked who came to the synagogue twice daily "and recited the *Shem'a* and prayed the *Tefillah* and performed *other mizwot* (commandments—italics mine)" will ultimately be saved from Gehenna.[178] One of Israel's virtues which, among others, causes God to weigh them to the side of merit is the fact that "Israel (rise early in the morning from their beds and?) proclaim My oneness twice every day continually" and that they go to synagogue daily.[179] Attendance at the synagogue for prayer, morning and evening, is one of the claims for divine favor to Israel in the powerful plea of our author.[180] And there is the story told approvingly by R. Joḥanan of the old woman whom he found in the synagogue praying, and who went from one city to another to pray, and who explained that she went "from city to city to pray in order to receive reward (therefor)." R. Joḥanan declared that he learned about "reward" from this old woman.[181]

Without doubt the Rabbis were well aware of all the tendencies toward mere ritualism lurking in these prescribed prayers. The very fact that they were prescribed and that thus they were become "commandments," together with the element of reward associated with this term, tended to render them stereotype phrases, uttered as ritual, and lacking the glow of devotion that warm personal experience enkindles in spontaneous prayers.

177 P. 13.

178 P. 15.

179 "Additions," p. 37. See above p. 149, note 162, where the text of this homily is corrected.

180 P. 110; in the expanded form, p. 112.

181 "Additions," p. 22.

Yet the aim of the Rabbis was to supply expression to the devotional moods of all Israel alike, even to those of the common man who lacks the gift of putting his feelings—gratitude for daily bounties, concern for Israel, adoration of God, desire for moral improvement, and the like—into words; and to arouse, also, by means of harmonious expression these devotional attitudes in the hearts of those men who might otherwise be insensible to them. They are not prayers recited only at public worship, in the synagogue, though this was most desirable, but are obligatory on the individual wherever he may happen to be. In mood and theme, as we have moreover observed, they conform to the types of prayer uttered by individuals. For these reasons the term "public prayer" has been avoided here throughout and "prescribed prayer" used instead.

The Rabbis tried to overcome the tendency to mechanize the prescribed prayers by laying down certain rules calculated to stimulate the devotional attitude or to avoid distractions. One should not pray where passersby may disturb him, nor among women, lest he be disturbed by thoughts of sex.[182] "One should sanctify his camp four ells in all directions," except he be in his house, and one should stand at the side of a tree or stone in prayer (when on a road).[183] There is also the separatistic injunction that one should not stand in the valley in prayer, as the (Gentile) nations do.[184] The very tone used in prayer may indicate whether the latter is true worship: "He that recites the *Ḳeri'at Shem'a* so that his ears hear his voice, he is praising himself (משתבח); he that prays (the *Tefillah*) so that his ears hear his voice is testifying false testimony, and some say, lacks faith."[185] To be properly attuned to prayer, let one first engage in Torah that he may create the mood of communion: " 'Worship the Lord in the beauty of holiness' (Ps.

[182] P. 46. [183] Ibid.

[184] Ibid.

[185] P. 140. "The injunction against praying aloud seems to be directed against a common custom in Palestine." (L. G.). On the divergence between Palestine and Babylon in this regard, see Ginzberg, Legends VI, p. 217, note 11. Here is another indication of the Palestinian locale of homilies in our Seder.

29:2)—From this they taught: Let no man stand in prayer (בתפילה) until he has studied (at least) one halakah or one verse (of the Bible)."[186] Rules of this kind were designed to prevent prescribed prayer from becoming "a fixed task."

Seder Eliahu also contains a number of passages very much akin to prayers which we shall designate as "contemplations." Without being couched in the form of prayer—of a direct appeal to God or laudation of Him in which He is addressed—these contemplations nevertheless possess the other characteristics of prayer. The mood is most frequently that of praise, and the themes are the same as those of the true prayer-types. They arise from the contemplation of the ordinary phenomena of life and of history (as the Rabbis knew it), hence the name by which they are here designated. Although these contemplations may perhaps be distinguished from prayer in that many, by no means all, close with an exhortation, one senses that they too have been a means of communion with God, the communion that accompanies reflection if not that expressed in prayer. There is evident a pondering over the details of man's and Israel's existence and a warm comprehension of their meaning, an ascent, as it were, into the mind and purpose of God; that is why these contemplations may justly be regarded as true communion.

The following contemplation is one where praise and thanksgiving is the mood, and the theme the daily miracles of man's existence; it closes with an implied exhortation for man to be careful of his deeds: "I will tell of the righteous and loving deeds of God that He does for Israel every single hour and every single day: Every day man is sold and every day he is redeemed (this refers to the Evil *Yeẓer*—Friedmann); every day the spirit of man is taken from him and given to its Owner, and in the morning it is returned to him, as it says 'Into Thy hand I commit my spirit' (Ps. 31:6); every day they perform for him such miracles as occurred to those that went out of Egypt; every day they bring about for him a redemption such as occurred to those that went out of Egypt; every day they provide him

[186] P. 12.

with food (as) from his mother's breast; every day they punish him as the master punishes the child, because of his deeds."[187] Another selection concludes in a similar vein with an exhortation to thank God for the blessing of life: "Hear me, my brethren and my people, that you may not come to arrogance of spirit: A man should search into himself and realize that after a while is death. He should lift up his eyes to heaven and say, 'Who created the sun, moon, stars and planets, the four winds of heaven and all the work of creation? For through His wisdom and understanding each one is dependent upon the word of His lips . . .' Further, one should observe the works of the hands of the Holy One blessed be He, man, beast, fowl of the heaven and fish of the sea, the provisions of each one of whom are in His hands, and whose lives are in His charge . . . Therefore, I say, that one ought to bless and praise and exalt and magnify and sanctify the name of Him who spake and the world came into being for the spirit and soul that he returns to the Owner in the evening, and in the morning it is returned to him."[188] Here the mood is also praise and thanksgiving.

Humility is the theme of a number of contemplations. Against the glory, wisdom, might and power of God, man ought to recognize his own limitations. Be man as strong as Og, king of Bashan[189] or as Samson,[190] as wise as Moses,[191] or as rich as Ahab,[192] let him not glory in these things. But let God glory for all the might, all the wisdom, all the riches, are His.[193] At times it may be good for man to realize that he has a fate in common

[187] Pp. 8–9. See Friedmann, note No. 16. This passage is put into the mouth of King David. In a parallel passage on p. 199, which Friedmann (Introd. p. 48) thinks is a later interpolation, there is no reference specifically to Israel: "I will tell of God's kingship and greatness and might: For every day every man is created and every day every man is born; every day every man lives, every day every man dies; . . . every day he is fed like an infant at its mother's breast by the fruit of his hands." This passage is far more prosaic than the one cited above.

[188] Pp. 103–4. Friedmann's Introduction, pp. 126–7.

[189] "Additions," p. 43.

[190] Ibid., p. 44.

[191] Ibid.

[192] Ibid. [193] Ibid.

with the animals, and at death is not superior to them. Nay, in the laws of ritual uncleanness at death, man makes humans unclean for a longer time, and renders houses unclean and humans who have touched his body a source of ritual impurity, which the carcass of the beast does not. Though it is true that in life man distinguishes God's bounties and blesses Him for them, which the beast cannot do, when man reaches the point of death they consider how to dispose of his body as they consider also how to dispose of a carcass. And even after death, though a beast has rest, man is placed in judgment.[194] The conclusion to be drawn from these reflections is again suggested in another passage where the exhortation, as here, is only implied: "One should reflect on three occasions every day: when he attends to his natural wants, when he is being bled, and when he stands over the dead. When he attends to his natural wants, he is being told: See, thy way is like that of the animal; when being bled, he is being told: See, thou art only flesh and blood; and when he stands over the dead, he is being told: See whither goest thou. And yet he does not repent but sits and multiplies additional sins."[195]

Now it is true that in the last two selections, God is neither praised nor petitioned. But the communion that comes with reflection is sensed in these also, and in the last selection almost takes the form of communication. Implicit also is the recognition that man, after all, is different from the animal, that he possesses a different estate, for which he is held accountable, and for which, by very reason that he is otherwise like the animals, he should be thankful. What is implicit above is put clearly in this contemplation: "Hear me, my brethren and my people: He that hath eyes will see, (that hath) a heart will take wisdom, and (that hath) reins will understand that there is no difference between man and animals, and that it is a high estate for man that he is seated together with the King (שמושיבין אותו עם המלך בקרון). And he ought to search into his heart, his very self, and realize that the spirit(s) and soul(s) the Holy

[194] "Additions", pp. 42–3.

[195] P. 176. See above, p. 127, note 67.

One blessed be He hath created in the world from end to end, when they return to the dust, it is only Israel that will come back again; because of the love that He bears them and the joy that He takes in them, He will raise them from the dust upon their feet, and place them between His knees, and fondle them and embrace them and kiss them, and bring them to the life of the World to Come."[196] The mood here is one of thanksgiving, and the theme, again, the similarity between man and animal. The denial of future life for all non-Israelites is contradicted in other passages.[197]

Israel, Torah and God's justice are themes of contemplations. Besides the reference to Israel we have just read, there is a swift summary of Israel's history. After giving the number of years in each period—that of the period in the wilderness, of the period until the Temple was built, of the years of the First Temple, of the Babylonian exile, etc.—there is a statement of praise, either "How much did He fondle them, how much did He embrace them, how much did He kiss them," or "His hand was stretched over them, protecting them from adversary and enemy."[198] Torah is the theme of the exhortation, but God's power is the theme of praise, in the following contemplation: "A man should not say to himself: I have studied Bible and Mishnah today, I do not need to do this again tomorrow; I have done charities today (צדקות), I need not do this again tomorrow; I have done deeds of loving-kindness (גמילות חסדים), I need not do this again tomorrow. But he should look searchingly into himself and know that death comes after a while. He should lift up his eyes to heaven and say: Who created these? Heaven and earth, sun, moon, stars and constellations early and late (משכימין ומעריבין) do the will of their Creator. So must thou rise early in the morning and remain in the evening (תשכים ותעריב) for the words of Torah, to do the will of thy Creator every day. For it says, 'And let us know, eagerly strive to know

[196] P. 86—הרוח ונשמה. The kinship between the three contemplations and the prayer in the liturgy (S. P. B. p. 4) is obvious.

[197] See below in chapter on The World to Come.

[198] P. 163.

the Lord' etc. (Hosea 6:3)."[199] The contemplation praising the power and justice of God begins the same way: "A man should look searchingly within himself . . . He should lift up his eyes to heaven and say: Who created the stars in the firmament and gave to each of them its place, to each of them its way and path? How many towers did the kingdom of Rome build—who cut them down and flung them to the ground? How many towers did the kingdom of Media build—who cut them down and flung them to the ground? Who destroyed (lit. "kicked") the first Tower and put its top in one place and its body in another, twenty-one miles distant?"[200]

We can conclude, then, that the contemplations while not couched in the style of prayers do possess characteristics of true prayer-types. Though usually containing an exhortation, which is not a quality of prayer, their themes, most often of praise, are the same as the prayer-themes.

The organic unity of the four fundamental concepts is to be discerned with exceptional clarity in prayer. Israel, Torah and God's justice and love are not only themes of petition and praise but are frequently combined into one theme.[201] It is worthwhile, however, to trace the other ways in which these concepts are integrated in prayer. Torah, we have seen, is the authority for the prescribed prayers, and sets down their order.[202] Biblical prayers for health and material well-being—Ps. 71:9 and I Chron. 4:10—are interpreted as prayers for Torah.[203] The efficacy of a prayer of petition depends upon Torah, as witness the case of the prayer for rain.[204] The study of Torah is a necessary preparation for prayer.[205] And we even find that

[199] P. 195. "משכים ומעריב seems to refer to *Ḳeri'at Shem'a* which is recited morning and evening"—(L. G.). On p. 139 a parallel passage is found. It ends, however, "And thou wilt be like unto the sun that gives light to the multitudes (לרבים), and like unto the moon that gives light to the multitudes . . ." For passage on p. 195, compare prayer in S. P. B., p. 8.

[200] P. 118.

[201] Above, pp. 140–142.

[202] Above, p. 152.

[203] Above, p. 141.

[204] Above, p. 143.

[205] Above, p. 154.

prayer is employed as an alternative, if not a substitute, for Torah: A man felt sad that he learned neither Bible nor Mishnah, and answered in a loud voice the Trishagion of the leader in prayer. When asked why he had raised his voice, he replied, "Is it not enough that I haven't studied Bible and Mishnah? Now that I have permission, shall I not lift my voice and let my soul be bowed down (in humility)?"[206] As an alternative to the study of Torah which is communion with God, the man found prayer as the means of communion.

Israel is saved by prayer. Judges 5:2 carries the interpretation that God uses those men to punish the Nations of the World who come early in the morning to the synagogue and in the evening, and respond with "Amen," thereby blessing God; and Ps. 55:19 is interpreted to mean that he saves Israel in warfare who comes in the morning and in the evening to be the tenth man of the Congregation.[207]

God's justice, besides being invoked or extolled in prayer, is counted on when reward is expected for reciting prescribed prayers.[208] There are additional instances of how God's justice is associated with prayer: The man who knew no Bible and Mishnah and who raised his voice in prayer was rewarded when he went up to Palestine from Babylon by being made an officer of the emperor, appointed over all the fortresses of Palestine, and given a place to build a city in which he and, after him, his descendents dwelt.[209] The priest who "feared Heaven in secret" and prayed that his ten children be kept from sin was rewarded, also, by being brought up from Babylon by Ezra, and by being enabled to see in the fifty years before he died "High Priests and young priests from among his sons and sons' sons."[210] The man who thanks God for the sons He has given him will

[206] P. 66. "קדושת השם is undoubtedly what is usually called קדושה, the only part of the *Tefillah* which was recited by all present and not only by the reader"—(L. G.). תשוח נפשי is a quotation from Lam. 3:20; "While reciting the holiness of God my soul is bowed down in humility"—L. G.

[207] P. 52. The tenth man completes the quorum necessary for public worship.

[208] Above, p. 153.

[209] P. 66.

[210] P. 90.

have "his bed (or rest) perfect" and will gain for himself this world, the days of the Messiah and the World to Come.[211] The one who acts in behalf of Israel (in leading the prayers), "him will I give a good reward."[212] All these cases depict God's reward for prayer; He punishes, however, those who desecrate or condone desecration of the prayers. The story is told of a man "who was standing with his son in the synagogue." All the people responded "Hallelujah" after the leader in the prayers, but the son "responded with words of frivolousness (תיפלות)." When the people remonstrated, the father replied, "What shall I do to him. He is but a child. Let him play." Next day the child did the same, and again the people remonstrated. This continued for the eight days of the festival of *Sukkot*. It was reported that before three years had elapsed that man died and his wife and son and his son's son and fifteen members of the family altogether, and there remained only two sons, one lame and blind and the other half-wit and wicked.[213] The ethical attitude involved in this story will be touched upon again in the next chapter.

In this section we have discussed the moods of prayer, which are that of petition and praise, the themes of prayers, which range from health and well-being to moral rectitude and include Israel, Torah and God's justice, prescribed prayers and their special characteristics, and contemplations; and we have also shown how in prayer, too, the fundamental concepts weave a recognized pattern.[214]

[211] P. 31.

[212] "Additions," p. 42.

[213] Pp. 65–6.

[214] It is evident that there is much material in Seder Eliahu of interest to the student of the liturgy. Our Seder contains, besides parallels to prayers in the prayer book, a number of expressions that are found in the prayer book. It is hard to determine in every case, of course, which is the original source. Friedmann, in his Introduction pp. 78–81 has collected a number of these expressions, to which a few may be added. Expressions of the *Ḳaddish:* יתגדל ויתקדש שמו—pp. 56, 58; יתברך ... בזמן קרוב—p. 110; בעגלא ובזמן קריב (Aramaic)—p. 95; יהי שמו הגדול מבורך לעולם ולעולמי עולמים, the Hebrew of יהא שמה רבא מברך לעלם ולעלמי עלמיא is found very frequently—pp. 9, 11, 18, 25, 32, 33, 40, 51, 53, 56, 83, 84, 89, 100, 109, 113, 115, 121, 136, 139, 143,

156, 157, 180. Friedmann believes that since all expressions except one are in Hebrew that this proves that the *Ḳaddish* was originally in Hebrew, and brings the שבלי הלקט as support. See Friedmann's Introd. p. 79.

Other expressions collected by Friedmann:

P. 91: כל הבוטחים בשמך באמת לא יבושו—in the daily *'Amidah;* p. 69: אב הרחמים—used in prayer when scroll is taken from the Ark; p. 31: לא נאמר אהבה רבה אלא אהבת עולם, a reminder of the discussion in the Talmud—see Friedmann, Introd. p. 81; p. 173: לעמוד ולעשות רצונו בלבב שלם—(Ber. 17a), in ברוך אלהינו שבראנו לכבודו in קדושא דסדרא (also in מודים דרבנן).

There are three more expressions found also in the liturgy:

P. 168: ברוך ה' שבחר בכם משבעים לשונות ונתן לכם את התורה is similar to the blessing over the Torah; p. 31: (כדי) שתהא מטתו שלימה is found in the prayer before going to bed; p. 84 (and elsewhere): (חכמה) בינה, דעה והשכל—in the daily *'Amidah.*

Friedmann calls attention to a number of homilies used by *payyṭanim* (Introd. pp. 81–2): p. 115: אבינו שבשמים ששמינו כשמו ושמו נאה לו . . . מושבותיכם—used by Ḳalir (see Friedmann, Introd. p. 82); p. 65: אם אש אחזה בלחים מה יעשו יבשים—used by *payyṭan* for Day of Atonement *piyyuṭ* (See Friedmann, Introd. p. 81).

Other expressions found in the liturgy, as well as references and parallels to prayers, have been cited at the places the passages containing them have been used in the discussion.

CHAPTER VI

THE JUSTICE OF GOD

I

The Quality of Justice

The justice of God, like God's love which man relies upon both in the world of nature and in the moral sphere, embraces the whole world in its scope. In the Rabbis' vision, the justice of God was an infallible principle operating in the world of natural phenomena, deciding the fortunes of individuals, and determining the history of nations. And it must always be borne in mind that this infallibility of God's justice was not something the Rabbis felt was finally achieved only in the World to Come, but something they discerned in all the mundane affairs of this world, here and now. It is this principle, above all others, that reduces, or rather exalts, the world as it exists to a moral order, in which whatever befalls of good or evil is never fortuitous but only a just recompense for deeds done.

That the Rabbis believed the justice of God operates in the world of nature we had occasion to observe before: The sun and the moon are held guilty of countenancing idolatry;[1] heaven and earth, the sun and the moon, the stars and the constellations will be called to judgment on account of Israel;[2] and the beasts, birds and cattle were driven forth from Eden together with Adam.[3] These instances, to be sure, should probably be taken not altogether at their face value but rather as springing from the desire of the Rabbis to concretise their conviction that God's justice is world-wide in scope. The main application of God's

[1] Above, p. 77.

[2] Above, p. 88.

[3] P. 164. On animals possessing speech and other man-like qualities, comp. Ginzberg, Legends, V, p. 61.

justice, whence indeed it derives its meaning, is man. God's justice to man will be the burden of the present chapter.

The justice of God is an aspect or a quality of His character; it is called "The quality (or attribute) of justice" (מידת הדין).[4] The Rabbis felt that the character of God was projected in "His ways" with man, that is to say, that God's character was implied in the fortunes, vicissitudes, joys and achievements of men. "From the character of His ways (ממידת דרכיו) he (Moses) learned that His mercies in the world are manifold" is the opening statement of a homily which relates that Moses asked of God the "character by which the world is governed;"[5] and then there is revealed to him in the tetragrammaton and the thirteen *midot* "the quality of loving-kindness and the quality of mercy."[6] Moses' question, however, dealt really with the quality of justice, and later we shall consider it in full. What is pertinent here is that the Rabbis assumed that God's character or qualities are revealed in the things that happen to man and to the world: God acts toward man with the *Midat Ha-raḥamim*, the quality of mercy, and with the *Midat Ha-din*, the quality of justice. In other words, the character of God, as revealed in His governance of the world, is both merciful and just.

The term מידת הדין is given several connotations in Seder Eliahu. It is contained in a promise of judgment to come, here or in the World to Come: the ten generations from Adam to Noah did not fear it in this world;[7] and we are told to expect its operation at some future time.[8] It is also invoked to explain the troubles and wanderings of those who fear God. After a parable in which those who both fear and love God are shown superior to those who only fear Him, the midrash pronounces: " 'He hath given טרף unto them that fear Him' (Ps. 111:5)—that refers to the quality of justice."[9] טרף, in accordance with

[4] Pp. 68, 141, 190.

[5] הראיני מידה שהעולם מתנהג בה—pp. 182–3.

[6] P. 183. See above, p. 114.

[7] P. 190.

[8] P. 68.

[9] P. 141.

its analogous use in Bereshit Rabba 40,2 was understood as טרוף, "wandering":[10] the tribulations of those who but fear God were held to be a just punishment, a consequence of the quality of justice. So far the term מדת הדין is employed to denote an activity of God: He withholds just punishment for the time being, His judgment is assured for the future, He punishes now with perfect justice. But at times the Quality of Justice is detached and personified as an entity in itself, distinct from God. She is represented as engaging in a dialogue with God in which she assumes the role of prosecutor of Israel with God as the Advocate or Defender: "And each and every day the Quality of Justice strengthens itself and stands before the Holy One blessed be He and says to Him, 'Master of the universe, . . . Israel swear falsely, and covet their neighbors' wives, and relate evil gossip (לשון הרע) about their friends. Perhaps there is favoritism before Thee . . .'" God answers that Israel proclaim His oneness twice daily, that they study, pray and observe *mizwot* and that He has created repentance for them, all this to prove that He does not show them favoritism.[11] The same argument is repeated, again with the Quality of Justice claiming that God shows favoritism to Israel, and again with God in the role of Defender of Israel "who have merit which surrounds them as the sand does the sea."[12] R. Eliezer, the author of these homilies wherein the Quality of Justice is personified, applies to the dialogue Ps. 20:2, "The Lord (will) answer thee in the day of trouble;" and he sees in Song of Songs 5:4 a grateful recognition by the *Keneset Yisra'el* of God's enduring mercy, without which "I would not have the strength to stand before the Quality of Justice."[13]

Now we ought to notice that R. Eliezer personifies Israel as well as the Quality of Justice. If the Quality of Justice speaks with God so does the *Keneset Yisra'el*. R. Eliezer apparently exercised the poet's flair for personification, in order to gain for his homilies that vital quality abstract ideas acquire only when

[10] See Theodor, Bereschit Rabba, p. 382.

[11] "Additions," p. 37.

[12] Ibid, p. 40.

[13] Ibid. See Friedmann's note No. 5; also above, p. 121 for full quotation.

personified. This was no doubt a common device among the more imaginative Rabbis. We can safely say that the Rabbis soberly accepted the fact that the "Quality of Justice" was but an aspect of God's character, a term expressive of His activity and partially descriptive of His dealings with men and with the world. In imaginative flights, they allowed themselves the liberty of personifying it as well as other ideas.[14]

II

Distributive Justice: Individual and Corporate

God judges mankind.[15] In the oft-quoted midrash describing His activity throughout time, we are told: "Since the world was created down to the present hour . . . one-third of the day I judge the world . . ."[16] The visitation of reward and punishment, it must be again emphasized, is not postponed or confined to the hereafter only: "From the day the world was created down to the present hour each and every one is given his just recompense, whether good or evil."[17] It is not a passive judgment that God exercises over man but one that is daily executed and that is constantly affecting the lot of man for good or evil, according to his ways. He "judges the sons of men, each one according to his ways, and pays to every man according to his deeds,"[18] giving reward for each *mizwah* done and administering punishment for each transgression.[19] The close supervision of God so impressed the Rabbis that one of them declares, "Every day they punish him (every man) as the master punishes the child, because of his deeds."[20] Whether in relation to one individual or to a whole generation, the distributive justice of God never fails. Generations that have engaged in Torah are rewarded with good even as the individual who is engaged in Torah, and

[14] For a similar view see Moore, Judaism, Vol. I, p. 392.

[15] P. 5, end.

[16] Pp. 130, 62 (twice), 90, 162. For full quotation see above, p. 38.

[17] P. 40. [18] Pp. 98, 50.

[19] P. 174; p. 173.

[20] P. 9. See above, pp. 155–156.

generations that have done evil are punished with death even as is the individual who has done evil, and punishment like reward is meted out in measure to the deeds performed.[21] That the Rabbis looked upon all the incidents of life as proof and vindication of this belief that God's distributive justice is constantly exercised will soon become abundantly clear.

If it is God who is responsible for all that happens to man then to the religiously minded nothing that happens is either arbitrary or wantonly cruel; the harshest misfortune and smiling good fortune are alike the judgments of a just God. The introduction to the midrash last cited denies the supposition—Heaven forfend!—that God deals with the world "as a cruel man, all whose ways are those of wanton cruelty," and, after affirming that God is just in his dealings with entire generations as well as with individuals, closes with the proof-text "My people shall never be ashamed" (Joel 2:26).[22] Those who place their faith in God's justice, as did Israel, "are never ashamed" because they can never conceive it to fail to extend to each man his just deserts. To describe the absolute character of God's justice, the Rabbis apply to it the word "truth:" "All fear Thy judgment, which is a true (judgment);"[23] the plagues brought upon the Egyptians were just recompense "since all His ways are truth";[24] when God chastises a man, he ought to realize that He "chastises justly (לאמיתו)."[25]

The justice of God is universal, embracing Gentile as well as Israelite. Nothing can be more explicit. "There is no favoritism before Me: Whether Gentile or Israelite, whether man or woman, whether male-slave or female-slave, he that has done a *mizwah*,

[21] P. 115; also p. 4, where only reward is mentioned.

[22] P. 115.

[23] "Additions," p. 40. [24] P. 40.

[25] P. 96. Ginzberg emends לאמיתו to לאהבתן, and this would, of course, change the entire meaning of the passage. "I do not believe that לאמיתו is equivalent to 'just punishment;' nor has the reference to Deut. 8:5 any bearing on it. Read לאהבתן—'because of the love he bears for them.' And the verse (from the Bible) is quoted where it is said that God chastises Israel as a father his son; comp. Sifre, Deut. 32, p. 73b, ed. Friedmann." (L. G.).

On p. 39, David is depicted as praising God with the attribute of "Truth": but see above, p. 37.

the reward thereof is at hand (שכרה בצדה)."[26] According to the deeds done, taking no stock of station or sex, knowing no distinction between Israel and the Gentiles, God's distributive justice places the highest of spiritual gifts, the Holy Spirit, upon him who deserves it: "I call heaven and earth to testify for me," says one of our authors in reference as to why Deborah was chosen as leader and prophetess over Phineas, the son of Eleazar, the High Priest, who was still alive, "I call heaven and earth to testify for me: whether Gentile or Israelite, whether man or woman, whether male-slave or female-slave, according to the deed done thus does the Holy Spirit rest upon him!"[27] The vigorous phrases common to both homilies point, perhaps, to a single author, whose views on God's justice may not be typical of general rabbinic thought. Emphasis upon Israel is just as conceivable, since Israel and God's justice are both points of reference, and no doubt some Rabbis stress Israel at the expense of universal justice. The identical question, it may be recalled, arose in the preceding chapter in the discussion of repentance, when the rule of the righteous who does *Teshubah* was applied to the Gentile as to the Israelite.[28] At all events, here, the decided tone in which the second homily is uttered, even the similar style in both, testify to the deep conviction of the author and to his established habit of mind. Nor do these statements stand alone. In the course of this chapter instances of God's universal justice will be so plentiful as to indicate that this is a dominating view in Seder Eliahu. And what must not be lost sight of is that, as in the homilies quoted in this paragraph, God rewards, not only punishes, deserving Gentiles. We are surely far away indeed from any conception of justice that can be characterized as tribal.

Man begins to be judged when he is no longer a child, that is, when he reaches the age at which he is brought to school to study Bible and Mishnah.[29] Although God is just, indeed because

[26] P. 65. [27] P. 48. [28] Above, p. 125.

[29] P. 92. Friedmann's rendering here is very doubtful. "The passage is not quite clear to me; and Friedmann's emendation is not tenable, as the opening sentence הקב'ה מרחם requires something about their reward and not punishment"—(L. G.).

He is just, He takes into account the moral temper of the individual: "The righteous are punished for slight transgressions and the wicked for the grave ones." Examples are adduced from Moses and Aaron and Nadab and Abihu "who were punished but for slight transgressions," and from Jereboam, Ahaz and Manasseh "who were not adjudged guilty until they filled the entire world with transgressions."[30] The sequel to this selection is a parable which likens the righteous to those in the presence of the King, and the wicked to those that stand outside; but the parable and its application are soon confused, and there is lost that discriminating understanding of the difference in human temperaments that illumines the first half of the selection.

The personalness of God, so heavily drawn upon in the description of all the aspects of God's love, is not nearly so strikingly in evidence when God's justice is depicted. True enough, the Rabbis conceive God as affected by the actions of man; "He rejoices over him who does good and is angry with him who does evil;"[31] and sometimes He is moved to anger over man's deeds and in wrath "inflicts judgment upon the wicked," as when He punished Pharaoh because he oppressed Israel.[32] But by and large the justice of God is made manifest by the Rabbis without recourse to all those striking figures they found it necessary to employ in order to depict God's love. To assure man that God forgives his sins and that He accepts him in repentance, both purely abstract ideas, the Rabbis had to dilate upon the personalness of God to such an extent as to make these ideas take on concrete, almost phenomenal form. This they are not called upon to do here for the reason, maybe, that many examples of divine justice are taken from the ordinary things that happen to man, such as sickness and the loss of goods by fire, etc., where the hand of God need only be inferred, though to the Rabbis convincingly inferred. Moreover, the Rabbis employed the principle of divine justice as an explanation of the good or evil that befell individuals and nations, and as proof that God watches and decides the fate of men in accordance

[30] P. 11.
[31] P. 185.
[32] P. 40.

with their deserts. Explanations are made after the facts have occurred; and proofs of God's justice are perhaps more necessary in the ordinary affairs, fortunes and mishaps of life where divine regulation is not so patent than in dramatic catastrophes where God's hand may appear more manifest; whether it be as example or proof, therefore, the ordinary phenomena of individual or national life form the bulk of the demonstrations of God's justice. These considerations may account for the infrequency of the occasions when the personalness of God is drawn upon in the rabbinic delineation of the justice of God.[33]

In offering what were to the Rabbis concrete demonstrations of the justice of God, we shall be obliged to borrow some homilies that have already been referred to in previous chapters, particularly the immediately preceding one of God's loving-kindness, and many other homilies that will subsequently be dealt with in those chapters concerned with Torah, Good Deeds, Israel, the Nations of the World and the World to Come. The organic unity of the four fundamental concepts makes any other course impossible. God's justice is frequently affected by His love; it is integrated with Torah; it determines the history of Israel. All four enter into the concepts of the Nations of the World and the World to Come just as they decided the outlines of the concepts of *Ḳiddush Hashem* and *Malkut Shamayim*. We have been careful, however, to select only such passages also treated elsewhere as will give point to some of the conclusions stated above or else illustrate a new aspect of the justice of God.

God rewards him who does good deeds by protecting him from harm. "A man whose deeds exceed his wisdom" is compared to a foot protected by the shoe from all trouble and sorrow.[34]

[33] In the development of the Jewish philosophy of the middle ages, its wide divergence from rabbinic theology is most marked at this point. The denial of attributes to God involves also the negation of the attributes of love and justice as, for example, in Maimonides' Guide for the Perplexed, Part I, Chapter 54, and even in the Kuzari of Yehudah Halevy (of all the medieval Jewish philosophers perhaps the closest to the rabbinic view point), near the beginning of the second chapter.

[34] P. 84. The expression "whose deeds exceed his wisdom" is found in Abot 3:12.

And the reward, given in all cases, is greater the more self-control the performance of the *mizwah* exacts: If he that refrains from blood—referring to the prohibition against the blood of animals as food, and quoting the Mishnah (end of Makkot)—receives reward even though blood is not to man's taste, all the more will he receive reward that refrains from taking things illegitimately and from indulging in illicit sexual intercourse, which are matters man desires and lusts for.[35] The very effort that it takes to refrain from transgression is itself so praiseworthy that Rabbi Simon declares that he who does nothing but does not commit a transgression is given reward as he who performs *mizwot*.[36] That this reward may well take place in this world the first midrash cited in the paragraph indicates. The rewards of repentance, we ought recall, are in large part conferred in this world: It has the power to cause men to reign in the world (as was the case with David); to cure the sick; to save men from trouble and sorrow; to bring material prosperity; and to make certain that one's children be God-fearing and even, as with Rahab's, illustrious.[37] No less is it true that rewards of prayer are also explicitly concerned with this world. We have but to recall that the man who raised his voice in prayer was rewarded by being appointed over all the fortresses of Palestine by the emperor, and that the priest who "feared Heaven in secret" was enabled to see his own children as High Priests in the Temple.[38]

Frequently God uses men as His instruments to reward or punish, as the case may be. But here, too, the choice of His instruments is not haphazard, for "good (זכות) is brought about by means of the worthy, and evil (חובה) by means of those who are (themselves) guilty." And then there immediately follows a statement significantly affirming the universality of God's justice: "And this rule applies to all the families of the earth, both among Israel and among the nations."[39]

[35] P. 73.

[36] P. 69. Also a mishnah at the end of Makkot.

[37] Above, pp. 135–136.

[38] Above, p. 160.

[39] P. 184.

God brings all the evil that men suffer in this world as punishment for their bad deeds. This principle of the Rabbis confirms our conclusion that God's justice is manifest in this world, and, as we shall see later, partially solves for the Rabbis the problem of evil. Basing themselves on the Scripture, "Thus saith the Lord . . . that formed the earth and made it . . . He created not a waste, He formed it to be inhabited" (Is. 45:18), the Rabbis draw an analogy from the ways of man. A man builds a house that he may store fruit, furniture and other things in it, not in order to destroy it by fire. With a similar constructive purpose did God create the world; He built it for permanence and for the well-being of man; and if aught occurs that seems to negate this purpose it is only that "men are punished because of their ways."[40] Fruit and grain rot because of the ways of men, and for the same reason men come to shame. "Nor do the eyes of men fail them in their prime but because of their ways; nor are men made unclean by the plagues (בנגעים) but because of their ways," and again for the same reason women cause ritual uncleanness.[41] Widely diverse as man's misfortunes are, the basic cause for all is always his own evil actions. If a rich man becomes poor, the loss of his wealth is a punishment for sin.[42] Indeed, the Rabbis say that the wicked because of their deeds suffer poverty and remain poor to the day of their death.[43] It is thus that they account for the mention of the Hebrew slave in the Bible: The wicked who, being poor, turned thieves were sold to make good their theft.[44] Money that is gained by theft or cheating is forcibly taken away by an act of God, as in the story of the man who cheated a Gentile out of two measures of dates and bought a pitcher of oil for the money, only to have the pitcher break and the oil spilled.[45] Certain sources of gain were regarded as either undesirable or unworthy or unsafe, and hence money derived from them "will have no sign of blessing" (that is, will soon be lost): The remuneration of writers (of

[40] Pp. 175–6.
[41] P. 175.
[42] P. 181.
[43] P. 132.
[44] P. 120.
[45] P. 74–75.

Scripture), the remuneration of interpreters of the learned (to the public on the Sabbath), money gained from foreign travel, and the money received from a woman married for the sake of her money.[46] Elsewhere the Rabbis explain why writers of Scripture lose their money, and also say that the possibility of loss in ships sunk at sea always faces the one engaged in foreign commerce.[47] The same text declares that interpreters ought not receive money for what they do on the Sabbath.[48] If the interpreter and the one who marries for money lose their money, therefore, it is traceable to the wrong or unethical ways of their acquiring it.

God's justice is apparent in everything that happens to man. It punishes or rewards a man even for his motive in choosing a wife. He that marries a woman for fornication will in the end have "a stubborn and rebellious son;" that marries for social position (לשום גדולה), "in the end a member of that family will destroy his children;" that marries for money "will in the end come in need of his fellows;" and that marries for the sake of Heaven will have children who will save Israel in time of distress.[49] The righteous are not "forsaken" but are rewarded with children who are also righteous. When R. Dosa was told he was standing near R. Eliezer, the son of Azariah, he remarked, "Has Azariah our friend a son?" and applied to him Ps. 37:25, "I have been young and now am old, yet have I not seen the righteous forsaken."[50] That the poor usually are blessed with children was explained on the ground that God deliberately compensates them thus for being poor in worldly goods.[51] Again,

[46] "Additions," p. 9.

[47] b. Pesaḥim 50b. [48] Ibid.

[49] P. 177. The homily goes on to explain that the motive of fornication is found in Deut. 21:11. After marrying the captive, people will gossip about him; because of this he will marry another woman, and the first wife will become the hated one; and "because he love the one and hate the other in the end he will have 'a stubborn and rebellious son.' " On p. 9 of "Additions," the homily is repeated with the changes that the man who marries for money will lose it, and the one who marries for fornication will beget no children.

[50] P. 168.

[51] P. 99. "Read שאין הקב"ה נותן ... [אלא] במחשבה—the poor begot many children in accordance with the plan of God." (L. G.).

in these homilies it is plainly indicated that God's justice applies to the life here and now.

Evil traits, harsh dealing with one's fellows, and frivolous conduct do not go unpunished. They will cry "Woe" (Prov. 23:29) who are insolent and haughty with all men, who do not refrain from taking things illegitimately, or who do not remove themselves from a woman ritually unclean.[52] If either a father or son, or one of two brothers, or one of two partners, or one of two scholars deal harshly with the other, he will surely be punished;[53] "there is great punishment" for a man who has two wives and he supplies to one "her food, her raiment, and her conjugal rights," but not to the other;[54] if a man engage in frivolous conduct even with one so worthy as a priest, or a prophet, or a prince, all share in the retribution.[55] The penalty for some actions is declared to be forfeiture of life, which, conveyed in the picturesque phrase "uprooted from the world," may sometimes be merely an emphatic manner of voicing disapproval. One who is arrogant (or immodest or brazen) is an abomination unto God,[56] and is "uprooted from the world;"[57] he who tarries early and late with the wine "uproots himself (from the world) with his (own) hand."[58] That the Rabbis looked upon this penalty as really deserved only when sins had cumulatively multiplied would appear from this midrash: "The scholars have declared: The sins of a man are not only bad enough in themselves but they lead to unseemly things and to things that are not proper, and (thus) he uproots himself with his (own) hand from this world and from the World to Come."[59]

Two stories in Seder Eliahu vividly illustrate the complete confidence of the Rabbis in God's justice in this world. We have related above the story of Miriam, the daughter of Tanḥum and her seven sons.[60] When the emperor asked the youngest son

[52] P. 80. [53] Pp. 67–8.

[54] P. 68. The phrase regarding women's rights is from Exod. 21:10.

[55] P. 65.

[56] P. 159 גסות רוח.

[57] P. 158.

[58] P. 79. [59] P. 13.

[60] Above, p. 47 and p. 53.

why, if God has power, He did not save the brothers, the boy replied, "Fool that you are! You are not worthy that miracles be performed through you. We had incurred the penalty of death. Would you not kill us, the Omnipresent has many (other) slayers—many bears, many leopards, many snakes, many scorpions, many lions, that would have struck us down."[61] Can any statement be plainer in its absolute affirmation of the infallibility of God's justice in this world? And the statement attributed to R. Ishmael is equally plain. R. Simon and R. Ishmael were seized, and were about to be slain. When R. Simon wept in despair over the inscrutability of God's justice which condemned them to the fate of those who transgress and those who desecrate the Sabbath, R. Ishmael replied, ". . . There were times when we sat as judges over cases and did not decide correctly; and (there were times) when false witnesses came and testified before us and they (the defendants) were found guilty by us (on this false testimony); and (there were times) when we entered the bath and took time to eat and drink, and orphans and widows came to plead for their sustenance and the sexton told them, 'They are busy just now.' See how great is the punishment for this!"[62] Question and answer both reveal that the two Rabbis regarded their tragic fate as a just punishment by God for their sins, R. Ishmael having only quieted the mind of his comrade by finding specific grounds for it. To us, the question of the historicity of the two stories we have cited is irrelevant, for whether historically true or not, they are incorporated in our text for ethical edification, and therefore express the ethical outlook of rabbinic theology. From that ethical outlook, all events that happen to man are not the haphazard accidents of chance, or the apportionments of an inscrutable fate, but all alike are meted out by a just God who pays to each and every one in this world according to his deserts.

This outlook, we have had so many occasions to notice, allows the Rabbis to attach an ethical meaning to all of life. Every event has its ethical coloring. Since years of good fortune

[61] P. 152. The term for God here is מקום.

[62] P. 153. והן נתחייבו מיתה seems to refer not to the witnesses but to the defendants—(L. G.).

indicate ethical worth and bad fortune the opposite, the Rabbis draw the conclusion that "when one good year has befallen anyone close to his old age, it is a good sign for him; when one bad year has befallen anyone close to his old age, it is a bad sign for him," and the example from history is Jacob.[63] "A good sign" is their way of stating that the life led, taken as a whole, was the good life. That whatever may happen is for the best is a corollary of such an ethical doctrine: If a man met a lion and was not eaten or other wild and dangerous animals and was not harmed, he ought to thank God, for he may have been designed for such an end but God took pity on him. Wounded in a fleshy part, he ought to thank God that he escaped wounds in arteries and bones.[64] Naturally, where every event has an ethical significance, any escape from danger can be viewed only as God's kindness in saving a man from what was justly in store for him. Finally, even after the worst has taken place, this outlook acts as solace to those who have suffered. The wife of one of the learned who died in his prime was inconsolable, going from one of her late husband's colleagues to the other, and, half-demented, asking how the death of her husband, who had studied Torah so diligently and fruitfully, could be justified. One of our authors, questioning her, at last discovered that her husband had infringed upon a law regulating sex-relations when the woman is ritually unclean; and thereupon he bids her take comfort in the reflection that a *miẓwah* always brings with it reward and a transgression punishment.[65]

We have purposely omitted here what is often very prominent in the discussions of the justice of God, the reward and punishment of men in the hereafter. The Rabbis taught, of course, that after death man is placed in judgment upon his deeds.[66] But, although we shall refer to this in a later section of this chapter, its full discussion will be reserved for the chapter on the World to Come, where it properly belongs. The notion that the Rabbis believed that the justice of God was to be infal-

[63] P. 30.

[64] P. 97.

[65] P. 76. The "reflection" is a quotation from Abot 4:2.

[66] "Additions," p. 43.

libly manifest only in the future, that they envisioned it as absolute only in eschatology, we have seen to be erroneous. Life after death and the World to Come are, as we shall see, a fulfillment and a continuance, in a way, of life on earth now. The justice of God is always manifest, in this life as in the life to come, except that the conditions of this life and the one to come are totally different. Full justice, the complete and final measure, can be gauged only when the whole of life, here and in the hereafter, will be limned. But the justice of God has no single point of gravity: it is as apparent now to him who has religious insight as it will be clear to all of humanity in the hereafter. Perhaps this element in rabbinic ideology, namely, that God's justice will be *seen* and *acknowledged* by *all* of humanity only in the World to Come, coupled with our own tacit assumption that chance rules much of our lives, is responsible for the wrong notion that with the Rabbis the point of gravity in God's justice was in the World to Come.

There are two additional aspects of the justice of God that need to be explained. One is merely an elaboration of the kind of distributive justice described above, and can almost literally be summed up in the phrase "measure for measure." "Thou art righteous and dost judge the sons of men according to their ways, and payest to every man according to his deeds—the measure that a man metes out is meted out to him."[67] The phrase itself —"the measure that a man metes out is meted out to him"— is not always employed wherever instances of this kind of distributive justice are given. Sometimes it is embodied in the homily: "Notice that the measure a man metes out is meted out to him: A man gives charity to his fellow in this world, intending thus that he should live and not die; so also the Holy One blessed be He wills that its giver should live and not die." And he who has wherewith to do charity and save lives but does not do so brings death upon himself, as was the case with Nabal.[68] At other times the idea of measure for measure, recognizable in the form of the reward or punishment meted out, is also contained in the supporting proof-text. The learned commiserated

[67] P. 98; also on p. 50.
[68] P. 170.

with a priest whose wealth had been destroyed by fire, until they found out that the priest had fed his cattle with *terumah* which, if not eaten by priests, should by law be burned.[69] Since he did not burn unused *terumah*, his property was burned; and although the phrase we have translated "measure for measure" does not occur in this connection, the Scriptural verse "He that diggeth a pit shall fall into it" (Koheleth 10:8), which is applied, conveys the same idea. There are times, also, when the idea is expressed by the style in which the homily is couched: "Just as the slaughterer pulls the flesh away from the neck, thus committing *hagramah* and making the meat unfit for food, so his wealth will be pulled away from him and given to others."[70] Finally, there are occasions when the idea of measure for measure is recognizable only in the poetic justice that characterizes the reward or the punishment.

The Rabbis like to employ the idea of measure for measure to supply ethical causes for afflictions mentioned in the Bible. The plagues mentioned in Leviticus are sent, the Rabbis say, as punishment for sins. The plagues on the body because of which one is obliged humbly to warn off those who would approach his unclean body are sent primarily for acting haughtily and insolently towards family or teachers or any man;[71] and the plague on clothes for being fond of taking things illegitimately (גזל).[72] The plague on houses comes as punishment for lying to a poor man who asked for a loan of wheat or barley or dates by declaring that these are not in the house; and the neighbors detect the lie when they raze the plagued house to the ground after taking the goods outside. "Blessed be the Omnipresent, blessed be He, who sanctifies His great name in the open forever!"[73]

[69] Pp. 66–7. *Terumah* is the tithe given to the priests and may be eaten by them and their families.

[70] P. 73. *Hagramah* is one of the prohibited ways of slaughtering an animal, and was apparently indulged in by some sectarians who wished to save the flesh at the side of the neck. See Friedmann's note No. 7.

[71] Pp. 76–7.

[72] P. 77.

[73] Ibid. See above in Chapter III, section on *Ḳiddush Hashem*, particularly pp. 70–71, where it is explained how the manifestation of God's justice constitutes sanctification of the Name.

And the plague of gonorrhea is sent upon men[74] and women[75] for failing to adhere to prescribed sex ritual. In all these cases the Rabbis appear to argue that the plague does not appear for naught, and on the basis of measure for measure, discover the sin for which it has been sent as punishment. The belief that everything that happens to a man in this world is in accordance with his deeds certainly testifies to the ethical sensitiveness of the Rabbis, an attitude that frequently determines their interpretation of Scripture. We have already pointed out that in this interpretation God's love is more poignantly expressed than in the Bible itself.[76] Now we notice that God's justice is interpreted into biblical texts. Apparently the Rabbis have a heightened awareness of God's love and justice as these are manifested toward the individual.

If this be so, the last aspect of distributive justice we shall consider, corporate justice, is at first all the more difficult to comprehend. Here the fine sense for the justice due the individual seems to be blunted. We have called corporate justice the conception that the reward or punishment for the deeds of an individual is visited by God not only upon him but upon others as well. Now, when we read that all humanity is saved from destruction by the merit of those who are to be found in the houses of prayer and study and that the righteous are like pillars supporting the whole world,[77] it may appeal to our feeling that all humanity is one. But our sense of justice is jarred when we are told, also, that others are punished because of the sins of the guilty. "Pray for the heads of families (בעלי בתים) in Israel because of the *Derek Ereẓ* they possess . . . for the heads of families in Israel are uprooted from the world and descend into the earth only because of the arrogant."[78] Just as the righteous save the world, so the wicked bring evil upon it. All who engage much in levity and blasphemy "bring wrath upon the world;

[74] P. 78.

[75] P. 79. All of the plagues are withdrawn for those who repent. See above pp. 135–136.

[76] Above, pp. 110–112.

[77] P. 182.

[78] P. 103.

in the end the crops diminish through them, and because of them many troubles and evils come upon the world, and severe decrees are renewed, and the youth of Israel are killed, and orphans and widows cry out and are not answered."[79] Moreover, if the one who engages much in levity and blasphemy lives within a family, or neighborhood, or courtyard, which find joy in him, in the end he causes that family, neighborhood, or members of the courtyard to be exiled.[80] Above we read of a whole family being severely punished because the father had not chided his child for frivolousness at prayer in the synagogue.[81] Another story is related of the death of a teacher and that of his wife and son and son's son as well as that of his two hundred pupils because of the wicked ways and a bad sexual practice indulged in by the latter.[82]

Yet we must not suppose, on the other hand, that the conception of corporate justice dominated the minds of the Rabbis. Enough has surely been said here regarding their extreme sensitiveness for the justice due the individual. And there is evidence that this sensitiveness struggled to express itself even while they held on to the conception of corporate justice. When Israel sinned with the golden calf, Moses, according to the Rabbis, pleaded with God, ". . .'For the sake of three thousand who served (the idol) with a whole heart shall six hundred thousand die—and those who are twenty years old and below, and those who are eighteen and fifteen and two and one, and how many proselytes and slaves that joined them? There is no end to the matter!' Thereupon the compassion of the Holy One blessed be He was moved and He was reconciled to them at that time."[83] No stronger plea could be made against the conception of corporate justice than is contained in these very words. If, for one reason or another, the Rabbis could not surrender the idea of corporate justice, they were by no means blind to the ethical difficulty it involves. Another homily clearly reflects a struggle

[79] P. 64.

[80] Ibid.

[81] Above, p. 161.

[82] Pp. 100–1.

[83] P. 17.

in the minds of the Rabbis between the conception of corporate justice and the justice due the individual: They ask how it is that the ten tribes were exiled during the reign of Hoshea, the son of Elah, and not before; and they explain that from Jereboam the son of Nebat until Hoshea the sin of idolatry "was bound up with an individual" (i. e., idolatry, though engaged in by the mass, was the king's responsibility, for the king prevented the people from going up to Jerusalem), "and it was difficult for the merciful Father to exile a community for the iniquity of an individual." When Hoshea became king, however, he abolished all the guards who had hitherto prevented the people from going to Jerusalem, and announced, "Every one who wishes to go up to Jerusalem may go up," but he did not say, "Everybody *should* go up to Jerusalem." "And he slipped the guilt (קולר) from his own shoulders and hung it on the shoulders of the many. From this (instance) they taught: Every one who performs a *miẓwah* but does not complete it forfeits his life and that of all who belong to him, and buries his wife and sons."[84] The contradiction between the statement that God will not punish the many for the iniquity "bound up with an individual" and the conclusion of the midrash is obvious; but it should be regarded as a conflict between two conceptions of distributive justice rather than as a contradiction, the Rabbis wishing to stress the justice due to the individual while holding on to the conception of corporate justice.

It is not hard to find an explanation for the Rabbis' belief in corporate justice, now that we are aware that the Rabbis

[84] P. 188. "He did not say, 'Everybody should . . .' " is not in the text, but is found in the Yalḳuṭ, par. 234, and renders the meaning clear. Friedmann, note No. 13, suspects that the last phrase of the midrash, "and buries his wife and sons" is an interpolation, but it is found in all the three parallels he brings, except that since these omit the word "two" before "sons," I have done likewise.

"I cannot see how the reading in the Yalḳuṭ is an improvement. By adding: 'He did not say' etc., the king's guilt is emphasized and exactly the opposite is expected"—(L. G.). It appears to me, however, that the Rabbis do intend partly to emphasize the king's guilt, as can be seen from the conclusion: "From this instance they taught: Everyone who performs a *miẓwah* but does not complete it . . ."

themselves occasionally depart from it. The belief in corporate justice is based on the belief in corporate responsibility. And corporate responsibility is something that we, too, can sympathize with, providing it involves benefits for humanity but rarely otherwise. The Rabbis, however, found no exceptions to corporate responsibility—particularly as it applied to Israel—be the outcome good or bad for those who themselves had neither performed the good nor done the evil. Nevertheless, even though the conception of corporate justice is applied both in reward and punishment, the Rabbis, no less than ourselves, had qualms about the inclusion of innocent people, wives and children in the fate of the guilty, and therefore voice an opposite opinion.[85]

Corporate responsibility, then, is the assumption behind corporate justice. But it is probably not the only reason for the wide prevalence of the latter conception. Once an idea gains acceptance, it grows and ramifies. Corporate justice branched out and became a complicated ethical concept which could be made to explain many phenomena in personal life and human history. Corporate justice could be extended in time as well as space: The deeds of the fathers reflected upon the children and affected them, and vice versa. That this explanation should be turned around, and that the ethical relation between fathers and children, in time, lead to a similar conception of that between individuals and Israel or humanity, in space, is also possible. In either case, the Rabbis were committed to a number of ethical concepts all based on the idea of corporate justice, and these naturally helped to determine its hold on their mind and the wide use to which the idea was put. One receives the impression, however, after all is said and done, that the Rabbis preferred to employ the conception of distributive justice as it applied to individuals rather than that of corporate justice.[86]

Corporate justice, as we have said, causes the parents' deeds to affect the children's welfare and the children's deeds to affect

[85] An instance of corporate responsibility more harsh to us than out-and-out corporate justice is vicarious atonement, for there only the innocent suffer. See above, p. 134.

[86] The question is taken up again from another angle below, on pp. 203–207.

the parents' welfare. He that refrains from taking things illegitimately and from illicit sexual intercourse stores merit for himself and for the generations after him "until the end of all generations."[87] Men may have hope because of their deeds and "because of their fathers' deeds."[88] Not only are rewards visited upon the children because of their fathers' deeds but punishments also. Certain people—among them gamblers, informers, apostates, and those that profane the name of God—do not leave inheritance to their children; and if they do leave it to their children, then not to their children's children. This midrash closes with the significant text, "That which is crooked cannot be made straight" (Koh. 1:15).[89] The wife of a man decides by her actions the fortunes and abilities of her children. If she is modest, "in the innermost parts of thy house" (Ps. 128:3), she will have children among whom some will know Bible or Mishnah, some will be men of affairs, and some will be learned and wise. On the other hand, if she is a gadabout, or regards herself higher than her husband or curses his forbears to his face, she herself causes her children to be cripples; if she does not observe the law regarding the first of the dough, and makes vows but does not keep them, then she will find no satisfaction in the world, and because of her bad deeds one of her sons will limp, one will be blind and one will be witless and wicked.[90] The iniquity of the fathers is visited "upon the children unto the third and fourth generation" (Exod. 20:5). The Rabbis take this text to account for four generations of poor men one after another, the great-grandfather having been wealthy and become poor (דל) because of his deeds.[91] And because a man commits many transgressions death is decreed concerning him and his children unto the fourth generation.[92] When the righteous sin, their children die young,[93] and R. Joḥanan declared that he

[87] P. 73.
[88] P. 183.
[89] P. 77.
[90] P. 92. The law regarding the first of the dough is in Numbers 15:20-1.
[91] P. 182 and p. 181.
[92] Pp. 21, 22.
[93] P. 191.

expected to come up for judgment both for his sons and for the death of his children.[94] Another midrash has it that when children die young it is because of the sins of the parents, but the righteous knowing this take care lest they come to sin, whilst the wicked, also knowing this, are hard-hearted, slaying their children through their sins.[95]

The virtue of the children affects the fate of the father. R. Joḥanan, the son of Zakkai, tells, according to Seder Eliahu, of having met a man gathering wood, who proved to be a dead man, and who, together with his companion had been sentenced to burning in Gehenna. He begged the Rabbi to train his son and then to take the boy to the synagogue. "When he says 'Blessed be God who is to be blessed,' they will bring me up from the judgment of Gehenna."[96] The learned son of an *'am haareẓ* (ignorant man) will save his father, who caused him to be taught Torah, from the judgment of Gehenna.[97] The same homily contains, at the end, an obscure reference to Jacob's rescuing Abraham, a reference that is made clear in parallel passages which say that although Jacob was yet to be born, nevertheless his virtue (or merit) caused Abraham to be saved from the fiery furnace.[98] Corporate justice allows the merit of the children to react on the fathers.

We have endeavored in this section to demonstrate that the Rabbis believed that the distributive justice of God operates infallibly in this world and that it is universal in its scope, reward and punishment issuing to Gentiles as well as Israelites; to account for the infrequency with which the Rabbis draw here on the personalness of God; to describe the conception of measure for measure; and in some degree to indicate how the idea of corporate justice is employed, particularly the manner in which it is used to show that the fathers' good deeds or sins affect the children's welfare and vice versa. All the ideas con-

[94] P. 43 of "Additions."

[95] P. 111.

[96] "Additions," p. 23. See above, p. 150.

[97] P. 194.

[98] Ibid. The parallels quoted by Friedmann, note No. 9, are b. San. 19b; Gen. R. Chapter 63; and Lev. R. Chapter 36.

nected with the rabbinic belief in God's distributive justice, individual and corporate, are applied to Torah, Israel, the Nations of the World, and the World to Come, as we shall see when we shall consider these topics.

III

Justice in History

By means of the ideas discussed in the preceding section, the Rabbis explain the events of history as recorded in the Bible, the great changes that took place since the Bible, and the history of their own day. Their belief in God's distributive justice to the individual, in the divine law of measure for measure and in God's corporate justice enabled them to find an ethical cause for every historical event that came under their purview. Human history revealed to them that the justice of God operated infallibly in this world.

In the rabbinic perspective of history the events related in the Bible loom so large as almost to block out subsequent history except for the few decisive changes in Israel's fortunes. When, therefore, the Rabbis undertake to demonstrate that God's justice can be unfailingly discerned in history, the events chosen are largely from the Bible. Where the biblical story illustrates the justice of God, the story is elaborated and given more ethical coloring; and where the biblical event seems to have no ethical background, the Rabbis supply it. The Rabbis, one may say, abhor an ethical vacuum for that would negate entirely their belief in the justice of history.

The justice of God extends over Gentiles as over Israelites. Nations and individuals must conform to basic moral laws; only when they do not conform are they destroyed. "Because of eight things is the world destroyed: Injustice in the courts, idolatry, incest, murder, the profanation of God's name, because of foul things a person utters, arrogance, and the evil tongue (scandal-monging), and some say also because of covetousness." Examples from history, of nations and individuals who had done these things and were therefore destroyed are the First

Ten Generations, the men of the Generation of the Division, the people of Sodom, Pharaoh, Sennacherib and Nebuchadnezzer. On the other hand, "Civilization is established (העולם מתישב) because of four things: Charity, justice, truth and peace." The last statement, as well as the first, in the homily applies to all, Gentiles and Israel alike.[99]

The Rabbis account for the great leaders of Israel by ascribing ethical deeds to their forbears. Amram married "for the sake of Heaven," hence there went out from him Moses, Aaron, and Miriam.[100] Boaz likewise married "for the sake of Heaven," hence he was the forbear of David and Solomon "who caused Torah and *mizwot* to increase in Israel."[101] The reward for Elkanah's good deeds was Samuel, his son; the punishment for Hezekiah's deed was Manasseh, his son.[102] Deborah became prophetess and leader because of her own deeds. Because she and, following her advice, Barak her husband made thick wicks for the Temple at Shiloh, she deserved from God "who pays to every man according to his ways" that the Holy Spirit rest upon her.[103] Successful achievements of wicked leaders in Israel are laid to single specific good deeds performed by these men: The ten tribes were given to Jereboam, the son of Nebat, because he gave Solomon a proper retort;[104] and Jereboam, the son of Joash, was given such wide borders, "from the entrance of Hamath unto the sea of the Arabah" (II Kings 14:25), as were not given even to Joshua and David. For, although Jereboam, the son of Joash, was an idol-worshipper, he "honored the prophets;" he refused to listen to Amaziah's slander against Amos, and rebuked him, saying, "God forbid! That prophet did not utter such a prophecy, and if he did thus prophesy it

[99] P. 74. See Friedmann's note No. 15. "ישוב העולם is the nearest equivalent to our term 'civilization.' "—(L. G.).

[100] P. 177.

[101] P. 178.

[102] P. 48.

[103] Pp. 48 and 50. "Wicks" the Rabbis derive from the word לפידות (p. 18). They could not conceive of Barak and Deborah as co-leaders unless they were man and wife; and they seem to notice a resemblance between ברק and לפידות. On Barak, see Ginzberg, Legends, VI, pp. 195–196.

[104] P. 125.

was not his own prophecy but it was from Heaven."[105] From the fact that the Bible records no assenting reply on the part of Jereboam to Amaziah's message, the Rabbis apparently infer that the king disagreed with Amaziah and rebuked him.

The Bible narrates that evil also befell the Patriarchs and Israel. The Rabbis ascribe the evil to definite sins. Because Jacob listened to Joseph's tales he was punished through Joseph for twenty-two years.[106] Moses and Aaron were punished because of the matter of the waters of Meribah,[107] but here there is good biblical warrant. Basing themselves on the inference from "the people mourned greatly" (Num. 14:39) that the people of Israel were punished by thirty days of *niddui* (a kind of excommunication) because they were swayed by the spies, the Rabbis, declaring that he who is excommunicated for thirty days below "is never released from Above," account for the divine decree that the generation die in the wilderness.[108] The slaying of the people of Nob and later that of Saul and his son Jonathan were in punishment for their having refused bread to David.[109] Because Jehoshaphat allied himself in marriage with Ahab in order, say the Rabbis, to enhance his prestige, Ahab's daughter, Athaliah, slew the members of Jehoshaphat's family.[110] These are a few examples of rabbinic interpretations of biblical events, taken at random, which illustrate how the Rabbis account in terms of reward and punishment for the course of Jewish history.

In the same terms the Rabbis explain the history of all mankind. They account for the statement "For thee have I seen righteous before Me in this generation" (Gen. 7:1) by saying that it was Noah's reward for rebuking the generation of the flood all those one hundred and twenty years before what

[105] P. 184. "God forbid" is a translation of חס ושלום. A briefer midrash on the same theme, with exactly the same wording of Jereboam's rebuke, is on p. 88. The king does not reply to Amaziah in the biblical account—Amos 7:10–11.

[106] P. 65. [107] Ibid.

[108] Pp. 145–6. The period for mourning is thirty days. *Niddui* could be imposed by a court.

[109] P. 60. "I am sure that יהונתן בן שאול must be read (for אחימלך בן אחיטוב)" —(L. G.). Comp. b. Sanhed. 104a.

[110] P. 177.

he had predicted came to pass.[111] Esau shed two tears before his father Isaac, therefore "they gave him Mt. Seir where the beneficent rains never fail."[112] The children of Seir who received the children of Esau cheerfully likewise were rewarded—by being mentioned in the Bible (in Gen. 36:20); he receives reward for Torah that, knowing neither Bible nor Mishnah, reads but this verse consisting only of names.[113] The serpent who ruined the entire world, Adam and Eve who transgressed the divine command, Cain who killed Abel, Ham who did not honor his father, all were punished, (as the Bible tells us).[114] The same midrash asserts that Lamech received reward for mourning over his father's father and that Shem was rewarded for honoring his father;[115] but what the reward was is not mentioned in either case. Frequently the utterances of the wicked, as given in the Bible, furnish the Rabbis with the causes of their later downfall. These wicked men were destroyed, "uprooted from the world," because they were arrogant: Pharaoh, who said, "Who is the Lord . . .?" (Exod. 5:2); Sennacherib, who said, "Who . . . that the Lord should deliver Jerusalem out of my hand?" (II Kings 18:35); Nebuchadnezzer, who said, ". . . I will ascend into heaven" (Is. 14:13).[116] The same arrogance and brazenness

[111] P. 174. See Friedmann's note No. 24.

[112] Ibid; pp. 65, 125.

[113] Pp. 174–5. In the same pages it is mentioned that Shem, Ishmael, Isaac, Jacob, the twelve tribes (the sons of Jacob), and again Abraham, Isaac and Jacob together, received reward for their good deeds, but the reward is not mentioned, for the text is corrupt (Friedmann, note No. 27). On p. 65, the reward of Ishmael for the modicum of respect he showed Abraham is that God allowed no nation or kingdom to rule over his descendants; on p. 114, Abraham is said to be the reward of Shem's prophesying for four hundred years to an unreceptive world. See below, p. 191.

[114] P. 174.

[115] Ibid. Lamech's mourning consists of the Song of Lamech, Gen. 4:23–4. "Read אבי אביו (for אחי אביו). Cain is meant who was mourned by his grandson (i. e., descendant), Lamech, (Comp. Legends I, pp. 116–117); and Lamech's reward was that his daughter Naamah became the mother of mankind by her marriage to Noah; comp. Legends V, p. 147, note 45."—(L. G.). Friedmann, note No. 22, tries to account for אחי אביו.

[116] P. 158. Other causes for Pharaoh's downfall, and for the plagues, are given on p. 40, and discussed in the chapter on The Nations of the World.

(נסות רוח) the Rabbis find in the men of the Tower of Babel, who also wanted to build to heaven.[117]

When the Bible itself relates of the justice of God, the Rabbis often enlarge upon the text, adding numerous and vivid details. The First Ten Generations (from Adam), the Rabbis say, feared neither the government nor retribution nor judgment by God. They would eat and drink and sate themselves and say, "Depart from us . . ." (Job. 21:14). "They descended to violence and robbery, as it says 'And the earth was filled with violence' (Gen. 6:11); they descended to incest, as it says, 'For all flesh had corrupted their way . . .' (Gen. 6:12); they descended to murder, as it says, 'And God saw the earth, and behold, it was corrupt' (*ibid*)."[118] The men of the period of the Deluge were brazen: they would take off their clothes and walk naked in the market-place; therefore, God made them float like skin-bags upon the waters of the Deluge.[119] The men of Sodom were arrogant and brazen, and were therefore "uprooted from the world:" " 'The men of Sodom were wicked and sinners against the Lord exceedingly' (Gen. 13:13)—'wicked' refers to robbery, 'sinners' to incest, 'against the Lord' to profanation of the Name, 'exceedingly' to deliberate sinning. When Lot spoke to them courteously, they said 'Stand back' (Gen. 19:9), and when he spoke discourteously, they said, 'This one fellow came in to sojourn' etc. (*ibid*)."[120] By supplying details where the Bible makes only a general accusation and by introducing more dramatic elements, as in the reference to Lot, the Rabbis add interest to the stories, but what is more, they render the punishment visited upon the men of the Deluge and the men of Sodom more clearly to be recognized as just.

The principle of measure for measure is invoked by the Rabbis to explain why the ten plagues were sent upon Egypt.

[117] P. 158.

[118] P. 190.

[119] P. 190 and p. 158. As Friedmann, p. 158 note No. 9, says, נסות רוח may also mean brazenness, immodesty. "Comp. Ekah R. IV, 17, ed. Buber, 152, where נודות, the Hebrew equivalent for זיקים (talmudic) is used in the very same way—" (L. G.).

[120] P. 158.

Whereas in the biblical account, it is God that hardens Pharaoh's heart, here every plague is found to have had its own justification. The water of the Egyptians was turned to blood because the Egyptians had withheld water from Israel in order to prevent the Israelites, who abided by the law requiring ablutions for sex ritual, from cohabitation; the plague of frogs was brought because the Egyptians used to compel the Israelites to bring them frogs and other insects for the purpose of cruel sport; similarly, for every single plague the Rabbis supply a reason characterized by poetic justice.[121] Another instance where the principle of measure for measure has been applied in history is in connection with Ahitophel the Gilonite. This midrash, incidentally, also explains why Uzzah, whose intentions from the biblical account seem to have been good, should have perished. Ahitophel the Gilonite was learned "and there was Torah in him." When David wished to bring up the Ark, the people, having forgotten the law that only the sons of Amram are to carry it (Num. 7:9) and recalling that it had come from the Phillistines in a wagon, took the Ark and placed it in a wagon. "But the Ark hung between heaven and earth, neither going up nor going down." Uzzah standing near stretched forth his hand and took hold of the Ark, whereupon the wicked among Israel remarked that were it not for Uzzah's holding up the Ark it would have fallen down. Uzzah died and the Ark was seen to hang unsupported. Now Ahitophel knew the law but held it back in his throat, "therefore did he die by strangling, one of the four deaths handed over to the *bet-din* (court)."[122]

The principle of corporate justice, particularly that form of it wherein the fathers' deeds are made to affect the welfare of the children, accounts for many major incidents in history. The original sin of Adam which consisted of eating of the fruit of the tree of knowledge is the cause for the death that overtakes every living being. Calling the tree of knowledge "the tree of death," one homily states that because Adam ate of its fruit, God "decreed death upon him and upon his generations

[121] Pp. 40–3. On measure for measure as applied to Egypt, comp. Ginzberg, Legends V, p. 427, note 172.

[122] P. 157. See Friedmann note No. 4.

coming after him until the end of all generations."[123] This is by no means, however, the only view of the matter. If we accept Friedmann's interpretation of another homily, Adam's sin is responsible, not for death in the world but for the suffering that precedes death, for were it not for Adam's sin man would depart this life after a life-time of joy.[124] Still another midrash refuses to regard death as a calamity, and without assigning it to Adam's sin, declares that death is a necessary moral purgative for the world—"Were it not for the Angel of Death what would we not have done against our Father in heaven!"[125] It is not safe to conclude, therefore, that the prevailing idea, basing itself on biblical grounds, regarded death as the penalty visited on all mankind for Adam's sin. The second homily cited seems to stress God's love for mankind, and the third His corrective justice. Different interpretations of the same fact, we have noticed before, are due to stressing one or another of the points of reference.[126]

Abraham came into the world because of the merit of Shem who prophesied four hundred years to a world that would not hearken to him.[127] Abraham, though he broke all the idols of the world, sinned in one respect. He asked "O Lord God, whereby shall I know that I shall inherit it (the land)?" (Gen. 15:8). "In punishment for that wonderment his children went down into Egypt."[128] Thus is the long period of slavery accounted for. But Abraham's deeds also stood his descendants in very good stead: During the forty years in the wilderness, God gave Israel a well which always bubbled up where Israel camped, and He surrounded them with seven clouds of glory, and He gave them manna (which tasted like whatever the eater desired), and He gave them quail twice, and He accompanied and led Israel all

[123] P. 24. In contrast to the "tree of life" which the Rabbis identify with Torah.

[124] P. 175. Friedmann note No. 3.

[125] P. 81. See above, p. 92.

[126] Cf. above, pp. 33, 125. A very suggestive discussion of the different views taken of Adam's sin and its effects is in Ginzberg's Legends, V, 129–130.

[127] P. 114.

[128] Pp. 174, 65.

those forty years like a father his son—every kindness of God corresponding to an act of Abraham's when he entertained the angels.[129] The merit of Abraham and Isaac, we have seen above, is recalled by God when anybody, Israelite or Gentile, recites the verse "*Ẓafonah* before the Lord" (Lev. 1:11), and that merit treasured with God, descends upon the one who invokes it.[130]

Lines of High Priests and kings in Israel owe their rise or fall to the deeds of their ancestors. Because Phineas had not acted well, the High Priesthood was given to the sons of Ithamar; because the sons of Eli sinned, it was returned to the sons of Eleazar, father of Phineas.[131] Jehu and four generations after him sat on the throne of the Northern Kingdom, the longest line in its history. The Bible relates that Jehu destroyed the prophets of Baal and was careful to avoid killing the prophets of God (II Kings 10:18ff); the Rabbis say that "he was a man who feared Heaven and did not go after the golden calves that Jereboam the son of Nebat made, but after he reached unto power and attained to kingship he corrupted his ways." But because he was originally a good man, he was rewarded "unto the fourth generation," and his line became extinct only after this dictum, expressive of corporate justice, was fulfilled.[132] Zechariah, the fifth of the line, was a wicked man, and, no longer protected by the merit of his ancestor, was killed after a very short reign.[133]

The same principle was applied to the Nations of the World. The descendants of Ishmael, the Arabs and their neighbors, roamed free; why? "Because of the modicum of respect Ishmael showed his father, the Holy One blessed be He allowed no nation or sovereign power to rule over his children."[134] The Greek Empire was brought about in reward for Japheth who covered his father's nakedness; and the Median Empire (Persia) in

[129] Pp. 59–60. When the fountain delayed several hours, the small boys and the learned would say עלי באר בזכות אברהם יצחק ויעקב . . . בזכות משה אהרן ומרים. The conception of the זכות of the righteous is discussed in the chapter on the righteous and the wicked.

[130] See above, pp. 133–4.

[131] P. 57.

[132] P. 184.

[133] P. 88; II Kings 15:8ff.

[134] P. 65.

reward for Cyrus who wept and grieved when the nations destroyed the Temple.[135] Wicked men and nations who used their power to harm Israel owed their existence and their power to the good deeds of their forbears. Amalek issued from Eliphaz the Temanite in reward for the latter's honoring his father.[136] Sennacharib came into the world in reward for Ashur, who was a righteous man and an adviser to Abraham, our father;[137] Nebuchadnezzer, in reward for Merodach who honored our Father in heaven;[138] and Haman, in reward for Agag who wept and grieved in prison, fearing his seed would be utterly destroyed.[139]

The Romans who caused such disaster to Israel were identified by the Rabbis as the progeny of Esau. The Roman Empire, they declared, was brought about in reward for Esau who wept and grieved because Isaac blessed Jacob.[140] Another midrash states that in reward for going off and not harming Jacob, Esau was given a hundred lands (Rome).[141] Persecuted and buffeted about by the later Roman Empire, Israel, repentant and having forgotten its early sins, wondered at the justice of God until it was recalled to them that Rome's power was the reward of Esau's having wept two tears before his father.[142]

It has become clear in this section that the Rabbis believed that God's justice is manifest throughout history. It is manifest here and now and in the fortunes of the Nations of the World as well as those of Israel. What we ought particularly to keep in mind is that the Rabbis take pains to explain the course of history so that it should be seen to conform to the infallible justice of God. When they supplement biblical narratives it is most often in order to make clear the operation of God's distributive justice, the workings of the law of measure for measure, and the application of God's corporate justice to history.

[135] P. 114.
[136] P. 125.
[137] Pp. 114, 115.
[138] Pp. 115, 125.
[139] P. 115.
[140] P. 114. On the rabbinic identification of Esau and Edom with Rome, see Ginzberg, Legends, V, p. 272, note 19.
[141] P. 65. Friedmann, note No. 49.
[142] P. 155.

IV

Chastisement (Corrective Justice)

God brings afflictions upon man not only to punish but to correct him. Afflictions which a man should recognize to be correction by God are called יסורין, chastisements. "The Holy One blessed be He says to man . . . 'See what you have done; therefore have chastisements come upon you.' For chastisements come upon a man only for his own good, to save him from the consequences of his own acts."[143]

The idea that a man should regard his afflictions as chastisements of God is a necessary consequence of the belief in the infallibility of God's justice. Nothing that befalls individuals and nations is an arbitrary act of God or a haphazard incident of chance. One may be certain that there are some things in the past that he has not done well or else omitted to do. "A man has done what he has done; chastisements have come upon him for his good and to save him from the consequences of all that he has done."[144] The moral experience of the vast majority of mankind, the consciousness of possibilities for good not exploited, lent to this belief more than mere plausibility. Evil fortune, illness, even death of near ones, are chastisements of God sent in order to cause the sinner to change his ways. Chastisements bring the convert who has reverted to his old practices back into the fold.[145] When they are sent upon Israel it is only for their own good and because God loves them. They have sinned and God would thus restore them to moral health.[146]

In consonance with the belief that misfortunes were chastisements of God is the idea that their effect was ennobling, purifying man of sin. An old man who met one of our authors argued that the fact so many heads of families in Israel were childless proved that they did not marry for the sake of having

[143] P. 67. להוציא מידו מה שעשה. On p. 96 (twice) and on p. 146 (twice) the expression is ולהציל מידו מה שעשה; I have, accordingly, translated the phrase similarly here.

[144] P. 96 (twice).

[145] P. 146.

[146] P. 191.

children. Our author argued, however, from the examples of Abraham, Rebecca, Rachel and Hannah, that God loves these householders in Israel, and withholds children from them only "to purify them (by suffering) (ומצרפן), (and) in order that they should pray much before Him."[147]

A tragedy, repeatedly witnessed in ancient civilizations, where bad sanitary conditions prevailed and the knowledge of medicine was crude, was the death of little children. Since this fact could not be explained on the ground that these children deserved to die, the moral onus was put upon the parents. Above we have cited several homilies which state that the little children die because of the sins of the fathers; and R. Joḥanan declared on his death-bed that he would be placed in judgment over the loss of his children.[148] But another midrash lays such a loss, among the righteous, to the "chastisings of love:" "And which are the chastisings of love (ייסורין של אהבה)? These (occur) when the children of the learned die young and they (thus) atone (ומכפרין להן) their sins (i. e., of the learned), and (the learned) come in purity to the *'Olam Habba*. Even though Scripture says (i. e., applies this verse to them), 'Also in thy skirts is found the blood of the souls of the innocent poor' etc. (Jer. 2:34), Scripture returns and placates them (ורצה ביניהם), 'Even as a father the son in whom he delighteth' (the second half of the verse 'For whom the Lord loveth He correcteth even . . .') (Prov. 3:12)."[149] The verses used show the quandary the Rabbis were in: The fact of the death of young children among the righteous could not be gainsaid, and it had to be accounted for on the grounds of God's justice; if the fault be the parents', then the learned are guilty of killing innocents (Jer. 2:34), and that would be contrary to what one should expect from those devoted to Torah; the difficulty is resolved by including the deaths among the chastisements of love (Prov. 3:12). Here again misfortune has a purging, purifying

[147] P. 99. "For the use of צרף, comp. the oft-quoted saying: . . . לא נתנו . . . אלא לצרף (Comp. for instance Tanḥuma 81)—the ennobling effect of the fulfillment of God's will—" (L. G.).

[148] Above, pp. 183–4.

[149] P. 191.

effect: the chastisements of love wipe off the sins of the righteous.[150]

Chastisements, then, are sent by God in order to correct and to purify. If men take the chastisements to heart, they forestall further and greater evil. "Men are punished because of (infringements of) *Derek Ereẓ* in order that they may be saved from the day that comes to meet them."[151] After describing how dear Israel is to God as compared with other nations, and how the destruction of King Josiah is accounted in His eyes as great a loss as the destruction of the whole empire of wicked Rome, the midrash states: "The Holy One blessed be He hastens to bring chastisement upon Israel in order to forestall retribution."[152] Thus, no doubt, Israel comforted themselves in affliction by reflecting that they merely suffered chastisement which forestalled the even greater evils their sins deserved.

The ethically significant factor in chastisement is the attitude with which one bears it. "He should not say, 'I am righteous, I am upright—should chastisement come upon me? I have given food to the hungry and drink to the thirsty—should chastisement come upon me?' But one ought not to prattle things where one cannot speak . . . Let him gaze within himself; and he will realize that the Holy One blessed be He even to Himself has not shown favor." For Israel is God's first born (Exod. 4:22), yet He chastized them, and does any one wish to harm his son? "When He chastizes them, he chastizes them justly (לאמיתו)."[153] Hence, two reflections are urged upon the afflicted man: One, that no one can really tell what evil he has done or what good he has left undone; second, that God loves him and would never harm him for naught. " 'My son, despise not the chastening of the Lord' etc. (Prov. 3:11), and it says,

[150] R. Joḥanan would insist that the death of his children was purely an act of God's justice which He visited upon the father; the homily we have considered here would seem to argue it was a manifestation of God's love in wiping off the sins of the learned. We should consider it a cruel love indeed were it not that the whole dialectic is an explanation *after* the fact.

[151] P. 176.

[152] P. 26—להעביר את הפורענות.

[153] P. 96. Ginzberg reads לאהבתן—see p. 167, note 25.

'For whom the Lord loveth He correcteth, even as a father the son in whom he delighteth' (Prov. 3:12)."[154]

The man who knows Torah is bound to accept the judgment of God as righteous; "his heart is at rest," for his knowledge enables him to realize that, whether he is aware of them or not, there are specific causes for his misfortunes. It is only the man who is unversed in the words of the Torah "whose heart is bitter." But he who knows the Torah, "if he be hungry, should say, 'Thus and thus is it written in the Torah as regards hunger;' if he be thirsty, he should say, 'Thus and thus is it written in the Torah as regards thirst;' if he remain naked, he should say, 'Thus and thus is it written in the Torah as regards nakedness'—'Therefore shalt thou serve thine enemy whom the Lord shall send against thee, in hunger, and in thirst, and in nakedness, and in want of all things' (Deut. 28:48, an example in the Torah of the justification for God's chastisement). Alive and existing on the face of the earth (one should say), 'Blessed be the Omnipresent, blessed be He, who has given life unto me in this world.' " And thus indeed did David find appeasement in the words of the Torah when chastisements came upon him; were it not for the Torah, he would have uprooted himself from the world: "Unless Thy Torah had been my delight I should then have perished in mine affliction" (Ps. 119:92).[155]

The virtuous attitude is therefore one of complete trust in God and in His justice, no matter what befall. "Happy is he who feareth Heaven in secret and leans upon Him who hath protection to offer, for thus we find to be the case with David, who, even though chastisements came upon him, leaned upon Him who hath protection to offer."[156] It is this virtue which one of our authors extols when he finds it in his day among the learned in Israel.[157] On the other hand, objection to chastisement is worse than useless; the only result is that he who objects (lit. "kicks") to the chastisements visited upon him has them doubled.[158]

[154] P. 191.

[155] P. 137. See above, Chapter I, p. 2. There is a similar homily, in lengthened form, but in a different context, on p. 3 of "Additions."

[156] P. 90.

[157] P. 110. [158] P. 12.

Merely to accept chastisements as just is not yet the height of virtue. Since they are brought for our good, to correct and purify, one ought to acknowledge them gratefully, indeed, to thank God for them (הודאת הייסורין); "and one should rise at midnight and should bless and praise and exalt and magnify and sanctify the name of Him who spake and the world came into being."[159] In fact, the prophet's vision that God will be exalted is realized, the Rabbis say, when thanks are given for chastisement: "And ye shall say 'The Lord is great' (Mal. 1:5)—that refers to the thanksgiving for chastisement."[160] Naturally, those who receive chastisement in this wise, those who rejoice in them, will be rewarded[161] and will be given life in this world and the life that is without end in the World to Come.[162]

Nevertheless, with all that has been said, chastisements are decidedly unpleasant. The Rabbis literally made a virtue out of necessity. There is a way by which chastisements can be avoided altogether. "If you see that chastisements are about to come upon you, run to the words of the Torah, and immediately the chastisements will flee from you. As it says, 'Come, my people, enter thou into thy chambers' (Is. 26:20)."[163] Thus, in the very means taken to avoid chastisement there is reliance on the justice of God. In passing, our attention may well be directed to the organic unity of the concepts, Torah being interlaced in several places with the concept of chastisement.

There is no difference in kind between afflictions that are chastisements and those that are explained to be acts of God's distributive and corporate justice. Both are punishments by God. The difference consists in the purpose, if one may define as such an attitude of mind that is surely one of sincere belief, behind the explanation. The purpose informing the exposition of God's distributive justice is to inculcate confidence and faith in the unfailing supervision and governance of God to the end that man be meticulously careful in every ethical and religious

[159] P. 96.
[160] P. 68—אילו הודיות הייסורין.
[161] P. 78.
[162] P. 17.
[163] P. 32.

obligation.[164] The purpose behind the concept of chastisement is to induce man to accept evil fortune with equanimity, to feel on such occasions that all is not lost, and to turn them into moments of keener religious apprehension and ethical stimulation.

V

The Problem of Evil

That this section is so much smaller than we should expect from one devoted to this profound theological problem is due to the fact that we have already discussed important aspects of this problem. The evil that befalls man is a just dispensation by God, we have learned. On the basis of distributive justice, individual and corporate, and that of corrective justice, the Rabbis find that man's misfortunes are just recompense for his sins. The presence of wicked men in the world is accounted for by a good deed of their forbears, which, on the grounds of corporate justice, entitles these wicked men to their existence. Nevertheless, a few details of the problem of evil still agitated the Rabbis' minds, and these we shall now consider.

If God is both good and the Creator of everything, how is it that He created evil, wrong-doing and falsehood? This is one of the stock puzzles of scholastic philosophy. Philosophy approaches the problem in devious ways in order to answer the speculative question raised with regard to God's omnipotence. The Rabbis, aware of the difficulty, do not see it eye to eye with the philosophers. The Rabbis are concerned with the question not because it raises doubts with regard to God's omnipotence but because it raises doubts regarding God's goodness. Their answer is calculated to allay the latter not the former.

"The Holy One blessed be He," says Seder Eliahu, "created everything in His world except the quality of falsehood (שקר), which He did not create; and the quality of iniquity (or wrong-doing עול), which He did not make. For it says, 'The Rock, His

[164] This will be discussed in detail in the chapter on motives, when we consider the conception of fear of God.

work is perfect; for all His ways are justice; a God of faithfulness and without iniquity (עול), just and right is He' (Deut. 32:4)."[165] It is this assurance that prompts the objection to the statement in Lam. 3:38: "It says, 'Out of the mouth of the Most High proceedeth not evil and good?' "[166] How, then, do the Rabbis account for the existence of falsehood, evil and wrong-doing? God did create the possibility of wrong-doing in man, the Evil *Yeẓer*—the impulses for evil in man—and He immediately regretted that it was created.[167] The definite acts of wrong-doing and falsehood, are, therefore, the works of man, who is incited by his evil impulses.[168] Now man is not foreordained to domination by the Evil *Yeẓer*: It is only like a high iron wall, in the figure of the parable, which the righteous do overcome.[169] Thus is the evil in the acts of men explained. How is the evil that God sends forth as punishment to be accounted for, if God is the source of only that which is good? "No evil measure (מידה) issues from Him but only good measures issue from Him; and (only) because of the corrupt deeds of men does an evil measure (decree מידה) issue upon them."[170] The objection to the statement in Lamentations is now answered: "Say thus: Good does not issue to him that does evil, and evil does not issue to him that does good, but good for good and evil for evil."[171] And God, leaving man thus to decide his fate, and wanting good for man, not evil,[172] hopes that he will do the good and not the evil;[173] when man does good He rewards it joyfully, and when He must punish man for evil done, it is "with sighing" (reluctantly).[174]

[165] P. 175. Other proof-texts are Zeph. 3:5 and Job 34:10–11.

[166] P. 176.

[167] P. 62.

[168] Ibid.

[169] P. 193.

[170] P. 40. This statement, incidentally, is in connection with the plagues brought on Egypt, another proof, if we need it, of the universality and complete fairness of God's justice.

[171] P. 176.

[172] P. 98.

[173] P. 3.

[174] Pp. 98–9.

The argument, then, runs as follows: God is the source only of good; the evil in man is the result of the evil impulses, which God did create; these impulses can be overcome by man, as among the righteous, or they can incite to evil deeds; specific evil deeds are thus the work of man, who has free-will; evil fortune to man, in a sense, is not God's doing—it is certainly not His intention—but is, as it were, forced from Him as the result of man's evil deeds.

Religion and philosophy ask the same question, but how widely the answers differ. It may be truthfully stated that philosophy in the past regarded it as its business to attempt to solve the logical contradictions arising from the conclusions of religious experience; its method was rational and speculative. But when a question comes to the fore in religious thought, it is only apparently speculative. The answer is necessarily a confirmation of religious and moral experience since it must contain only the concepts evolved by that experience. Conclusions of rabbinic religious experience we have discussed throughout this chapter are: Man engages in evil and wrong-doing; some men, the righteous, are relatively free from wrong-doing; hence, it is the Evil *Yeẓer*—the evil impulses—that incites to wrong-doing, and it is possible for man to dominate it. Here, then, is a fact of their experience. Man is free (-willed), not condemned to wrong-doing. A stubborn fact everywhere observed is that men suffer; the religious conclusion was that they suffer in punishment for their wrong-doings, and this conclusion became so much a part of their mental outlook as to become an important element in their religious experience. On the other hand, it is an equally patent fact that man gets along, obtains his sustenance, gets joy out of the world; hence that God loves man was a strong element in their religious experience. How can these two things—that God loves man and sends evil upon him, in his heart and in external fortune—be reconciled? Why, in the very terms their experience propounded the question: Definite acts of wrong-doing are the product of men themselves as the result of the Evil *Yeẓer* God implanted; and God, who is the source of good, is forced to punish men for their sins.

Finally, we must notice one more thing. The entire argument

neither intends to nor does it allay man's intellectual doubts; it appeals to man's craving for assurance in his spiritual strivings. The problem of evil is solved by emphasizing God's goodness. Man can absolutely rely on God's enduring love and goodness, just as he must with all his strength endeavor to live blamelessly. He is punished for doing wrong, but he can repent, the very fact that God implanted the Evil *Yeẓer* in him being sufficient ground to ask for God's forgiveness.[175] Serenity in suffering, hope for the future, reliance, ethical sensitiveness—are the fruits of the conclusions of rabbinic religious experience.

What happens to the questions philosophy sees bristling in the problem of evil? What of God's omnipotence and omniscience as opposed to His justice? What of man's freedom of will? The Rabbis, it would seem, would grant a loss to His omniscience,[176] perhaps, would they take up the question. But they would never take it up, for that would introduce concepts not the products of their experience. Freedom of the will they merely affirm as a fact of their experience, but they would do little else than affirm it. For rabbinic theology is essentially an affirmation of a religio-moral experience. It is not a speculative philosophy which may occupy the mind a fraction of the day, but a complex of concepts which constituted the mind of the Rabbis itself, mental habits so deeply ingrained as to be inseparable from the daily, hourly facts of life they interpreted.

We are prepared to find the Rabbis solving concrete questions involved in the problem of evil in much the same fashion as they resolve the problem generally. R. Joshua proves to the emperor that the lame, the blind and the deaf from birth have already been judged and therefore afflicted because "a man's deeds are revealed to Him, whether they will be good or bad,

[175] P. 62.

[176] Not only did God regret that He created the Evil *Yeẓer*, but it was His original intention not to give speech to animals, to divide the world into seventy tongues immediately after Noah, to give the priesthood only to the sons of Phineas, to give sovereignty in Israel only to David and his descendants, to give the Torah only to Israel (it was given also to Balaam). In all these cases, His not following His original intention resulted in evil—pp. 190–1. See above, p. 111.

before He intends to create (the man);" and proof is supplied in the instance of the duplicity of a certain blind man.[177] There are two matters here worthy of attention. One is that the question is asked by the emperor, a non-Jew; and this, no doubt, is a reflection of the frequent arguments the Rabbis had with Gentiles concerning the justice of God which may well have stimulated the interest of the Rabbis in the problem of evil. The other is that we have here something of an addendum to the solution of the general problem of evil. God not only implants the Evil *Yeẓer* but also knows whether it will dominate a certain man or not. This comes perilously close to determinism, but it is completely relieved by the concluding proof-text of the midrash: "Therefore it says, 'My Beloved put in His hand by the hole in the door' (Song of Songs 5:4),"[178] a verse that in the entire passage refers to God's anxiety to accept repentance. The blind man in the story, all those handicapped from birth, have only to repent to be cured. The justice of God is here again affirmed whilst room is left for freedom of the will, without which such an affirmation would be baseless.

We come now to what is most often in mind when we speak of the rabbinic version of the problem of evil—the question of "the righteous man to whom evil befalls and the wicked man to whom good befalls." That question has been answered, as we know, on the basis of God's corporate justice. Yet the Rabbis themselves were not completely satisfied with the answer. The struggle we have discerned above between their fine sense of the justice due the individual and their conception of corporate justice[179]—that struggle comes to the surface in the words the Rabbis put into the mouth of Moses. God unfolded to Moses the whole world's history, past and future, this world and the

[177] "Additions," p. 41. Comp. Tanḥuma, ed. Buber, I, 167, where there is a strong affirmation that God's judgments are not arbitrary, for all is revealed to Him.

On this see L. L. Mann, Freedom of Will in Talmudic Literature, in Year Book of C. C. A. R., Vol. XXVII, pp. 301–337.

[178] "Additions", p. 42. See Friedmann's note No. 25; see also above, p. 36, note 12, and p. 121.

[179] Above, pp. 180–181.

'Olam Habba. But Moses was not content: " 'Thou hast shown me the character of the world; show me the character (מידה) by which the world is governed. Behold, I see a righteous man to whom good befalls (and) a righteous man to whom evil befalls (צדיק וטוב לו צדיק ורע לו); a wicked man to whom good befalls (and) a wicked man to whom evil befalls; a wealthy man to whom good befalls (and) a wealthy man to whom evil befalls; a poor man to whom good befalls (and) a poor man to whom evil befalls.' He (Moses) said, 'Show me, I pray Thee, Thy glory' (Exod. 33:18)."[180] In the reply the Rabbis attribute to God, we see at once their own despair at solving the problem and their faith that God's goodness transcends even the principle of corporate justice. "The Holy One blessed be He answered him: 'Moses, thou canst not comprehend My qualities (or character מידותי), but I shall show thee part of My qualities; When I see men who neither because of their own deeds nor because of their fathers' deeds, can have any hope, yet becasue they stand and bless (Me) and ask for grace and pray much before Me, I hearken unto them and double their sustenance.' " What Moses witnessed was the quality of loving-kindness (מידה של חסד) and the quality of mercy (מידה של רחמים).[181]

Inner conflict there was, but the fact remains that the Rabbis did use the principle of corporate justice to explain why evil may befall the righteous and to account, in large part, for the justice of history. We must not imagine, however, that this solution was easy to accept, particularly when it was applied not to history but to their own experience. The sense of the justice due the individual was too highly developed, would not down. "And not only that, but Moses drew a lesson from himself. He said: 'Perhaps Israel will not want to stand in the ways of the Omnipresent (i e., will rebel at His meting out of justice), God forbid! He will then mete out severe decrees against them, and they will be flogged every little while.' "[182] That this midrash refers to corporate justice is evident from its following immediately on the statement that the righteous poor is in the category

[180] P. 183.

[181] Ibid; see above, pp. 126 and 164.

[182] P. 182. לעמוד בדרכיו של מקום—See Friedmann's note No. 2.

of the "righteous whom evil befalls,"[183] with which it is connected by the phrase "and not only that." The midrash mirrors, of course, the state of mind of the Rabbis and of the people to whom they preached; it is a warning to accept the principle of corporate justice, and that this warning was necessary is proof that the people, perhaps the Rabbis also, accepted it reluctantly.

Of real importance, the warning notwithstanding, was not so much the principle of corporate justice which is only an explanation of how God's justice functions, but rather the belief in God's justice itself; and the midrash continuing with a parable of a king (God) and his wife (Israel), closes "The King loves truth, loves peace, loves justice and righteousness."[184] Whether a man accepts the principle of corporate justice or not, he must continue to believe that God's ways, though they may be inscrutable, are just: "Thou hast learned that a man should not descend to bearing a grudge (תרעומת) (against God). When he sees two men, one a righteous man to whom evil befalls and the other a wicked man to whom good befalls, and he descends to bearing a grudge (against God for that), he forfeits his life. For it says, 'Suffer not thy mouth to bring thy flesh into guilt' (Koh. 5:5)."[185]

With all that we have learned regarding the difficulties the Rabbis encountered with the principle of corporate justice, it is pertinent once more to inquire why they nevertheless insisted upon it. Above we stated that the assumption behind this principle was the basic one of corporate responsibility, and that, moreover, the Rabbis were committed to it because they employed it, in one form or another, in their interpretation of the justice of history. They were apparently committed to the principle of corporate justice also because it is explicitly stated in Exod. 34:7—"visiting the iniquity of the fathers upon the children, and upon the children's children, unto the third and unto the fourth generation"—but this does not prevent them

[183] P. 182 and p. 181. "The wicked to whom good befalls," on p. 184 and p. 88.

[184] P. 182.

[185] P. 189. Friedmann's note No. 1.

on occasion from interpreting it away, and from turning the verse into an expression of God's beneficence, as we have observed above in the chapter on God's love.[186] There must have been something more fundamental than any reason we have thus far assigned which compelled them to employ this conception.

The struggle between the sense of the justice due the individual and the principle of corporate justice, whence arises the real problem of evil as the Rabbis knew it, is at bottom a struggle between two conceptions of individuality, both clamoring for expression in rabbinic theology. The Rabbis had a conception of the individual person similar to ours, hence the emphasis on distributive justice towards the individual person. But, at the same time, they had also a different conception of individuality, wherein the individual person was merged into a kind of corporate personality of which he was only one link, as it were. The Rabbis actually speak of Eliphaz and his son Amalek, of Nebuchadnezzer and his father Merodach, of Haman and his ancestor Agag, as though father and son were the same person. "What can these be likened to—Esau the wicked, Eliphaz the Temanite and his son Amalek, and Jereboam the son of Nebat, and Nebuchadnezzer king of Babylon, and Haman the Agagite? To one who found a garment in the way near a city, took it and brought it into the city and cried out, saying, 'Whom does this lost article belong to? Whom does this lost article belong to?' All the townspeople gathered to greet him and said, 'Have you noticed so and so, how righteous he is, how pious he is, how upright he is?' And they made him forthwith the head and prince of the town. In a year or two or three, he destroyed all the states and the whole land. To this may Esau the wicked, Eliphaz the Temanite and his son Amalek, and Nebuchadnezzer king of Babylon and Jereboam the son of Nebat and Haman the Agagite be likened." The midrash then proceeds to tell us that in reward for Eliphaz who honored his father, Amalek went forth from him into the world; because Jereboam gave a proper retort to the king, he was given the ten tribes; because Merodach honored God, Nebuchadnezzer went forth from him into the

[186] Above, p. 115.

world; and that Haman owed his existence to the fears expressed by his ancestor Agag.[187]

Now this homily attempts to explain the presence of wicked, godless men in the world. The reason given is that the father or ancestor performed something of merit. But notice that in the analogy, *the descendants*, not the fathers in most cases, are spoken of as the man who originally performed the meritorious act which led the people to elect him as their chief: "To whom may . . . Amalek . . . Nebuchadnezzer . . . Haman the Agagite be likened?" Son and father are alike to them, rather, the son is the last link of the corporate personality of which the father was the first. Notice also that Jereboam is rewarded for his own deed, and that he, an individual person, is placed on a par with the corporate personalities. There were times when individual and corporate personalities were alike to the Rabbis' minds. This would certainly account for their belief in corporate justice, for corporate justice then would be tantamount, literally, to justice to the individual.[188]

Yet the Rabbis conceived also at other times of the individual person as a distinct personality by himself. Distributive justice to the individual personality and distributive justice to the corporate personality are thus two categories, both flowing from belief in the absolute justice of God toward the individual, but differing in the conception of the individual. That there should be moments of conflict between them is inevitable, since both were held by the same minds.

Despite the great pains the Rabbis take in proving that the

[187] P. 125. Part of this midrash was given as an example of corporate justice above, pp. 192–3.

[188] See above, p. 182. Compare also the remarks of Professor M. M. Kaplan on the awakening individual in his article, Jewish Philanthropy, in the collection, Intelligent Philanthropy, ed. Faris, Laune and Todd (U. of Chicago, 1930), p. 72. The idea of the individual as a link in a corporate personality was also suggested to me by Rabbi Aaron Abromowitz of the College of Jewish Studies, Chicago.

Professor Ginzberg takes a somewhat different view. "The national consciousness of the Jew made him feel part of a whole in which past, present and future is a unit, and hence the inconsistence in their conception of divine retribution which is individual and corporate!"—(L. G.).

justice of God is manifest in this world, they hold that the complete reckoning cannot be seen here. What takes place here together with what takes place in the hereafter is the sum of the justice of God. This matter will be dealt with fully later;[189] we are concerned now only with its bearing on the problem of evil. Man will be brought up for judgment after death.[190] The meed of justice due him will then be paid in full. And so, obviously, the solution to the problem of evil is further advanced. When Moses asks God to allow him his reward in this world, God replies that he will receive it only in "the future to come" (*L'atid labo*) at which time Abraham, Isaac and Jacob will also receive their reward.[191] The problem of "the righteous whom evil befalls and the wicked whom good befalls" is now resolved in this wise: "From the chastisements of the righteous (in this world) thou dost learn the measure of retribution of the wicked in Gehenna; from the tranquility of the wicked in this world thou dost learn of the reward of the righteous in the World to Come."[192]

The tremendous emphasis on the justice of God in this world on the part of the Rabbis shows that they did not care to avail themselves altogether of the easier solution that all will be rectified in the hereafter. All will not be "rectified" for the simple reason that what has taken place in this world is also "right." "The chastisements of the righteous" are not for naught, nor is "the tranquility of the wicked." However much the belief in the World to Come meant to the Rabbis—and it meant very much—they never lost their hold upon the realities of this life. This life, its joys and sorrows, its vicissitudes and triumphs, the history of Israel and the history of nations, had to be accounted for here and now. Only thus could they and the people they taught, who occupied themselves with the practical concerns of life in this world, come to rely upon a God who governs it.

[189] Below in chapter on The World to Come.

[190] "Additions," p. 43.

[191] "Additions," p. 44.

[192] P. 120.

VI

Mercy in Judgment

Mercy in judgment is an expression of God's love. It is almost needless now to repeat the statement that God's love and justice often interlace with one another;[193] they are so frequently inextricably interlaced, as we have observed throughout this chapter. God's love manifest in the moral sphere has been discussed in the preceding chapter: He is merciful, judging His creatures with forbearance; He is forgiving, receiving man, even the most wicked, in repentance; He Himself provides the means whereby man may atone for his sins and be reconciled with Him; He rewards those who repent and punishes those who do not.[194] He hears prayer and answers it, and rewards for prayer and punishes blasphemy.[195] He is distressed over man's sins; He hopes that man will do good not evil; He rewards good deeds with joy on His part and punishes evil "with sighing;" even when the judgment itself is meted out, He is moved to the profoundest sorrow.[196] And when He punishes man, chastising him, it is only because He loves man and wants him to correct his ways.[197]

Were God to exercise absolute justice untempered with mercy, the world would soon be destroyed. Rigorous justice may demand that one who commits a sin be killed immediately, but God has pity even on the most wicked, and thus saves, oftentimes, their righteous children for the world: "If thou wilt say that as soon as a man commits a transgression, he should die immediately, the entire world would be destroyed. And how do you know this is so? Go learn from Manasseh, the son of Hezekiah, king of Judah, who left no idol in the world that he did not worship, yet the Holy One blessed be He pitied him and did not slay him. Why? Because of the righteous that are destined to issue from him."[198] But this reason for the wicked being saved

[193] Above, p. 108.
[194] Above, pp. 114–18.
[195] Above, pp. 137–162.
[196] Above, pp. 117–118.
[197] Above, p. 196. [198] P. 189.

holds only if they do not repent; the homily goes on to say that if one repents, no matter how many be the sins committed or how grave—even blasphemy—he is forgiven and saved (in his own right).[199]

The decree of corporate justice wherein the sins of the fathers are to be visited upon the children is on occasion either annulled or not applied. It is annulled, we have seen, when the wicked repents and studies Torah—"even though a hundred decrees were made concerning him, the Holy One blessed be He removes them from him."[200] It is also apparently annulled when men "who have no hope" pray for grace.[201] And it was not applied to the First Ten Generations. It was God's "(original) intention to visit the sins of the parents upon the children (in those generations). But He did not do so; instead, the Holy One blessed be He made each one king over his wife and children and members of his household."[202] God's mercy, in that instance, went for naught; but at least the Deluge when it came was brought about by the sins of every man who perished in it.

When God does come to pass judgment upon men, He judges them "on the side of merit," finding, if only possible, a good interpretation to every act. R. Joshua, walking with his pupils, entered the house of a Roman matron. When he returned, although he had performed a number of suspicious actions, his pupils' faith in him enabled them to interpret every one of his actions "on the side of merit." "By the Temple service!" exclaimed the Rabbi, "Thus indeed it was! And just as you have judged me on the side of merit so will the Holy One blessed be He judge you on the side of merit."[203] Indeed, God takes particularly into account the deeds of kindness and compassion a man has to his credit, even if He have cause to be very angry with him: " 'In wrath remember compassion' (Hab. 3:2)—even in wrath Thou rememberest the compassion of a man (toward others)."[204]

[199] P. 189.
[200] P. 22. But see p. 128, above.
[201] P. 183; see above, p. 204.
[202] P. 190.
[203] "Additions," p. 7.
[204] P. 194.

There are times when God's mercy delays the punishment or affects its form. After "the grave matter that happened to Israel on account of the spies," Moses pleaded with God to forgive them, and God Himself recalled to Moses the kind of plea he should make. "Although He forgave, the decree stood in force:"[205] God, it is true, did not kill off the generation at that time but they died, nonetheless, in the wilderness. God takes care to deal with sympathy even while He administers punishment, as is illustrated by the story of the Tower of Babel. The men of the Tower of Babel were arrogant, and were therefore uprooted from the world. But when God punished them, he spoke to them in the very words they employed, not in sarcasm, but to make them feel better, like the man in the parable who was exiled and, "when he found a fellowman speaking with him in his own tongue," felt better for it. The word used by the men of the Tower and later employed by God was "come" (Gen. 11:4 and 7).[206] Using the idea of exile in the parable and rendering God's kindness a matter of language is, incidentally, particularly apt in a story that has for its theme the dispersion of the human race and the confusion of tongues by which this was achieved.

At the very last, when the punishment has been meted out, God's sorrow is most profound. He went into mourning after He brought the Deluge.[207] He weeps with the wicked whom He has punished.[208]

No scholastic dialectic decides for the Rabbis just where God's justice ends or His mercy begins. It is sufficient for them to know that He judges every act. It is comforting for them to feel that He is kind, that He forgives all, understands all, is merciful in His judgment. To define further is needless, and may become intellectual sport; to assume less is to rob morality of its sanction and to displace hope with despair.

[205] P. 144.
[206] P. 158.
[207] P. 162; see above, p. 110.
[208] P. 87. Above, p. 118.